D1442317

1000 Recipes
Cook's Bible

igloobooks

igloobooks

Published in 2013
by Igloo Books Ltd
Cottage Farm
Sywell
NN6 0BJ
www.igloobooks.com

Copyright© 2013 Igloo Books Ltd

LEO002 1113
4 6 8 10 9 7 5
ISBN 978-1-78197-174-1

Food photography and recipe development: PhotoCuisine UK
Front and back cover images © PhotoCuisine UK

Printed and manufactured in China

1000 Recipes
Cook's Bible

CONTENTS

EGGS

1

MAKES 16

Pancakes with Chocolate Sauce

PREPARATION TIME 25 MINUTES

COOKING TIME 20 MINUTES

INGREDIENTS

225g / 8 oz / 1 cup plain (all purpose)
flour
2 tsp baking powder
1 tsp caster (superfine) sugar
Pinch salt
300ml / 10 fl oz / 1 ¼ cups milk
2 eggs
1 tsp vanilla extract
Vegetable oil
Mixed berries such as blueberries,
raspberries and strawberries

FOR THE CHOCOLATE SAUCE
1 jar Nutella (200g)
100ml / 3 ½ fl oz / ½ cup double
cream

- Mix together the flour, baking powder, sugar and salt in a bowl.
- Whisk together the milk, eggs and vanilla extract.
- Mix the wet ingredients into the dry ingredients to a thick smooth batter then leave to rest for 15 minutes.
- Heat a thin film of vegetable oil in the pan and add large dollops of batter to the pan to make circles around 5cm across. Cook until they bubble on top, then turn over and cook for another 1-2 minutes.
- Remove from the pan and keep warm while you make the rest.
- Heat the Nutella with the cream in a small pan to make the chocolate sauce, then serve with the pancakes and berries.

Pancakes with Chocolate Cointreau Sauce

2

- Add 2 tbsp of Cointreau or orange liqueur to the Nutella and cream while heating.

3

SERVES 4

Toasted Muffin with Scrambled Egg

PREPARATION TIME 5 MINUTES

COOKING TIME 8 MINUTES

INGREDIENTS

4 English muffins, split horizontally
6 eggs
40g / 1 oz / ¼ cup butter
6 tsp double cream
Salt and pepper

- Crack the eggs into a bowl and beat lightly.
- Heat most of the butter in a pan until foaming, then stir in the eggs.
- Cook gently, stirring thoroughly with a wooden spoon moving the eggs around the pan until lightly cooked with some liquid egg still left.
- Stir in the cream and season.
- Serve immediately with the toasted muffins.

Toasted Muffin with Herby Scrambled Eggs

4

- Stir in ½ bunch chopped chives or chervil with the cream.

5

SERVES 4

Ham, Tomato & Chive Omelette

- Heat the oil in a large frying pan and cook the tomatoes for a few seconds.
- Season the eggs, then pour into the pan. Swirl the pan to move the eggs into all the corners and coat everything.
- Top with the ham and sprinkle over the chives.
- Place under a hot grill for about 5-6 minutes to set the frittata – keep checking it to ensure nothing burns.
- Allow to cool a little then cut into wedges and serve.

PREPARATION TIME 5 MINUTES

COOKING TIME 8 MINUTES

INGREDIENTS

1 tbsp olive oil
3 slices prosciutto, torn into strips
6 eggs, lightly beaten
Salt and pepper
8 cherry tomatoes, halved
1 bunch chives, chopped

Ham Mushroom Chive Omelette

6

- Cook 8 quartered button mushrooms for 5 minutes as a substitution for the tomatoes.

7

SERVES 4

Scotch Eggs

- Place 4 eggs in a pan of simmering water. Cook for 1 minute, then cover with a lid, remove from the heat and leave for 5 minutes exactly.
- When the time is up, remove from the heat and chill.
- Mix together the meat, herbs, salt and pepper, mustard and mix well. Divide into quarters.
- Peel the boiled eggs. Place the beaten eggs, flour and breadcrumbs in dishes in a line.
- Lay a piece of clingfilm on the work surface and cover with a quarter of the forcemeat. Lay another piece on top and squish until large enough to coat the boiled egg.
- Roll an egg in the flour then place in the centre of the forcemeat. Encase the egg in the meat. Dip each egg into the flour, then beaten egg then breadcrumbs. Repeat for all 4.
- Heat the oil and cook the eggs 2 at a time for 6-7 minutes until crisp and golden.

PREPARATION TIME 25 MINUTES

COOKING TIME 6-7 MINUTES

INGREDIENTS

4 eggs + 2 eggs beaten
200g / 7 oz / ¾ cup sausagemeat
200g / 7 oz / ¾ cup minced pork
1 tbsp parsley, finely chopped
½ tbsp sage, finely chopped
½ tsp ground mace
1 tbsp grain or Dijon mustard (optional)
2 tbsp plain (all purpose) flour
100g / 3 ½ oz / ½ cup fine breadcrumbs, seasoned with a pinch of Cayenne
Vegetable oil

Black Pudding Scotch Eggs

8

- Substitute the minced pork for an equal amount of crumbled black pudding for an earthier treat.

9

SERVES 4

Cherry Tomato, Coriander & Feta Tortilla

PREPARATION TIME 30 MINUTES

COOKING TIME 30 MINUTES

INGREDIENTS

6 eggs
1 tbsp crème fraîche
8 cherry tomatoes, halved
100g feta cheese, cubed
6 sprigs coriander (cilantro), chopped
Olive oil
Salt and pepper

- Preheat the oven to 180°C (160° fan) / 350F / gas 5.
- Beat the eggs with the creme fraîche in a large bowl.
- Add tomatoes, feta, coriander and season then mix together carefully.
- Oil a large frying pan, then pour the mixture in and bake for about 35 minutes until puffed and golden. The egg should be cooked through.
- Cut into squares and serve warm or cold.

Cherry Tomato, Parsley & Goats Cheese Tortilla   10

- Try goats cheese instead of feta and substitute the parsley for coriander.

11

SERVES 4

Eggs Benedict

PREPARATION TIME 10 MINUTES

COOKING TIME 3-5 MINUTES

INGREDIENTS

4 eggs
4 thick slices ham
4 English muffins
30g / 1 oz butter

FOR THE HOLLANDAISE SAUCE

175g / 6 oz / ¾ cup butter
1 tbsp white wine vinegar
2 tbsp lemon juice
3 egg yolks
Pinch salt

- Melt the butter in a pan. Place the vinegar and lemon juice in another pan and boil.
- Place the egg yolks and salt in a food processor and whiz briefly, then with it still running, very gradually add the hot lemon juice and vinegar.
- Again very very slowly add the melted butter until the sauce emulsifies. Keep warm in a bowl over hot water while you cook the eggs.
- Poach the eggs in boiling water for about 3 minutes for a runny yolk. Remove to kitchen paper and leave to drain.
- Cut the muffins in half horizontally and lightly toast the cut sides, then butter.
- Place the muffins on a plate and lay over the slices of ham.
- Top with the poached eggs and hollandaise sauce.

Eggs Benedict with Watercress   12

- Wilt a small bag of chopped watercress in a little butter then serve under the poached egg for a peppery hit.

Eggs Florentine with Mornay Sauce

SERVES 4 · 13

Eggs Florentine with Tomato Sauce · 14

- Instead of making a mornay sauce, simply simmer a can of chopped tomatoes until reduced, season well and pour over.

Eggs Florentine with Bacon · 15

- Add 2 rashers of chopped streaky bacon to the pan before you wilt the spinach.

Eggs Florentine with Baked Mushrooms · 16

- For low-carb addicts, serve the poached egg and spinach on top of a buttery oven-baked field mushroom.

PREPARATION TIME 5 MINUTES

COOKING TIME 8 MINUTES

INGREDIENTS

2 handfuls spinach leaves
1 tbsp butter
4 eggs
4 slices bread, toasted

FOR THE MORNAY SAUCE
150ml / 5 fl oz / ⅔ cup milk
150ml / 5 fl oz / ⅔ cup single cream
1 tsp Dijon mustard
1 tbsp plain (all purpose) flour
1 ½ tbsp butter
50g / 1 ¾ oz / ¼ cup Cheddar, grated
1 tbsp Parmesan, grated
½ bunch parsley, chopped
Squeeze of lemon juice
Salt and pepper

- To make the Mornay sauce, whisk the milk, cream, mustard, flour and butter in a pan over medium heat until smooth and thick.
- Whisk in the cheeses and stir to melt, then cook the sauce over a low heat for 5 minutes or so to cook out the flour.
- Add the parsley, season well, set aside and keep warm.
- Poach the eggs in boiling water for about 3 minutes for a runny yolk. Remove to kitchen paper and leave to drain.
- Wilt the spinach in a pan, then squeeze out any excess moisture and stir in the butter to melt.
- Toast the bread and top with the spinach. Place an egg on top, then spoon over the Mornay sauce.

SERVES 4

Baked Eggs with Mushrooms

Herby Baked Eggs

18

- Serve with a scattering of chopped tarragon before serving for a herbal twist.

Baked Eggs with Ham

19

- Line the ramekin with a slice of thickly cut ham before adding the eggs and butter.

Garlicky Baked Eggs

20

- Scatter over a finely chopped clove garlic before baking.

PREPARATION TIME 10 MINUTES

COOKING TIME 15 MINUTES

INGREDIENTS

60g / 2 oz / ¼ cup butter
100g / 3 ½ oz / ½ cup mushrooms, finely sliced
4 eggs
2 tbsp
Salt and pepper

- Preheat the oven to 190°C (170° fan) / 375F / Gas 5.
- Cook the mushrooms in foaming butter in a pan until golden in patches.
- Butter 4 ramekin dishes generously and crack the eggs into the ramekins.
- Spoon the mushrooms around and top with a little butter and seasoning.
- Place the ramekins in a roasting tin, pour in enough boiling water to come halfway up the sides of the ramekins and bake in the ven for 15 minutes or until the eggs are just set.

21

SERVES 4

Poached Eggs with Aurore Sauce

- Heat the butter in a pan and when melted, whisk in the flour to make a paste.
- Pour in the stock and whisk until smooth and thickened, then leave to cook very gently for 10 minutes.
- Stir in the tomato puree, crème fraîche and chives and season. Keep warm.
- Poach the eggs in boiling water for about 3 minutes for a runny yolk. Remove to kitchen paper and leave to drain.
- Spoon the sauce over the eggs to serve.

PREPARATION TIME 5 MINUTES

COOKING TIME 18 MINUTES

....

INGREDIENTS

FOR THE SAUCE
1 tbsp butter
1 tbsp plain (all purpose) flour
300ml / 10 fl oz / 1 ¼ cups hot vegetable or chicken stock
2 tbsp tomato puree
2 tbsp crème fraîche
½ bunch chives, finely chopped
Salt and pepper
4 eggs

Poached Eggs with Tomatoes

22

- Simmer a can of chopped tomatoes with seasoning and a rosemary sprig until thickened then spoon over the poached eggs.

23

SERVES 4

Scrambled Eggs on Toast

- Crack the eggs into a bowl and beat lightly.
- Heat most of the butter in a pan until foaming, then stir in the eggs.
- Cook gently, stirring thoroughly with a wooden spoon moving the eggs around the pan until lightly cooked with some liquid egg still left.
- Stir in the cream and chives and season.
- Serve immediately with the toast.

PREPARATION TIME 5 MINUTES

COOKING TIME 8 MINUTES

....

INGREDIENTS

6 eggs
40g / 1 oz / ¼ cup butter
6 tsp double cream
Salt and pepper
1 tbsp chives, chopped
4 thick slices bread, toasted and buttered

Luxury Scrambled Eggs

24

- Stir in a couple of slices of finely sliced smoked salmon just as the eggs are cooked.

25

SERVES 4

Stuffed Tomatoes

PREPARATION TIME 10 MINUTES

COOKING TIME 10-15 MINUTES

INGREDIENTS

6 eggs, lightly beaten
40g / 1 oz / ¼ cup butter
6 tsp double cream
Salt and pepper
1 tbsp parsley, chopped
4 large tomatoes

- Preheat the oven to 200°C (180° fan) / 400F / gas 7.
- Heat most of the butter in a pan until foaming, then stir in the eggs.
- Cook gently, stirring thoroughly with a wooden spoon moving the eggs around the pan until lightly cooked with some liquid egg still left.
- Stir in the cream and parsley and season.
- Core the tomatoes and scoop a little of the flesh from inside, then spoon the egg into the cavity.
- Place in a roasting and cook for 10-15 minutes or until the tomatoes have softened.

Mushroom Stuffed Baked Tomatoes

26

- Add 6 button mushrooms, finely chopped to the pan before the eggs.

27

SERVES 4

Vanilla Baked Egg Custard

PREPARATION TIME 10 MINUTES

COOKING TIME 50-60 MINUTES

INGREDIENTS

500ml / 1 pint / 2 cups milk
1 tsp vanilla extract
40g / 1 ½ oz caster (superfine) sugar
3 eggs, lightly beaten
Grated nutmeg

- Preheat the oven to 180°C (160° fan) / 350F / gas 5.
- Heat the milk and vanilla in a pan until nearly at boiling point then set aside to cool for a minute.
- Meanwhile whisk the sugar with the eggs.
- Pour the scented milk over the eggs, whisking continually until thickened and smooth.
- Strain into a buttered ovenproof 1 pint baking dish. Bake for 50-60 minutes until just set.
- Serve with freshly grated nutmeg over the top.

Rose Egg Custard

28

- Add 2 drops of rosewater to the custard mixture for a scented version of this classic.

29
SERVES 6 Courgette, Tomato and Feta Frittata

- Preheat the oven to 180°C (160° fan) / 350F / gas 5.
- Beat the eggs with the crème fraîche in a large bowl.
- Add the courgettes, tomatoes, feta, thyme leaves and season then mix together carefully.
- Oil a large frying pan, then pour the mixture in and bake for about 35 minutes until puffed and golden. The egg should be cooked through.
- Cut into squares and serve warm or cold.

PREPARATION TIME 30 MINUTES

COOKING TIME 35 MINUTES

INGREDIENTS

8 eggs
1 tbsp crème fraîche
2 courgettes (zucchini), finely diced
Handful sun dried tomatoes, finely chopped
100g feta cheese, cubed
6 sprigs thyme
Olive oil
Salt and pepper

Courgette, Tomato and Taleggio Frittata
30

- Substitute melting Taleggio cheese for the cubed feta for an oozing frittata.

31
SERVES 6 Green Asparagus Frittata

- Preheat the oven to 180°C (160° fan) / 350F / gas 5.
- Beat the eggs with the crème fraîche in a large bowl.
- Snap the woody ends off the asparagus and discard. Cut the asparagus into short lengths.
- Fry the onion gently in 2 tbsp olive oil until deep gold and soft – about 20 minutes
- Pour the egg mixture in, add the asparagus and distribute evenly.
- Bake for about 35 minutes until puffed and golden. The egg should be cooked through.
- Cut into squares and serve warm or cold

PREPARATION TIME 30 MINUTES

COOKING TIME 35 MINUTES

INGREDIENTS

8 eggs
1 tbsp crème fraîche
1 bunch asparagus
1 onion, peeled and thickly sliced
Olive oil
Salt and pepper

Asparagus and Ham Frittata
32

- Add 2 chopped slices of ham just before baking to set off the sweet flavour of the asparagus.

33

SERVES 4

Onion & Mint Omelette

Onion Parsley Omelette
34

- Substitute the mint for parsley and add 1 finely chopped clove garlic.

Red Onion Omelette
35

- Use red onions instead of white for a sweeter taste.

Cheesy Onion Omelette
36

- Omit the mint, but add 50g/ 1 ¾ oz grated cheese such as gruyere just before grilling.

PREPARATION TIME 5 MINUTES

COOKING TIME 8 MINUTES

INGREDIENTS

1 tbsp olive oil
1 tbsp butter
1 onion, very finely sliced
4 eggs
Salt and pepper
½ bunch mint leaves, finely chopped

- Heat the oil and butter in a large frying pan and cook the onions slowly until golden and sweet.
- Meanwhile crack the eggs into a bowl and beat lightly. Tip into the pan and swirl gently to cover the base of the pan and help it set.
- When the omelette is nearly set, sprinkle over the mint and seasoning and flash under a hot grill to set it completely.
- Remove from the pan and serve.

37
SERVES 6 Breakfast Frittata

- Preheat the oven to 180°C (160° fan) / 350F / gas 5.
- Beat the eggs with the crème fraîche in a large bowl.
- Heat the oil in a pan and cook the sausage chunks and bacon until golden,
- Add the mushrooms and cook briskly until all the liquid evaporates then add the tomatoes.
- Pour the egg mixture in and distribute evenly.
- Bake for about 35 minutes until puffed and golden. The egg should be cooked through.
- Cut into squares and serve warm or cold

PREPARATION TIME 15 MINUTES

COOKING TIME 35 MINUTES

INGREDIENTS

8 eggs
1 tbsp crème fraîche
2 tbsp olive oil
4 good quality pork sausages, meat removed from the skins and cut into small chunks
4 rashers smoked streaky bacon, chopped
100g/3 ½ oz / ½ cup button mushrooms, thickly sliced
12 cherry tomatoes, quartered
½ bunch parsley, chopped
Salt and pepper

Breakfast Frittata with Black Pudding
38
- Add small chunks of black pudding for a real meat feast.

39
SERVES 4 Fried Egg

- Heat the fat in a pan over a medium heat, then crack in the eggs.
- Cook until done to your liking, basting the top of the egg every so often with the fat to help the yolk set and add flavour.
- When cooked to your liking season and serve.

COOKING TIME 5 MINUTES

INGREDIENTS

4 eggs
2-3 tbsp groundnut oil, dripping or bacon fat
Salt and pepper

Fried Duck Egg
40
- Duck eggs are a richer taste and worth trying for a weekend treat.

41

SERVES 4

Spanish Style Scrambled Eggs

PREPARATION TIME 5 MINUTES

COOKING TIME 15 MINUTES

INGREDIENTS

1 tbsp groundnut oil
1 red pepper, deseeded and finely sliced
6 eggs
40g / 1 oz / ¼ cup butter
6 tsp double cream
Salt and pepper
1 tbsp chives, chopped
4 slices Serrano or prosciutto ham, torn into strips
4 thick slices bread, toasted and buttered

- Heat the oil in a pan and cook the peppers until softened and sweet.
- Crack the eggs into a bowl and beat lightly.
- Add the butter to the pan, then stir in the eggs.
- Cook gently, stirring thoroughly with a wooden spoon moving the eggs around the pan until lightly cooked with some liquid egg still left.
- Stir in the cream and chives and ham and season.
- Serve immediately on toast.

Spanish-Style Cheesy Eggs

42

- Add 2 tbsp finely shaved Manchego cheese on top just before serving.

43

SERVES 4

Scrambled Eggs & Mushrooms on Toast

PREPARATION TIME 5 MINUTES

COOKING TIME 10 MINUTES

INGREDIENTS

40g / 1 oz / ¼ cup butter
80g / 2 ½ oz / ⅓ cup button mushrooms, halved
6 eggs
6 tsp double cream
Salt and pepper
1 tbsp parsley, chopped
4 thick slices bread, toasted and buttered

- Heat the butter in a pan and cook the mushrooms until golden and all the excess moisture has evaporated.
- Crack the eggs into a bowl and beat lightly.
- Stir the eggs into the pan and cook gently, stirring thoroughly with a wooden spoon moving the eggs around the pan until lightly cooked with some liquid egg still left.
- Stir in the cream and parsley and season.
- Serve immediately with the toast.

Scrambled Eggs and Mushrooms with Bacon

44

- Fry a rasher of back bacon and place on the toast under the mushrooms for a more substantial meal.

45

SERVES 4

Baked Egg with Garlic & Tomato

Spicy Baked Eggs
46
- Add ½ finely chopped red chilli over the tomato before the egg for a real livener.

Baked Eggs with Cheese and Tomato
47
- Sprinkle a handful of cheese over the top of the eggs 5 minuts before the end.

Baked Eggs on Toasted Bread
48
- Five minutes before the end, gently toast 4 slices of bread and spread with a little butter. Slide the eggs on top and serve.

PREPARATION TIME 10 MINUTES

COOKING TIME 15-20 MINUTES

INGREDIENTS

60g / 2 oz / ¼ cup butter
2 tomatoes, halved
1 clove garlic, crushed
4 eggs
30g / 1 oz butter
Salt and pepper

- Preheat the oven to 190°C (170° fan) / 375F / gas 5.
- Butter 4 ramekin dishes generously and place a tomato half in the bottom topped with a little garlic and salt and pepper.
- Crack the eggs into the ramekins on top of the tomato and dot with butter.
- Place the ramekins in a roasting tin, pour in enough boiling water to come halfway up the sides of the ramekins and bake in the oven for 15-20 minutes or until the eggs are just set.

49

SERVES 4

Poached Egg with Mushrooms

Poached Egg with Field Mushrooms

50

- If you can't source wild mushrooms, place the poached egg on top of a field mushroom baked with butter and seasoning for about 20 minutes.

Poached Egg with Mushrooms and Spinach

51

- Stir in 2 large handfuls of baby spinach leaves into the mushrooms just before they are cooked.

Poached Eggs on Sourdough Toast

52

- To make this even more substantial and not to waste any good juices, serve alongside toasted sourdough for dunking and wiping.

PREPARATION TIME 5 MINUTES

COOKING TIME 10 MINUTES

INGREDIENTS

60g / 2 oz / ¼ cup butter
100g / 3 ½ oz / ½ cup mixed wild mushrooms
Salt and pepper
4 eggs

- Heat the butter in a pan and when foaming, add the mushrooms.
- Cook until tender and any excess moisture has evaporated. Season and keep warm.
- Poach the eggs in boiling water for about 3 minutes for a runny yolk. Remove to kitchen paper and leave to drain.
- Serve the egg on a bed of mushrooms.

53

SERVES 4

Hard Boiled Eggs with Béchamel Sauce

- Place the eggs in cold water, bring to a simmer and cook for 6 minutes.
- Place in cold water to stop the cooking, then peel carefully.
- Meanwhile make the sauce: melt the butter in a pan, stir in the flour to make a paste.
- Whisk in the milk a bit at a time, stirring until the sauce is smooth and thick. Add the bay leaf and leave to cook for 10 minutes, stirring occasionally. season
- Cut the eggs in half and place in a dish. Spoon over the bechamel and grill until golden and bubbling.

PREPARATION TIME 20 MINUTES

COOKING TIME 5 MINUTES

....

INGREDIENTS

4 eggs at room temperature

FOR THE BÉCHAMEL SAUCE
1 tbsp butter
1 tbsp plain (all purpose) flour
300ml / 10 fl oz / 1 ¼ cups milk
1 bay leaf
Salt and pepper

Hard Boiled Eggs
with Mornay Sauce

54

- Substitute the mornay sauce on p9.

55

SERVES 4

Egg Florentine Breakfast

- Wilt the spinach in a frying pan covered with a lid.
- Squeeze out the excess moisture.
- Place back in the pan with seasoning, a little grated nutmeg and the butter and stir until melted.
- Make small wells in the spinach and crack the eggs into them, then cover with the lid and cook for 5-6 minutes until the eggs are cooked to your liking.
- Serve with bread for dipping.

PREPARATION TIME 5 MINUTES

COOKING TIME 10-12 MINUTES

....

INGREDIENTS

1kg/ 2 ¼ lb / 4 ¼ cups spinach leaves, washed thoroughly
Salt and pepper
Grated nutmeg
4 tbsp butter
4 eggs

Egg Florentine Breakfast
with Tomatoes

56

- Chop up 2 vine ripened tomatoes and stir into the spinach, then proceed as above.

57

SERVES 4

Tuna and Courgette Tortilla

PREPARATION TIME 10 MINUTES

COOKING TIME 20 MINUTES

INGREDIENTS

4 tbsp olive oil
1 courgette (zucchini), quartered
and sliced
6 free-range eggs
200 g / 7 oz canned tuna, drained
and flaked
oregano, to garnish

- Heat half the oil in a non-stick frying pan and fry the courgettes for 5 minutes.
- Meanwhile, gently beat the eggs in a jug to break up the yolks. When the courgettes are ready, stir them into the eggs with the tuna and season with salt and pepper.
- Heat the rest of the oil in the frying pan then pour in the egg mixture.
- Cook over a gentle heat for 6 – 8 minutes or until the egg has set round the outside, but the centre is still a bit runny.
- Turn it out onto a plate, then slide it back into the pan and cook the other side for 4 – 6 minutes.
- Leave to cool for 5 minutes then cut into wedges and serve, garnished with oregano.

Salmon Courgette Tortilla   58

- Use canned salmon instead of tuna.

59

SERVES 6

Mixed Pepper Tortilla

PREPARATION TIME 30 MINUTES

COOKING TIME 35 MINUTES

INGREDIENTS

1 red pepper, deseeded and cut in
half
1 yellow pepper, deseeded and cut
in half
4 tbsp olive oil
1 clove garlic, crushed
8 eggs
1 tbsp crème fraîche
½ bunch parsley, chopped
Olive oil
Salt and pepper

- Preheat the oven to 200°C (180° fan) / 400F / gas 7.
- Place the pepper halves in a roasting in, drizzle with oil and roast for about 30 minutes or until soft and blackened.
- Remove from the tin, place in a freezer bag and leave to steam.
- Once cooled, remove the skins from the peppers and roughly chop the flesh.
- Beat the eggs with the crème fraîche in a large bowl.
- Add the peppers, garlic and parsley and season then mix together carefully.
- Oil a large frying pan, then pour the mixture in and bake at 180°C / 350F for about 35 minutes until puffed and golden. The egg should be cooked through.
- Cut into squares and serve warm or cold.

Mixed Pepper and   60
Serrano Ham Tortilla

- Stir in slivers of Serrano ham before baking for a meaty twist.

61

SERVES 4

French Toast

French Toast with Bacon & Maple Syrup 62

- Omit the vanilla extract and serve with fried or grilled rashers of streaky bacon or prosciutto and maple syrup.

Savoury French Toast 63

- Omit the vanilla extract and add some finely chopped chives to the egg/milk mixture.

Cheesy French Toast 64

- Omit the vanilla extract and add 50g/1 ¾ oz finely grated Parmesan to the egg/milk mixture.

PREPARATION TIME 15 MINUTES

COOKING TIME 10 MINUTES

INGREDIENTS

1 thick slice white bread per person (or more if you're hungry...)
2 eggs, beaten
300ml / 10 fl oz / 1 ¼ cups full fat milk or single cream
1 tsp vanilla extract
½ tsp ground cinnamon
2 tbsp vegetable oil

- Whisk together the eggs, milk, vanilla and cinnamon and pour into a bowl.
- Lay the bread into the mixture, soaking it thoroughly for a few minutes.
- Heat the oil in a pan and gently fry the bread triangles 2 at a time until golden and crisp on each side.
- Serve hot.

SAUCES AND STOCKS

65

MAKES 100ML Mustard Vinaigrette

- Whisk together the vinegar, mustard and salt until thick.
- Add the sugar, then whisk the olive oil in slowly to make a thick emulsion.
- Adjust the seasoning if necessary then serve with salad.

PREPARATION TIME 5 MINUTES

INGREDIENTS

1 tbsp red wine vinegar
1 tbsp Dijon mustard
Pinch salt
Pinch sugar
6 tbsp extra virgin olive oil
Black pepper

66

MAKES 100ML

Pesto

PREPARATION TIME 10 MINUTES

INGREDIENTS

2 handfuls pine nuts
1 clove garlic, peeled and chopped
2 bunches basil
80g / 3 oz / ⅓ cup Parmesan, grated
Extra virgin olive oil
Salt and pepper

- Add the pine nuts to a frying pan over medium heat and lightly toast for a few seconds until golden.
- Place in a food processor with the garlic, basil and Parmesan.
- Whiz the ingredients in a food processor until roughly blended, stirring in enough olive oil to loosen.
- Store in the refrigerator for up to 3 days.

67

MAKES 275ML

Mint Mayonnaise

PREPARATION TIME 10 MINUTES

INGREDIENTS

2 egg yolks
½ clove garlic, crushed
1 tsp mustard powder
1 tsp salt
Black pepper

130ml / 4 ½ fl oz / ½ cup groundnut oil
130ml / 4 ½ fl oz / ½ cup olive oil
White wine vinegar
½ bunch mint leaves, finely chopped

- Place the egg yolks in a bowl with the garlic, mustard powder, salt and pepper. Whisk well.
- Using an electric whisk or hand whisk, pour in the oils one drop at a time, whisking each one in thoroughly.
- Once the mixture begins to thicken, then add the oil a little faster, whisking well.
- After half the oil has been added, stir in 1 tsp of vinegar. Add the remaining oil in a thin trickle, constantly whisking. Season and add the mint.
- If the mixture curdles, put an egg yolk in a clean bowl, add the curdled mixture drop by drop whisking it in, then continue with the remaining oil.
- Store for up to 7 days in the refrigerator.

68
MAKES 100ML Mustard & Mint Vinaigrette

PREPARATION TIME 5 MINUTES

INGREDIENTS

1 tbsp red wine vinegar
1 tbsp Dijon mustard
Pinch salt
Pinch sugar
6 tbsp extra virgin olive oil
Black pepper
½ bunch mint leaves, finely chopped

- Whisk together the vinegar, mustard and salt until thick.
- Add the sugar, then whisk the olive oil in slowly to make a thick emulsion.
- Whisk in the mint leaves.
- Adjust the seasoning if necessary then serve with salad.

Mustard Tarragon Vinaigrette 69

- Substitute tarragon for the mint leaves for a French twist.

70
SERVES 4-6 Béarnaise Sauce

PREPARATION TIME 5 MINUTES

COOKING TIME 15 MINUTES

INGREDIENTS

1 tbsp tarragon, chopped
1 shallot, finely chopped
6 black peppercorns, crushed
2 tbsp white wine vinegar
150ml / 5 fl oz / ⅔ cup dry white wine
3 egg yolks
1 tsp mustard powder
25g / 1 oz butter at room temperature
180g / 6 oz / ¾ cup butter, melted
Salt

- Put the tarragon, shallot, peppercorns, vinegar and wine in a small pan and reduce by a third until there are about 3 tbsp liquid left. Strain.
- Whisk the egg yolks and mustard together in a bowl over a pan of barely simmering water.
- Whisk in the vinegar reduction, add a tbsp water and whisk.
- Beat in the 25g butter a little at a time, then slowly trickle in the melted butter a drop at a time, continually whisking, until the sauce has emulsified and thickened.
- Season and keep warm until needed.

Choron Sauce 71

- Whisk ½ tbsp tomato puree into the sauce at the end.

Classic Hollandaise Sauce

72

SERVES 4

- Place the vinegar, water, onion, mace, bay leaf and peppercorns in a small pan and reduce to about 1 tbsp. Strain into a bowl, add 1 tbsp water.
- Whisk the egg yolks into the reduction.
- Place the bowl over a pan of barely simmering water and add a little of the butter, whisking until it has melted.
- Add the butter a little at a time, whisking continually, until the mixture emulsifies and thickens.
- Cook very gently for 2 minutes, then add a little lemon juice and season.

PREPARATION TIME 5 MINUTES

COOKING TIME 10-15 MINUTES

INGREDIENTS

2 tbsp white wine vinegar
2 tbsp water
1 slice onion
Pinch ground mace
1 bay leaf
6 black peppercorns, left whole
3 egg yolks
180g / 6 oz / ¾ cup butter at room temperature
Squeeze of lemon juice
Salt and white pepper

Herb Hollandaise

73

- Stir in ¼ bunch finely chopped chervil, tarragon or parsley at the end of cooking.

Tartare Sauce

74

MAKES 200ML

- Finely chop the shallot and gherkins.
- Place all of the ingredients into a bowl, adding the mayonnaise last.
- Mix well to combine all of the ingredients.
- Adjust the seasoning to taste using salt and pepper and serve.

PREPARATION TIME 10 MINUTES

INGREDIENTS

200g / 7 oz / ¾ cup mayonnaise
1 shallot
2 gherkins (cornichons)
2 tbsp capers, drained
½ bunch parsley, chopped
½ lemon, juiced
Salt and pepper

Sauce Gribiche

75

- Stir in 1 finely chopped hard boiled egg.

MAKES 275ML # Aioli

Herb Aioli 77
- Stir in ¼ bunch finely chopped parsley.

Tomato Aioli 78
- Stir in ½ tbsp tomato puree.

Saffron Aioli 79
- Soak a few saffron threads in 1 tsp warm water then whisk into the mayonnaise.

PREPARATION TIME 10 MINUTES

INGREDIENTS

2 egg yolks
4 cloves garlic, crushed
1 tsp mustard powder
1 tsp salt
Pepper
130ml / 4 ½ fl oz / ½ cup groundnut oil
130ml / 4 ½ fl oz / ½ cup olive oil
1 tsp White wine vinegar
½ bunch mint leaves, finely chopped

- Place the egg yolks in a bowl with the garlic, mustard powder, salt and pepper. Whisk well.
- Using an electric whisk or hand whisk, pour in the oils one drop at a time, whisking each one in thoroughly.
- Once the mixture begins to thicken, then add the oil a little faster, whisking well.
- After half the oil has been added, stir in 1 tsp of vinegar. Add the remaining oil in a thin trickle, constantly whisking. Season and add the mint.
- If the mixture curdles, put an egg yolk in a clean bowl, add the curdled mixture drop by drop whisking it in, then continue with the remaining oil.
- Store for up to 2 days in the refrigerator.

80
SERVES 4 Madeira Sauce

- Melt the butter in a large pan and sweat the onion, carrot and celery. Stir in the flour to make a paste.
- Whisk in the beef stock, canned tomatoes and parsley stalks until thickened. Reduce the heat and simmer until the consistency is similar to double cream – perhaps 1 ½ - 2 hours. Sieve the sauce, discarding the vegetables.
- Add the mushrooms and the next amount of beef stock and reduce the liquid slowly by half. When reduced, sieve into a clean pan.
- Add the Madeira, butter and season. This is now a demi-glace and can be frozen or stored.
- To serve, measure out the required amount of the demi-glace and add the final amount of Madeira. Reduce by half, adjust the seasoning and whisk in the cold butter to make a smooth shiny sauce.

Smoky Madeira Sauce
81
- Fry 50g/1 ¾ oz cubed pancetta or smoked streaky bacon with the vegetables for a smokier flavour.

PREPARATION TIME 20 MINUTES

COOKING TIME 3-3 ½ HOURS

....

INGREDIENTS

80g / 2 ½ oz / ⅓ cup butter
1 onion, peeled and chopped
1 carrot, peeled and diced
1 stick celery, diced
80g / 2 ½ oz / ⅓ cup plain (all purpose) flour
2 L / 4 pints / 8 ½ cups beef stock
1 x 400g can chopped tomatoes
1 bunch parsley stalks, tied
50g / 1 ¾ oz / ¼ cup mushrooms, chopped
1 L / 2 ¼ pints / 4 ¼ cups beef stock
120ml / 4 fl oz / ½ cup Madeira
50g / 1 ¾ oz / ¼ cup butter
100ml / 3 ½ fl oz / ½ cup Madeira
Salt and pepper
1 tbsp butter, cold

82
MAKES 1 PINT Vegetable Stock

- Place the vegetables in a pan and cover with 570ml – 850ml (1-1 ½ pints) cold water.
- Bring to the boil, reduce the heat and simmer for 30 minutes.
- Strain. The stock is ready to use.

PREPARATION TIME 5 MINUTES

COOKING TIME 30 MINUTES

....

INGREDIENTS

2 sticks celery, chopped
1 onion, peeled and chopped
2 carrots, chopped
2 bay leaves
10 black peppercorns
1 bunch parsley stalks, tied
Salt

Consomme
83
- Once strained, use the stock to simmer pasta ravioli and serve together as a rich broth.

84
SERVES 4

Green Peppercorn Cream Sauce

PREPARATION TIME 5 MINUTES

COOKING TIME 12 MINUTES

INGREDIENTS

1 tbsp butter
1 shallot, finely chopped
50ml / 1 ¾ oz / ¼ cup dry white wine
300ml / 10 fl oz / 1 ¼ cups double
(heavy) cream
1 tsp brine from green
peppercorn jar
1 tbsp green peppercorns
Salt and pepper

- Heat the butter in a pan and when foaming sweat the shallot until translucent.
- Add the wine and reduce until nearly evaporated, then stir in the cream.
- Bubble up till it thickens, then add the peppercorns and the brine.
- Season and adjust if necessary – the brine will add sharpness but you may want more.

Mixed Pepper Sauce   85

- Adding 2 good pinches of freshly ground white pepper will increase the heat.

86
MAKES 500ML

Butter Sauce

PREPARATION TIME 5 MINUTES

COOKING TIME 25 MINUTES

INGREDIENTS

250ml / 9 fl oz / 1 cup dry white wine
120ml / 4 fl oz / ½ cup white wine
vinegar
1 tbsp shallot, finely chopped
500g / 1 lb / 2 cups butter, cold
Salt

- Heat the wine, vinegar and shallot in a pan until bubbling, then reduce the heat slightly and cook until the liquid has reduced to 2 tbsp.
- Cut the butter into small cubes, but make sure they stay fridge-cold.
- Strain the liquid, return to the pan, then whisk in the cubes of butter one at a time, whisking continually while the mixture emulsifies and thickens.
- Remove from the heat once the butter has nearly all been used and continue whisking, then whisk in the final couple of cubes.
- Taste and serve warm.

Herb Butter Sauce   87

- Use delicate herbs such as tarragon, basil or chervil to enhance the flavour, whisking them in at the end.

SERVES 6

Tzatziki

88

Tzatziki with Dill
89

- Stir in ½ bunch of chopped dill.

Avocado Tzatziki
90

- Mash 1 ripe avocado and stir into the tzatziki. Omit the mint for this one.

Coriander Tzatziki
91

- Add ¼ bunch finely chopped coriander.

PREPARATION TIME 40 MINUTES

INGREDIENTS

1 cucumber
500g Greek yoghurt, strained
4 cloves garlic, crushed
4 tbsp extra-virgin olive oil
Bunch mint leaves, finely chopped
1-2 tbsp red wine vinegar
Salt and pepper
Hot pitta breads
Crudités, to serve

- Grate the cucumber on the coarse side of a grater. Place in a sieve, sprinkle with a little salt and leave to drain for 30 minutes.
- Squeeze the excess water from the cucumber then stir into the yoghurt.
- Add the garlic to taste then whisk in the oil and mint.
- Add a little red wine vinegar at a time, tasting in between each addition, to achieve a rounded sharpness against the creamy yoghurt.
- Season and refrigerate for at least 1 hour.
- Serve with toasted pitta breads and raw vegetable crudités to dip.

92

SERVES 4

Apple Sauce

PREPARATION TIME 5 MINUTES

COOKING TIME 10-15 MINUTES

INGREDIENTS

250g / 9 oz / 1 cup Bramley apples
250g / 9 oz / 1 cup Cox apples
1 tbsp sugar (optional, depending
on tartness of apples and usage)
2 cloves
2 tbsp water

- Peel and core the apples and cut into chunks.
- Place in a pan with the sugar, cloves and water and cover with a lid.
- Cook over a low heat for 10-15 minutes, checking occasionally, until the apples have 'exploded' to a fine puree and are soft.
- Beat to a puree, remove the cloves and serve.

Spicy Apple Sauce **93**

- A pinch of mixed spice adds a kick.

94

SERVES 4

Mint Sauce

PREPARATION TIME 5 MINUTES

INGREDIENTS

1 bunch mint leaves
1 tbsp cider or white wine vinegar
1 tbsp olive oil
½ tsp sugar
½ tsp English mustard
Salt and pepper
3-4 tbsp natural yoghurt (optional)
1 clove of garlic, minced

- Chop the mint leaves finely and place in a food processor with the vinegar, garlic, oil, sugar and mustard.
- Whiz to make a thick sauce.
- Season and serve with roast lamb. Add the yoghurt if you want a creamier style sauce.

Garlicky Mint Sauce **95**

- Adding a crushed clove garlic with the yoghurt makes this a sauce to serve with barbecued lamb.

96

SERVES 4 # Béchamel Sauce

- Melt the butter in a pan, stir in the flour to make a paste.
- Whisk in the milk a bit at a time, stirring until the sauce is smooth and thick. Add the bay leaf and leave to cook for 10 minutes, stirring occasionally.
- Season and remove the bay leaf before serving.

PREPARATION TIME 5 MINUTES

COOKING TIME 15 MINUTES

INGREDIENTS

1 tbsp butter
1 tbsp plain (all purpose) flour
300ml / 10 fl oz / 1 ¼ cups milk
1 bay leaf
Salt and pepper

Mornay Sauce   97

- Add 75g/2 ½ oz grated cheddar makes this a cheese sauce for cauliflower and so on.

98

SERVES 8 # Horseradish Sauce

- Peel and grate the horseradish and place in a bowl.
- Whisk in the vinegar, mustard and sugar and leave to soften for 10 minutes or so.
- Stir in the crème fraîche and season.
- This will keep for 2 days in the refrigerator.

PREPARATION TIME 20 MINUTES

INGREDIENTS

100g / 3 ½ oz / ½ cup fresh horseradish root
2 tsp red wine vinegar
1 tsp English mustard
Pinch sugar
150g / 5 oz / ⅔ cup crème fraîche
Salt and pepper

Horseradish Sauce with Capers   99

- Stir in 1 tbsp chopped rinsed capers for more of a kick.

100

SERVES 4

Cranberry Sauce

PREPARATION TIME 5 MINUTES

COOKING TIME 10-15 MINUTES

INGREDIENTS

500g / 1lb / 2 cups fresh cranberries
200g / 7 oz / ¾ cup sugar (you may
need more)
Zest and juice of 1 orange
1 tbsp port or cassis

- Place the ingredients in a pan and add 4 tbsp water.
- Bring to a boil then reduce the heat and cook until the cranberries have burst and the sauce has thickened.
- Pour into a bowl and check if it needs more sugar – it will thicken further as it cools.

Cranberry Sauce with Mustard   **101**

- Stirring in 2 heaped tbsp grain mustard helps add depth and heat.

102

SERVES 4

Red Wine & Mushroom Sauce

PREPARATION TIME 5 MINUTES

COOKING TIME 30-40 MINUTES

INGREDIENTS

50g / 1 ¾ oz / ¼ cup dried
mushrooms
500ml / 1 pint / 2 cups beef or
chicken stock
25g / 1 oz butter
1 shallot, finely chopped
½ tbsp plain (all purpose) flour
100ml / 3 ½ fl oz / ½ cup red wine
1 bay leaf
1 sprig rosemary
Salt and pepper
25g / 1 oz butter, cold

- Soak the dried mushrooms in the stock while you get on with the sauce.
- Melt the butter in a pan and sweat the shallot until translucent.
- Stir in the flour to make a paste, then whisk in the red wine and cook until thickened.
- Add the mushrooms and the stock and herbs and simmer until reduced by half.
- Taste the sauce and reduce further if desired. Do not season until the sauce is the consistency you want it.
- Strain, return to the pan and whisk in the cold butter to enhance the shine. Serve.

Enriched Red wine Sauce   **103**

- A tbsp of cream at the end will add richness and creaminess.

Fish Stock

- Place everything in a large pan and bring to a simmer.
- Cook for 20 minutes, then strain and reserve the stock.

PREPARATION TIME 10 MINUTES

COOKING TIME 20 MINUTES

INGREDIENTS

450g / 1 lb / 2 cups fish trimmings
and bones
500ml / 1 pint / 2 cups water
150ml / 5 fl oz / ⅔ cup dry white
wine
1 onion, cut into quarters
2 sticks celery, chopped
Parsley sprigs
1 bay leaf
Salt and pepper

Roquefort Sauce with Poppyseeds

105
SERVES 2

PREPARATION TIME 5 MINUTES

COOKING TIME 10 MINUTES

INGREDIENTS

1 tbsp butter
1 shallot, finely chopped
50ml / 1 ¾ / ¼ cup dry white wine

300ml / 10 fl oz / 1 ¼ cups double
cream
75g / 2 ½ oz / ⅓ cup Roquefort
cheese
1 tsp poppyseeds
Salt and pepper

- Heat the butter in a pan and when foaming add the shallot and sweat until translucent.
- Add the wine and reduce until nearly evaporated.
- Pour in the cream and bubble up, then crumble in the cheese. Stir until melted.
- Stir in the poppyseeds and season carefully.

Tomato Celery Sauce

106
SERVES 4

PREPARATION TIME 10 MINUTES

COOKING TIME 30 MINUTES

INGREDIENTS

2 tbsp olive oil
1 onion, peeled and chopped
2 sticks celery, finely chopped
1 carrot, peeled and finely chopped

1 clove garlic, crushed
2 tbsp tomato puree
1 x 400g can chopped tomatoes
200ml / 7 fl oz / ¾ cup chicken stock
2 tbsp Worcestershire sauce
Pinch chilli flakes (optional)
Salt and pepper

- Heat the oil in a pan and cook the onion, celery and carrot until softened.
- Add the garlic and tomato puree and cook for 2 minutes.
- Add the tomatoes and stock and bring to a simmer. Cook for 20 minutes or until thickened and reduced.
- Whiz the sauce in a blender until smooth, then return to the pan and season with Worcestershire sauce, chilli and salt and pepper.

SERVES 6

Normandy Lemon Sauce

Normandy Lemon Sauce with Wine

108

- Add 50ml / 1 ¾ fl oz white wine before the fish stock and whisk to a paste. This will add depth of flavour.

Normandy Lemon Herb Sauce

109

- Stir in chopped parsley or dill to serve with fish.

Normandy Lemon Oyster Sauce

110

- If you have them, try adding the liquid from fresh oysters to the sauce before serving with seafood. It will add a real taste of the ocean.

PREPARATION TIME 10 MINUTES

COOKING TIME 15 MINUTES

INGREDIENTS

50g / 1 ¾ oz / ¼ cup butter
225g / 8 oz / 1 cup button
mushrooms, very finely chopped
50g / 1 ¾ oz / ¼ cup plain
(all purpose) flour
225ml / 8 fl oz / 1 cup fish stock
2 egg yolks
100ml / 3 ½ fl oz / ½ cup double
cream
½ lemon, juiced
Salt and pepper

- Melt the butter in a pan and add the mushrooms. Sweat for a few minutes until they release their liquid.
- Stir in the flour and cook for 2 minutes.
- Pour in the stock and bring to a simmer, stirring until thickened and smooth.
- In a small bowl beat the egg yolks with the cream, then add 1 tbsp of the stock. Stir then pour, whisking into the hot stock over a very low heat.
- Add the lemon juice, season and cook until hot but not boiling.
- Serve with fish or poultry.

111
MAKES 500ML Chicken Stock

- Place the bones in a large pan, add the vegetables and cover with water.
- Bring to the boil, then reduce the heat to a 'blip' and leave to cook uncovered for about 3 hours.
- Skim any fat or scum from the surface from time to time.
- When done, strain into a large bowl and chill. This will make any fat easy to remove.
- Store in the refrigerator until needed or freeze for up to 3 months.

PREPARATION TIME 5 MINUTES

COOKING TIME 3 HOURS

INGREDIENTS

1 chicken carcass, (cooked for better flavour) and broken up
1 stick celery
1 carrot, chopped
1 onion, peeled and halved and stuck with 2 cloves
6 black peppercorns
1 bouquet garni
1 leek, white part only, chopped

Speedy Broth   112

- Use to cook tiny pasta shapes or noodles and serve in the hot broth for a quick lunch.

113
SERVES 4 Four Cheese Sauce

- Heat the butter in a pan and sweat the shallot until translucent.
- Add the white wine and reduce until nearly evaporated.
- Pour in the cream, heat and stir in the cheeses to melt.
- Add the mustard powder and season carefully.

PREPARATION TIME 10 MINUTES

COOKING TIME 15 MINUTES

INGREDIENTS

1 tbsp butter
½ shallot, finely chopped
1 glass dry white wine
400ml / 13 ½ fl oz / 1 ½ cups double cream
100g / 3 ½ oz / ½ cup Gruyere, grated
100g / 3 ½ oz / ½ cup Parmesan, grated
50g / 1 ¾ oz / ¼ cup blue cheese, such as Roquefort crumbled
50g / 1 ¾ oz / ¼ cup Cheddar, grated
½ tsp mustard powder
Salt and pepper

Four Cheese Sauce with a Kick   114

- Adding a good tbsp of grain mustard and a pinch of cayenne pepper will give this sauce a kick.

SOUPS

Cream of Cauliflower Soup

SERVES 4

- Heat the butter in a pan and sweat the onion without colouring for about five minutes.
- Add the cauliflower florets and leaves, potato and garlic and cook for a further five minutes until softened.
- Add the stock and bring to the boil. Simmer for about 20 minutes until the cauliflower is completely tender.
- Liquidise in a blender, then return to the pan.
- Add the cheeses and cream and stir to melt, season carefully and reheat to serve.

PREPARATION TIME 10 MINUTES

COOKING TIME 35 MINUTES

INGREDIENTS

25g / 1 oz butter
1 onion, peeled and finely chopped
1 head cauliflower, divided into small florets, green leaves finely sliced
1 clove garlic, chopped
1 large potato, peeled and finely diced
500ml /1 pint / 2 cups vegetable stock
50g / 1 ¾ oz / ¼ cup Cheddar or blue cheese, crumbled
150ml / 5 fl. oz / ⅔ cup double cream

Indian Tomato & Lentil Soup

SERVES 4

PREPARATION TIME 15 MINUTES

COOKING TIME 35-40 MINUTES

INGREDIENTS

50ml / 1 ½ fl. oz / ¼ cup olive oil
1 large onion, finely chopped
2 cloves garlic, minced
3.5cm/1 inch piece of ginger, minced
1 tbsp ground coriander
2 tsp ground cumin
1 tsp Madras curry powder
½ tsp chilli powder
½ tsp turmeric
250g / 9 oz / 1 cup split lentils
4 large tomatoes, roughly chopped
1.4 l / 2 ½ pints / 5 cups vegetable stock
Coriander leaves, to garnish
Lime wedges

- Heat the olive oil in a large saucepan set over a medium heat. Sweat the onion, garlic and ginger for 6-8 minutes until soft.
- Add the ground spices and some salt and pepper. Stir well and cook for a few minutes over a reduced heat.
- Add the lentils and tomatoes, stir well then cover with the stock. Bring to the boil, skimming any scum that comes to the surface.
- Boil for 5 minutes, then reduce to simmer and cook for 20-25 minutes until the lentils have absorbed about half of the stock.
- Remove from the heat and puree roughly using a stick blender.
- Return to the heat and adjust the seasoning to taste. Ladle into serving bowls and garnish with coriander and lime wedges before serving.

Vegetable Soup

SERVES 4-6

PREPARATION TIME 15 MINUTES

COOKING TIME 20-25 MINUTES

INGREDIENTS

3 tbsp olive oil
1 large onion, chopped
2 carrots, roughly chopped
2 sticks celery, chopped 1 clove garlic, finely chopped
2 large potatoes, peeled and chopped
2 bay leaves
2 x 400g can chopped tomatoes
1.5L / 3 pints / 6 ⅓ cups vegetable stock
Large handful green beans, chopped
50g / 1 ¾ oz / ¼ cup peas
Salt and pepper
Extra virgin olive oil
Parmesan, to serve

- Heat the oil in a large pan and sweat the onion, carrot and celery until beginning to soften.
- Add the potatoes, garlic and bay leaves, cook for 3 minutes, then add the tomatoes and stock and bring to a simmer.
- Cook for 10 minutes then add the beans and peas and leave to simmer for another 6-7 minutes until all is tender.
- Season well.
- This soup is best served a little warmer than room temperature with extra virgin olive oil drizzled over and a generous grating of Parmesan.

118

SERVES 4

Minestrone

PREPARATION TIME 20 MINUTES

COOKING TIME 1 ½ HOURS

···

INGREDIENTS

2 tbsp olive oil
50g / 1 ½ oz / ⅓ cup pancetta or smoked streaky bacon
1 onion, peeled and finely chopped
2 celery stalks, finely chopped
2 carrots, peeled and finely chopped
2 cloves garlic, finely chopped
2 potatoes, peeled and finely chopped
1.5 L / 2 ½ pints / 5 cups chicken stock
200g / 6 ½ oz / ¾ cup greens, such as cavolo nero or Savoy cabbage, finely sliced
100g / 3 ½ oz / ½ cup macaroni pasta
Salt and pepper
Parmesan cheese
Extra virgin olive oil

- Heat the oil in a large pan and fry the pancetta until the fat runs and it starts to turn golden.
- Add the vegetables in the order given, giving each one a good 5 minutes to cook without colouring, stirring regularly, before adding the next one.
- Pour in the stock and bring to a gently simmer, then cook very gently for about an hour.
- Add the greens and the pasta and cook for a further 30 minutes.
- Adjust the seasoning.
- Serve hot, warm or even room temperature sprinkled with Parmesan and drizzled with olive oil.

Tomato Minestrone

119

- For a more familiar flavour, add 2 x 400g can chopped tomatoes before the stock.

120

SERVES 6

Gazpacho

PREPARATION TIME 1 HOUR 20 MINUTES

···

INGREDIENTS

800g / 1 ¾ lb / 3 ⅓ cups ripe tomatoes
10cm / 4 inch piece of cucumber, diced
½ bunch spring onions (scallions), finely chopped
2 cloves garlic, crushed
½ red pepper, finely chopped
1 bunch basil
100ml / 3 ½ fl oz / ½ cup extra virgin olive oil
1-2 tbsp red wine vinegar
300ml ice-cold water
Salt and pepper

FOR THE GARNISH

2 spring onions (scallions), finely chopped
10cm / 4 in piece cucumber, finely chopped
Croutons

- Cut a cross in the skin at the bottom of the tomatoes, place in a bowl of boiling water and leave for 30 seconds. This should help the skins slip off easily.
- Halve the tomatoes, deseed and chop the flesh and place in a food processor.
- Add the rest of the ingredients, then whiz until smooth.
- Pour into a bowl and adjust the seasoning if necessary.
- Chill thoroughly for at least 1 hour before serving. Check the seasoning again – it may need more as chilling dulls flavours and serve with the garnishes.

Roasted Pepper Gazpacho

121

- Roast a whole red pepper until blacked then peel carefully and process with the rest of the ingredients. This will give a sweeter, richer result.

122
SERVES 4

Pumpkin Soup with Hazelnuts

- Sweat the onion and garlic in the butter in a large pan until golden and soft.
- Add the squash and cook for five minutes, then add the thyme and stock.
- Simmer for about 20 minutes or until the squash is tender.
- Allow to cool a little, remove the thyme stems then blitz in a food processor or with a hand-held blender until smooth.
- Season and stir in the cream. Set aside.
- Toast the hazelnuts under a hot grill for a few seconds only. Sprinkle on top of the hot soup and serve.

PREPARATION TIME 10 MINUTES

COOKING TIME 40 MINUTES

INGREDIENTS

30g / 1oz butter
1 onion, peeled and sliced
2 garlic cloves, sliced
1 large butternut squash or pumpkin, peeled, halved, deseeded and cut into chunks
2 sprigs thyme
1 litre chicken or vegetable stock
Salt and pepper
100ml / 3 ½ fl oz / ½ cup single cream
100ml / 3 ½ fl oz / ½ cup hazelnuts (cob nuts), chopped

Pumpkin Soup with Rosemary Walnuts

123

- Toss halved walnuts in 1 tbsp finely chopped rosemary and oil and toast for a few seconds. Serve on top of the soup.

124
SERVES 4

Carrot Soup with Beetroot Crisps

- Heat the butter in a pan and sweat the onion without colouring until softened.
- Add the carrots and potato and cook for a further five minutes until softened.
- Stir in the cumin and coriander then cover with the vegetable stock. Bring to the boil and simmer for about 10 minutes until the vegetables are completely soft.
- Liquidise in a blender until smooth, then return to the pan. Add the seasoning and stir in the parsley.
- For the crisps, preheat the oven to 200°C (180° fan/ 400F / gas 7.
- Finely slice the beetroot with a vegetable peeler or on a mandolin. Toss with oil and seasoning, then lay on a baking sheet.
- Bake in the oven for 4-7 minutes, checking frequently, until golden brown.
- Serve the soup hot decorated with the beetroot crisps.

PREPARATION TIME 15 MINUTES

COOKING TIME 30 MINUTES

INGREDIENTS

25g / 1 oz butter
1 onion, peeled and finely chopped
500g / 1 lb / 2 cups carrots, peeled and finely chopped
1 large potato, peeled and finely diced
2 tsp ground cumin
1 tsp ground coriander
1 L / 2 ¼ pints / 4 ¼ cups vegetable stock
Salt and pepper
2 tbsp parsley, chopped
1 beetroot, peeled
Olive oil

Spicy Carrot Soup

125

- Add 1 finely chopped red chilli to the onion and carrots for a spicy twist.

126

SERVES 4

Cream of Asparagus Soup

Asparagus and Watercress Soup

127

- Puree a small bag of watercress with the ingredients.

Asparagus Soup with Parmesan

128

- Sprinle a handful of Parmesan shavings on top of the soup before serving. .

Asparagus Soup with Herby Croutons

129

- Toast small cubes of slightly stale bread with finely chopped rosemary and a crushed clove garlic until golden, then scatter over the soup.

PREPARATION TIME 5 MINUTES

COOKING TIME 25-30 MINUTES

INGREDIENTS

450g /1 lb / 2 cups asparagus, woody ends trimmed off and reserved, the rest chopped
1 potato, peeled and chopped
1 L / 2 ¼ pints / 4 ¼ cups hot chicken or vegetable stock
30g / 1 oz butter
100ml / 3 ½ fl oz / ½ cup single cream
Salt and pepper
1 tbsp parsley, chopped

- Add the asparagus ends to the stock and bring to the boil, simmering for about 15 minutes, then strain.
- Heat the butter in a pan, add the remaining asparagus and potato and cook for five minutes.
- Stir in the the strained stock, bring to the boil and simmer for five to ten minutes until the vegetables are tender.
- Liquidise in a blender until smooth then return to the pan.
- Add the single cream and reheat gently without boiling. Season and stir through the parsley before serving.

130

SERVES 4

Minted Pea Soup

- Heat the butter in a pan and sweat the onion and garlic for about five minutes without colouring.
- Add the peas, potato, stock and half the mint and bring to the boil.
- Simmer for five to six minutes until the peas are tender.
- Remove and discard the herb stalks and liquidise the soup in a blender until completely smooth.
- Return to the heat, season and pour in the single cream. Do not allow to boil.
- Serve in bowls, garnishing with a little chopped mint.

PREPARATION TIME 5 MINUTES

COOKING TIME 10 MINUTES

INGREDIENTS

25g / 1 oz butter
1 onion, peeled and finely chopped
1 garlic clove, finely chopped
250g / 9 oz / 1 cup peas, fresh or frozen
1 large potato, peeled and chopped
500ml /1 pint / 2 cups chicken or vegetable stock
¼ bunch mint leaves, chopped
150ml / 5 fl oz / ⅔ cup single cream
Salt and pepper

Pea and Spinach Soup
131

- Blend 2 large handfuls of wilted baby spinach with the rest of the ingredients.

132

SERVES 4-6

Mushroom Soup

- Heat the butter in a large deep pan and sweat the onion without colouring for 5-10 minutes or until softened.
- Add the mushrooms and garlic and cook for a further 5 minutes or until the mushrooms have softened.
- Stir in the flour and cook out for a few minutes, or until the flour has turned a biscuit colour.
- Pour over the stock, add the parsley stalks and bring to the boil, stirring constantly.
- Reduce to a simmer and cook for 10-15 minutes. Remove from the heat and allow to cool a little.
- Liquidise the soup in batches then return to the pan. Add the seasoning and cream and reheat the soup gently without boiling.

PREPARATION TIME 10 MINUTES

COOKING TIME 40 MINUTES

INGREDIENTS

50g / 1 ¾ oz / ¼ cup unsalted butter
1 onion, peeled and finely chopped
500g / 1 lb / 2 cups flat or wild mushrooms, finely chopped
1 clove garlic, crushed
50g / 1 ¾ oz / ¼ cup plain (all purpose) flour
1 glass dry white wine or port
1 L / 2 ¼ pints / 4 ¼ cups chicken or vegetable stock
Salt and pepper
100ml / 3 ½ fl. oz / ½ cup double cream
½ bunch parsley, chopped plus stalks

Mushroom Soup with Cheese Croutons
133

- Finely grate 80g / 2 ½ oz Parmesan and mound into 6 circles on a baking sheet. Bake until golden, leave to cool and harden and serve with the soup.

134
SERVES 4-6

Lentil Soup with Roasted Hazelnuts

PREPARATION TIME 10 MINUTES

COOKING TIME 1 HOUR

INGREDIENTS

2 tbsp olive oil
1 onion, peeled and finely chopped
2 carrots, peeled and diced
2 sticks celery, finely chopped
1 clove garlic, finely chopped
1 tsp ground cumin
1 tsp ground coriander
175g / 6 oz / ¾ cup orange lentils
1 x 400g can chopped tomatoes
1.5 L / 3 pints / 6 ⅓ cups chicken
or vegetable stock
Salt and pepper
2 tbsp hazelnuts (cob nuts),
lightly crushed
½ bunch coriander (cilantro),
roughly chopped

- Heat the olive oil in a large pan and sweat the onion, carrot and celery until soft.
- Add the garlic, cook for 2 minutes, then add the lentils and spices.
- Pour in the tomatoes and stock, bring to a boil, then reduce the heat and simmer for 50-60 minutes until the lentils are completely soft.
- Meanwhile lightly toast the hazelnuts in a dry frying pan or under a grill for a few seconds – watch them like a hawk.
- If desired, whiz half the soup in a blender for a smoother texture, then return to the pan.
- Season well and stir through the parsley before serving.

Orange Lentil Soup with Chorizo | 135

- Serve with 100g / 3 ½ oz chopped fried chorizo.

136
SERVES 4

Sweet Potato Soup

PREPARATION TIME 10 MINUTES

COOKING TIME 40 MINUTES

INGREDIENTS

30g / 1oz butter
1 onion, peeled and sliced
2 cloves garlic, sliced
500g / 1lb/ 2 cups sweet potatoes,
peeled and cut into chunks
2 sprigs thyme
1 tsp garam masala
Pinch dried chilli flakes
1 L / 2 ¼ pints / 4 ¼ cups chicken
or vegetable stock
Salt and pepper
100ml / 3 ½ fl oz / ½ cup single cream

- Sweat the onion and garlic in the butter in a large pan until golden and soft.
- Add the potato and cook for five minutes, then add the thyme, spices and stock.
- Simmer for about 20 minutes or until the potatoes are tender.
- Allow to cool a little, remove the thyme stems then blitz in a food processor or with a hand-held blender until smooth.
- Season and stir in the cream. Serve hot.

Sweet Potato Soup with Prawns | 137

- 150g/ 5 oz small defrosted cooked prawns will enhance the sweetness.

138
SERVES 4

Fish Soup

Fish Soup with Aioli 139

- Serve with large spoonfuls of the aioli on page 26 as is traditional in France.

Fish Soup with Parmesan Croutons 140

- Thinly slice pieces of baguette and cover with a spoonful of mayonnaise or aioli and grated parmesan. Grill until melted then serve floating on the soup.

Spicy Fish Soup 141

- Stir in a tbsp of harissa or a little chilli paste to make this a winter warmer.

PREPARATION TIME 20 MINUTES

COOKING TIME 50 MINUTES

INGREDIENTS

2 tbsp olive oil
1 onion, peeled and finely chopped
3 sticks celery, finely chopped
4 cloves garlic, finely chopped
3 beef tomatoes or 6 vine tomatoes, chopped
500g /1 lb / 2 cups potatoes, peeled and cut into small chunks
2 bay leaves
1-1.5 L / 2 ¼ - 3 pints / 4 ¼ - 6 cups vegetable stock
Pinch saffron
1 kg / 2 lb / 4 cups fresh fish and shellfish, scaled, gutted and cut into large pieces
1 lemon, juiced
Handful parsley, chopped
Handful dill, chopped
Salt and pepper
Extra-virgin olive oil

- Heat the olive oil in a large casserole and gently sweat the onion, celery and garlic without colouring for about 10 minutes.
- Stir in the tomatoes and potatoes and cook for a further 3-5 minutes.
- Add the bay leaves, stock and saffron, stir and bring to the boil. Simmer for 15 minutes.
- Add the fish only and cook gently for a further 15 minutes.
- Add the shellfish and cook for five minutes or until the prawns have turned pink and mussels have opened.
- If there is too much liquid, remove the fish and shellfish and bring the liquor to the boil. Simmer for another 10 minutes or so to reduce, then add the fish back in.
- Squeeze in the lemon juice and stir in the herbs. Check the seasoning and serve with a drizzle of extra-virgin olive oil.

142

SERVES 4

Parsnip Soup with Pancetta

PREPARATION TIME 10 MINUTES

COOKING TIME 35 MINUTES

INGREDIENTS

2 tbsp butter
1 onion, peeled and chopped
2 cloves garlic, sliced
6 parsnips, peeled and chopped
2 tsp garam masala
1 red chilli, deseeded and finely chopped
1 L / 2 ¼ pints / 4 ¼ cups vegetable stock
Salt and pepper
4 slices pancetta

- Heat the butter in a pan and cook the onion until sweet and golden.
- Add the garlic and parsnips and cook for a few minutes, then add the spices and chilli.
- Pour over the stock, bring to the boil and simmer for 20 minutes or until the parsnip is tender.
- Liquidise the soup in batches and return to the pan. Season and reheat.
- Grill the pancetta until crisp then use to decorate the soup when served.

Parsnip Soup with Parmesan

143

- Omit the pancetta and shave over parmesan for an equally meaty but vegetarian substitute.

144

SERVES 4

Cream of Tomato Soup with Basil

PREPARATION TIME 5 MINUTES

COOKING TIME 35 MINUTES

INGREDIENTS

500g / 1 lb / 2 cups ripe tomatoes, halved
Olive oil
Salt and pepper
Rosemary sprigs
4 cloves garlic
1 L / 2 ¼ pints / 4 ¼ cups vegetable stock
100ml / 3 ½ fl oz / ½ cup double cream
1 bunch basil leaves plus stalks

- Preheat the oven to 200°C (180° fan) / 400F / gas 7.
- Tip the tomatoes into a roasting tin and drizzle with oil. Season and tuck the rosemary and garlic cloves in and around.
- Roast in the oven until blackened and tender – about 25 minutes.
- Remove the rosemary sprigs and discard. Squeeze the garlic flesh from the skins into a blender and carefully tip in the tomatoes and their juices – you may need to do this in 2 batches – and the basil stalks.
- Add the stock and blend until smooth.
- Return the soup to a pan and heat through with the cream. Heat without boiling, then serve decorate with torn basil leaves.

Spicy Tomato Soup

145

- Stir in 1 tsp ground cumin and a large pinch dried chilli flakes for warming spice.

SERVES 4

Chicken, Vegetable & Basil Soup

- Heat the oil in a large pan and cook the onion, carrot and celery until softened.
- Add the garlic and potatoes and cook for 3 minutes.
- Add the chicken, turning the heat up a little and cook until golden in patches.
- Pour over the stock, add the bouquet garni and simmer gently for about 15 minutes.
- Add the peas and cook for 5 minutes.
- Season, stir in the basil and serve.

PREPARATION TIME 15 MINUTES

COOKING TIME 35 MINUTES

INGREDIENTS

2 tbsp olive oil
1 onion, peeled and finely sliced
2 sticks celery, finely chopped
2 carrots, peeled and finely chopped
1 clove garlic, crushed
2 floury potatoes, peeled and diced
4 chicken thighs, cut into fine strips
1 L / 2 ¼ pints / 4 ¼ cups chicken stock
1 bouquet garni
100g / 3 ½ oz / ½ cup frozen peas
½ bunch basil leaves
Salt and pepper

Chicken and Vegetable Noodle Soup

147

- Omit the potatoes, and instead cook noodles in the finished soup with the peas.

SERVES 4

Chinese Noodle Soup

- Heat the oil in a large pan and sweat the onion until translucent.
- Add the garlic, chilli slices and ginger and cook for 2 minutes, then add the remaining vegetables and cook for a few minutes.
- Pour over the stock and soy sauce and simmer for 10 minutes.
- Add the noodles and cook for about 5 minutes, until tender, then add the beansprouts.
- Adjust the seasoning and add the chilli sauce if liked.
- Serve sprinkled with fresh coriander, spring onions and a few drops of sesame oil. Add the lime slices to garnish.

PREPARATION TIME 10 MINUTES

COOKING TIME 25 MINUTES

INGREDIENTS

2 tbsp vegetable oil
1 onion, peeled and finely sliced
2 cloves garlic, finely sliced
1cm piece fresh ginger, finely sliced
2 carrots, peeled and sliced
1 courgette (zucchini), cut into matchsticks
1 red pepper, deseeded and sliced
1 yellow pepper, deseeded and sliced
1.5L / 3 pints / 6 ⅓ cups chicken or vegetable stock
3 tbsp soy sauce
2 nests dried noodles
Handful bean sprouts
Chilli sauce
Salt and pepper
2 tbsp coriander (cilantro), chopped
Sesame oil
1 red chilli, finely sliced into rings
Slices of lime, to garnish
2 spring onions, sliced diagonally

Noodle Soup with Prawns

149

- Add prawns at the same time as the onion and fry until cooked through, for a more substantial soup.

150

SERVES 6

French Onion Soup

PREPARATION TIME 15 MINUTES

COOKING TIME 1 HOUR 35 MINUTES

INGREDIENTS

60g / 2 oz / ¼ cup butter
1 tbsp olive oil
700g / 1 ½ lb / 3 cups onions, peeled and thinly sliced
1 tsp sugar
2 cloves garlic, crushed
1 tbsp plain (all purpose) flour
200ml / 7 fl oz / ¾ cup dry white wine
1.5L / 3 pints / 6 ⅓ cups beef stock
1 bay leaf
1 small glass Madeira or dry sherry

TO SERVE
6 slices French baguette
Gruyere cheese, grated

- Heat the butter and oil till foaming, then add the onions. Cook very slowly over a low heat for at least 30 minutes until deep golden. This is where you create the flavour, so ensure they are very sweet and deep gold.
- Add the sugar to caramelise, then stir in the garlic.
- Stir in the flour to make a paste, then pour in the wine. Stir until thickened then add the stock and bay leaf.
- Simmer for 1 hour very gently. Add the Madeira or sherry at the end of cooking.
- To serve, grill the bread slices loaded with cheese and launch them onto the soup.

Onion and Wild Mushroom Soup   151

- A few chopped ried mushrooms soaked in the hot beef stock before hand will add a punch of flavour.

152

SERVES 4

Leek & Potato Soup

PREPARATION TIME 10 MINUTES

COOKING TIME 40 MINUTES

INGREDIENTS

60g / 2 oz / ¼ cup butter
4 leeks, green ends discarded and finely sliced
2 floury potatoes, peeled and diced
2 sprigs thyme
850ml / 1 ½ pints / 3 ½ cups chicken or vegetable stock
250ml / 9 fl oz / 1 cup milk
Salt and white pepper
½ bunch chives, chopped

- In a large pan melt the butter and when foaming add the leeks. Cook gently over a low heat until soft and slithery.
- Add the potatoes and thyme and cook for a couple of minutes, then add the stock and milk, bring to a simmer and cook gently for 20-25 minutes, until the potatoes are soft.
- Remove the thyme stalks and whiz in a blender until smooth.
- Return to the heat and reheat, seasoning carefully. Serve with chives sprinkled on top.

Vichysoisse   153
(Cold Leek & Potato Soup)

- Serve very chilled for a refreshing summer starter.

154

SERVES 4

Cream of Asparagus Soup with Bacon

- Add the asparagus ends to the stock and bring to the boil, simmering for about 15 minutes, then strain.
- Heat the butter in a pan, add the remaining asparagus and potato and cook for five minutes.
- Stir in the the strained stock, bring to the boil and simmer for five to ten minutes until the vegetables are tender.
- Liquidise in a blender until smooth then return to the pan.
- Meanwhile grill the bacon until crisp and snap into shards.
- Add the single cream and reheat gently without boiling. Season and stir through the parsley before serving. Decorate with crisp bacon.

PREPARATION TIME 5 MINUTES

COOKING TIME 25-30 MINUTES

INGREDIENTS

450g /1 lb / 2 cups asparagus, woody ends trimmed off and reserved, the rest chopped
1 potato, peeled and chopped
1 L / 2 ¼ pints / 4 ¼ cups hot chicken or vegetable stock
30g / 1 oz butter
100ml / 3 ½ fl oz / ½ cup single cream
Salt and pepper
1 tbsp parsley, chopped
4 rashers smoked streaky bacon

Pea Gazpacho with Stilton

155

SERVES 4

PREPARATION TIME 5 MINUTES
+ CHILLING TIME

COOKING TIME 20 MINUTES

INGREDIENTS

25g / 1 oz butter
½ bunch spring onions (scallions), finely chopped

750g / 1 ¾ lb / 3 cups frozen peas
1 L / 2 ¼ pints / 4 ¼ cups vegetable or chicken stock
2-3 tbsp crème fraîche
Salt and pepper
60g / 2 oz Stilton cheese, crumbled

- Heat the butter in a pan and cook the spring onions gently.
- Add the peas and stock and cook for 10-15 minutes until soft.
- Liquidise in batches, then stir in the crème fraîche and season.
- Chill thoroughly for at least 1 hour before serving, then adjust the seasoning if necessary.
- Serve with stilton crumbled on top.

Broccoli Soup with Feta

156

SERVES 4

PREPARATION TIME 15 MINUTES

COOKING TIME 30 MINUTES

INGREDIENTS

25g / 1 oz butter
1 onion, peeled and finely chopped
1 clove garlic, finely chopped
1 stick celery, finely chopped

2 anchovy fillets
1 potato, peeled and chopped
1 head of broccoli, cut into florets
1 L / 2 ¼ pints / 4 ¼ cups vegetable stock
Salt and pepper
100ml/ 3 ½ fl oz / ½ cup single cream
100g / 3 ½ oz / ½ cup feta cheese, crumbled
Extra virgin olive oil

- Melt the butter in a pan and sweat the onion, garlic and celery for a few minutes until soft.
- Add the anchovies, potato and broccoli and cook for a few minutes, then pour over the stock.
- Cook at a simmer for about 20 minutes until the vegetables are soft.
- Liquidise in batches then return to the pan. Pour in the cream, season well and reheat gently.
- Serve with the feta crumbled on top and a drizzle of oil.

157

SERVES 4

Courgette Soup

PREPARATION TIME 15 MINUTES

COOKING TIME 30-40 MINUTES

INGREDIENTS

2 tbsp olive oil
1 onion, peeled and finely chopped
2 cloves garlic, finely chopped
1 kg / 2 ¼ lb / 4 ¼ cups courgettes
(zucchini), chopped
4 sprigs thyme
1 L / 2 ¼ pints / 4 ¼ cups chicken
or vegetable stock
Salt and pepper
Squeeze of lemon juice (optional)
60ml / 2 oz / ¼ cup single cream

- Heat the oil in a large pan and sweat the onion until softened and translucent.
- Add the garlic, courgettes and thyme and cook very slowly over a low heat until the courgettes have darkened to a khaki colour and are very soft.
- Add the stock and simmer for 20 minutes.
- Liquidise ⅔ of the soup, then return to the pan, reheat and season well. Add the lemon juice if you think it needs it.
- Stir in the cream, heat gently and serve.

Chunky Courgette Soup | 158

- Add a peeled, diced potato with the courgette, then when all is tender, roughly mash with a potato masher to keep the texture.

159

SERVES 4

Tomato, Pepper and Bean Soup

PREPARATION TIME 15 MINUTES

COOKING TIME 40 MINUTES

INGREDIENTS

4 tbsp olive oil
1 onion, peeled and finely sliced
2 cloves garlic, finely sliced
2 red peppers, deseeded and finely
sliced
2 yellow peppers, deseeded and
finely sliced
1 tbsp tomato puree
2 x 400g can chopped tomatoes
750ml / 1 ⅓ pints / 3 cups chicken or
vegetable stock
2 x 400g can cannellini beans,
drained
1 sprig rosemary
2 sprigs thyme
1 bay leaf
Salt and pepper
Extra virgin olive oil

- Heat the oil in a pan and cook the onion until golden.
- Add the garlic and peppers and cook until softened.
- Stir through the tomato puree and cook out for 2 minutes, then add the tomatoes, stock and beans. Throw in the herbs, bring to a simmer and cook for at least 20 minutes until rich and slightly thickened.
- If desired, crush the beans slightly with a potato masher to thicken the soup. Season well.
- Serve in deep bowls drizzled with extra virgin olive oil.

Tomato, Pepper and Bean Soup | 160
with Cured Sausage or Ham

- Stir in chunks of salami or slivers of cured ham for extra meaty flavour.

SERVES 4

Noodle Vegetable Broth

Pasta Vegetable Broth 〔162〕

- Instead of noodles, add the same amount of tiny-shaped pasta and cook in the same manner.

Noodle Squash Soup 〔163〕

- Roast cubed butternut squash in an oven until tender, then add to the soup.

Chicken and Vegetable Broth 〔164〕

- Add thinly sliced chicken breast at te same time as cooking the onion and garlic and heat until cooked through.

PREPARATION TIME 10 MINUTES

COOKING TIME 10 MINUTES

INGREDIENTS

1 tbsp groundnut oil
1 tsp sesame oil
1 red onion, peeled and finely sliced
2 cloves garlic, finely sliced
1cm piece fresh ginger, finely sliced
1 red chilli, deseeded (optional) and finely chopped
1 red pepper, deseeded and finely sliced
Handful green beans, topped and tailed
1 L / 2 ¼ pints / 4 ¼ cups chicken or vegetable stock
2 nests dried noodles
2 tbsp soy sauce
1 bunch coriander (cilantro), chopped
1 lime, juiced

- Heat the oils in a pan and sweat the onion, garlic and ginger until translucent.
- Add the chilli and vegetables and cook gently for 5 minutes or until starting to soften.
- Pour in the stock, simmer and add the noodles. Cook according to packet instructions.
- Season with the soy sauce and lime juice and sprinkle coriander over to serve.

PASTA

165

SERVES 4

Tagliatelle Carbonara

- Cook the pasta in boiling salted water according to packet instructions.
- Heat the butter in a pan and fry the pancetta until golden.
- Whisk the egg yolks and Parmesan into the cream.
- Drain the pasta, return to the pan and, working quickly, scrape the pancetta and butter into the pan and toss.
- Toss off the heat with the egg/cream mixture then serve immediately.

PREPARATION TIME 5 MINUTES

COOKING TIME 12 MINUTES

INGREDIENTS

500g / 1lb / 2 cups tagliatelle
2 tbsp butter
12 slices pancetta or smoked streaky bacon, chopped
4 egg yolks
100ml / 3 ½ fl oz / ½ cup double cream
2 tbsp Parmesan, grated

166

SERVES 4

Fresh Pasta Dough

PREPARATION TIME 1 HOUR

COOKING TIME 2 MINUTES

INGREDIENTS

600g / 1 lb 6 oz / 2 ½ cups '00' flour
6 eggs or 12 egg yolks

- Tip the flour into a bowl, make a well in the centre and crack the eggs into it.
- Using a fork, beat the eggs till smooth then mix together with the flour as much as you can.
- Flour your hands and bring the dough together into a ball.
- Remove from the bowl and knead until the dough is smooth and elastic. Cover with clingfilm and leave to rest in the refrigerator for 30 minutes.
- Roll the pasta out with a pasta machine to its thinnest setting.
- Cut vertically along the strip of dough to make lasagne sheets. Set aside, lightly dusted with flour until ready to use.

167

SERVES 4

Spaghetti Bolognese

PREPARATION TIME 15 MINUTES

COOKING TIME 40 MINUTES

INGREDIENTS

500g / 1 lb / 2 cups spaghetti
3 tbsp olive oil
2 onions, peeled and finely chopped
2 cloves garlic, chopped
1 pack pancetta or bacon lardons

500g / 1 lb / 2 cups minced beef
100g / 3 ½ oz / ½ cup chicken livers, finely chopped
1 glass dry white wine
2 x 400g can chopped tomatoes
4 tbsp double cream
100g / 3 ½ oz / ½ cup Parmesan, grated
1 bunch parsley, chopped
Salt and pepper

- Heat the oil in a pan and sweat the onion and garlic without colouring.
- Add the pancetta and fry until the fat runs.
- Add the mince and break it up with a wooden spoon, stirring frequently until browned.
- Add the chicken livers and cook until browned all over.
- Season, then add the wine, bubble up, then add the tomatoes. Partially cover and simmer for 20 minutes.
- Meanwhile cook the pasta in boiling salted water according to packet instructions. Drain and toss with a little oil.
- Stir the cream and parsley through the sauce, then toss the pasta in the sauce.

SERVES 4

Spiral Pasta with Tricolore Sauce

PREPARATION TIME 5 MINUTES

COOKING TIME 12 MINUTES

INGREDIENTS

500g / 1 lb / 2 cups spirali pasta
2 tbsp olive oil
1 clove garlic, finely sliced
2 x 400g can plum tomatoes
1 bunch basil
1 ball mozzarella
2 tbsp pitted black olives, chopped
Salt and pepper

- Cook the pasta in boiling salted water according to packet instructions.
- Meanwhile heat the olive oil in a pan until quite hot, throw in the garlic and the whole tomatoes without the juice. Cover with a lid as it will spit.
- When the spitting dies down, remove the lid and break down the tomatoes. Stir in the basil, season and remove from the heat.
- Drain the pasta and toss with the sauce.
- Stir in chunks of mozzarella and the chopped olives and serve.

Tricolore Pasta with Basil Oil 169

- Instead of stirring the basil into the sauce, simply whizz in a blender with a few tbsp olive oil until smooth then drizzle over the dish.

SERVES 6

Lasagne Bolognese

PREPARATION TIME 2 HOURS

COOKING TIME 40 MINUTES

INGREDIENTS

12 sheets of lasagne (see page 51)
4 tbsp of Parmesan cheese

FOR THE BOLOGNESE SAUCE
1 tbsp butter
Olive oil
1 onion, peeled and finely chopped
2 celery stalks, finely chopped
2 cloves garlic, finely chopped
2 carrots, finely chopped
120g / 4 oz / ½ cup pancetta, cubed
500g / 1 lb minced beef
120ml / 4 fl oz / ½ cup white wine
2 x 400g can chopped tomatoes
450ml / 1 pint / 2 cups beef stock
Salt and pepper

FOR THE BÉCHAMEL SAUCE
See page 31.

- Make the Bolognese sauce: heat the butter with a little oil in a pan and add the finely chopped vegetables, the carrots and pancetta and cook for about 10 minutes.
- Add the beef, breaking it up with a wooden spoon until cooked through. Season.
- Add the wine and stir for about 5 minutes until it has been absorbed. Add the tomatoes and half the stock and then lower the heat. Partially cover the pan and leave to simmer for about 1 ½ - 2 hours, adding more stock as it absorbs. Don't let it get too thick.
- Meanwhile, make the béchamel sauce (see page 31).
- Preheat the oven to 190°C / 375F / gas 5. Spread a third of the Bolognese sauce in the bottom of a baking dish, then a quarter of the béchamel, then 4 sheets of lasagne.
- Repeat twice more, then cover the top layer of lasagne with béchamel and sprinkle over the parmesan.
- Bake in the oven for about 40 minutes.

Lasagne Bolognese with Spinach 171

- Wilt 3 large handfuls of spinach and spread over the pasta before adding the sauce.

172
SERVES 4

Spinach & Ricotta Cannelloni

- Preheat the oven to 180°C / 350F / gas 5.
- Make the filling: heat the butter in a large pan with a little oil and cook the garlic for 2 minutes. Add the spinach and nutmeg and stir until wilted.
- Spoon into a sieve and press down firmly with a wooden spoon to extract as much liquid as possible. Once done, finely chop the spinach and leave to cool in a bowl.
- Stir in the ricotta, Parmesan and seasoning.
- Spoon into the tubes or onto the lasagne sheets and roll up to make 12 cylinders, then lay in a greased baking dish.
- Make the tomato sauce: heat the oil in a pan and add the garlic and tomatoes. Leave to simmer, topped up with ½ a can of water, for 10 minutes, then add the basil.
- Spoon over the cannelloni and bake for around 15 minutes until bubbling.

Spinach Mascarpone Cannelloni 173

- Substitute mascarpone for the ricotta for a creamier sauce, adding 2 tbsp grated Parmesan for flavour.

PREPARATION TIME 40 MINUTES

COOKING TIME 15 MINUTES

INGREDIENTS

12 cannelloni tubes or 12 sheets lasagne (see page 51)

FOR THE FILLING
2 tbsp butter
Olive oil
2 cloves garlic, chopped
¼ nutmeg, grated
1 kg / 2 lb / 4 ½ cups spinach leaves
400g / 13 ½ oz / 1 ½ cups ricotta
2 tbsp Parmesan, grated
Salt and pepper

FOR THE TOMATO SAUCE
2 tbsp olive oil
1 clove garlic, chopped
2 x 400g can chopped tomatoes
½ bunch basil, chopped

174
SERVES 4

Meat Cannelloni

- Preheat the oven to 190°C / 375F / gas 5.
- Make the filling: heat the butter with a little oil and cook the vegetables until soft.
- Add the beef and pork break it down with a wooden spoon, stirring until it is cooked through.
- Add the white wine and season and allow the wine to evaporate.
- Use a teaspoon to fill the cannelloni tubes with the beef mixture then lay in a greased baking dish.
- Lay the mozzarella slices over the pasta and smear with the tomato puree or passata.
- Bake in the oven for 10-15 minutes until bubbling and golden.

Meat Cannelloni with Tomato Sauce 175

- Before adding the mozzarella, top with tomato sauce, as in the recipe above.

PREPARATION TIME 20 MINUTES

COOKING TIME 10-15 MINUTES

INGREDIENTS

12 cannelloni tubes or 12 sheets of lasagne (see page 51)
2 balls mozzarella, sliced

FOR THE FILLING
1 tbsp butter
Olive oil
1 onion, peeled and finely chopped
2 celery stalks, finely chopped
2 cloves garlic, finely chopped
2 carrots, finely chopped
250g / ½ lb minced beef
250g / ½ lb minced pork
120ml / 4 fl oz / ½ cup dry white wine
3 tbsp tomato puree or passata
Salt and pepper

SERVES 2

Tortelloni in Creamy Tomato Sauce

Tortelloni in Tomato Sauce 177

- Omit the mascarpone if you're counting calories.

Tortelloni with Tomato Pancetta Sauce 178

- Add 50g 1 ¾ oz cubed pancetta to the pan with the onion.

Tortelloni with Tomato Mozzarella Sauce 179

- Stirring cubed mozzarella into the sauce just before serving makes it deliciously oozing and stringy.

PREPARATION TIME 5 MINUTES

COOKING TIME 15 MINUTES

INGREDIENTS

1 x pack fresh-made tortelloni, such as ham and cheese or spinach and ricotta

FOR THE SAUCE
2 tbsp olive oil
1 onion, finely chopped
1 clove garlic, finely chopped
1 x 400g can chopped tomatoes
Handful thyme leaves
100ml / 3 ½ oz / ½ cup mascarpone
Salt and pepper

- Heat the oil in a pan and sweat the onion and garlic without colouring.
- Add the tomatoes and a splash of water and simmer for 10 minutes, then stir in the thyme leaves and mascarpone and season.
- Cook the pasta in boiling salted water according to packet instructions. Drain.
- Toss the pasta with the sauce and serve.

Penne with Ham & Cream Sauce

180

SERVES 4

- Cook the pasta in boiling salted water according to packet instructions.
- Drain, hiving off a cupful of the cooking water and reserve.
- Meanwhile heat the butter in a pan and sweat the onion and garlic till translucent.
- Add the chopped ham and cream, season and add a little grated nutmeg.
- Toss the pasta into the cream sauce with a little of the cooking water to loosen.
- Serve sprinkled with parsley and parmesan.

PREPARATION TIME 5 MINUTES

COOKING TIME 15-20 MINUTES

INGREDIENTS

500g / 1 lb / 2 cups penne pasta
1 tbsp butter
½ onion, peeled and finely chopped
1 clove garlic, finely sliced
3 thick slices ham, chopped
300ml / 10 fl oz / 1 ¼ cups double cream
Salt and pepper
Grated nutmeg
½ bunch parsley, chopped
Parmesan, grated

Penne with Mushroom Sauce

181

- For meaty flavour without the ham, simply stir in a large handful quartered chestnut mushrooms with the butter until golden.

Papardelle in Creamy Chive Sauce

182

SERVES 4

- Cook the pasta in boiling salted water according to packet instructions.
- Drain thoroughly after hiving off a cupful of the cooking water.
- Heat the mascarpone in a pan with the chives, a little lemon juice and seasoning.
- Add the pasta and a little cooking water to loosen, toss well and serve.

PREPARATION TIME 5 MINUTES

COOKING TIME 10 MINUTES

INGREDIENTS

400g / 13 ½ oz / 1 ½ cups pappardelle pasta
225g / 8 oz / 1 cup mascarpone
½ bunch chives, chopped
Squeeze of lemon juice
Salt and pepper

Pappardelle with Creamy Cheese Chive Sauce

183

- Stir in 50g / 1 ¾ oz grated gruyere or parmesan.

184

SERVES 4

Asparagus Tagliatelle

PREPARATION TIME 10 MINUTES

COOKING TIME 12 MINUTES

INGREDIENTS

500g / 1 lb / 2 cups tagliatelle pasta
½ bunch asparagus, woody ends
snapped off and cut into short
lengths
60g / 2 oz / ¼ cup butter
1 clove garlic, sliced
¼ lemon, grated zest
Salt and pepper

- Cook the pasta in boiling salted water according to packet instructions.
- Add the asparagus 3 minutes before the end of the cooking time.
- Meanwhile heat the butter and garlic in a pan, then add the zest and toss together.
- Drain the pasta, reserving a little of the water and toss with the butter sauce, adding 1-2 tbsp of reserved cooking water to amalgamate the sauce.
- Season and serve.

Asparagus and Broad Bean Tagliatelle

 185

- Add 60g / 2 oz double podded cooked broad beans to the pasta.

186

SERVES 4-6

Tagliatelle with Meatballs

PREPARATION TIME 50 MINUTES

COOKING TIME 30 MINUTES

INGREDIENTS

350g / 12 oz / 1 ⅓ cups tagliatelle
Parmesan, grated to serve

FOR THE MEATBALLS
400g / 14 oz / 1 ½ cups minced beef
1 egg
2 tbsp parsley, chopped
1 clove garlic, crushed
½ lemon, grated zest
Salt and pepper
1 thick slice of white bread, crusts
removed soaked in 2 tbsp milk
3 tbsp olive oil
1 x 400g can chopped tomatoes
400ml / 14 fl oz / 1 ½ cups beef stock
1 tsp sugar

- Place the meat in a large bowl with the egg, garlic, lemon zest and 1 tbsp parsley and season.
- Mulch the bread in your fingers and crumble into the mix. Mix everything together with your hands to become smooth and sticky.
- Roll into small walnut-sized balls with cold wet hands, place on a tray and chill for 30 minutes.
- Heat the oil in a pan and fry the meatballs in batches until brown.
- Add the tomatoes and stock, then add the sugar and season and bring to the boil. Lower the heat and simmer for about 20 minutes.
- Meanwhile cook the pasta in boiling salted water according to packet instructions.
- Drain and tip into a large bowl. Pour the sauce over the pasta, sprinkle over the parsley and Parmesan and serve.

Tagliatelle with Lamb Meatballs

187

- Substitute minced lamb for the beef and add ½ tsp ground cinnamon and 1 tsp ground cumin to the mixture.

188

SERVES 4

Seafood Tagliatelle

Tagliatelle with Squid

189

- Try adding thawed squid rings in with the seafood.

Tagliatelle with Dill Aioli

190

- Stir chopped dill into the aioli recipe on P26 and serve on top of the seafood tagliatelle.

Seafood Tagliatelle a Bianco

191

- Omit the canned tomatoes, but use a glass of dry white wine and reduce by a third before adding the seafood and cooking juices.

PREPARATION TIME 15 MINUTES

COOKING TIME 15-20 MINUTES

INGREDIENTS

500g / 1 lb / 2 cups tagliatelle
2 tbsp olive oil
1 shallot, finely chopped
2 cloves garlic, finely chopped
Pinch dried chilli flakes
1 x 400g can tomatoes
2 sprigs thyme
200g / 7 oz / ¾ cup raw prawns (shrimp), shelled
8 scallops, sliced in half horizontally
250g / 9 oz / 1 cup mussels, cleaned
Salt and pepper

- Cook the pasta in boiling salted water according to packet instructions. Drain the pasta and toss with a little oil.
- Heat the oil in a pan and sweat the shallot and garlic with chilli flakes without colouring.
- Add the tomatoes with a splash of water and leave to simmer for 10 minutes.
- Meanwhile, cook the mussels in a separate pan with a splash of water for about 5 minutes or until they have opened. Discard any that remain closed.
- Drain over a bowl to catch the cooking juices. Remove the meat from the mussels once cool.
- Add the thyme, prawns and scallops to the tomato mixture and leave to cook until the prawns are pink and the scallops just opaque.
- Add the mussels and a little of their cooking liquor and season. Toss the tagliatelle through the sauce and serve.

192

SERVES 6

Conchiglie stuffed with Crab & Pesto

PREPARATION TIME 20 MINUTES

COOKING TIME 20 MINUTES

INGREDIENTS

1 kg / 2 lb / 4 cups giant conchiglie shells
300g / 10 oz / 1 ¼ cups crabmeat
2 large bunches basil, chopped
75g / 3 oz / ⅓ cup pine nuts
5 cloves garlic, chopped
Extra virgin olive oil
3 tomatoes, finely chopped
100ml / 3 ½ fl oz / ½ cup vegetable stock
Salt and pepper

- Cook the pasta in boiling salted water according to packet instructions. Drain and toss with olive oil.
- Place the basil, garlic and pine nuts in a pestle and mortar and crush to make a paste then pour in enough oil to loosen.
- Add the crab and tomatoes to the pesto and mix gently. Season.
- Preheat the oven to 150°C / 300F / gas 2.
- Stuff the pasta shells with the pesto mixture and place in a buttered baking dish. Pour the stock into the bottom of the dish and cover with foil.
- Bake for 10 minutes then serve.

Conchiglie Stuffed with Prawns and Pesto

193

- Use the same amount of cooked chopped prawns.

194

SERVES 4

Macaroni Cheese

PREPARATION TIME 15 MINUTES

COOKING TIME 25 MINUTES

INGREDIENTS

2 tbsp butter
2 tbsp plain (all purpose) flour
500ml / 1 pint / 2 cups milk
1 bay leaf
1 tsp mustard powder
Pinch Cayenne
Grated nutmeg
150g / 5 oz / ⅔ cup strong Cheddar cheese, grated
Salt and pepper
320g / 11 oz / 1¼ cups macaroni pasta

- Preheat the oven to 180°C (160° fan) / 350F / gas 4.
- Melt the butter in a pan, add the flour and stir to form a paste. Cook out for a couple of minutes, then gradually whisk in the milk to form a smooth sauce.
- Stir in the seasonings and ⅔ of the cheese and simmer very gently for 10-15 minutes to cook out any traces of flour.
- Cook the pasta in boiling salted water according to packet instructions. Drain thoroughly, retaining a little of the cooking water.
- Tip the pasta into 4 individual ramekins and cover with the cheese sauce, adding a little of the cooking water to each to loosen.
- Scatter over the remaining cheese and bake for 20-25 minutes until bubbling and golden.

Macaroni Cheese with Tomatoes

195

- Slice 4 ripe tomatoes and lay in rows over the top of the macaroni. Sprinkle with a little dried oregano and sugar and bake as above.

196

SERVES 4

Farfalle with Sausage and Vegetables

- Cook the pasta in boiling salted water according to packet instructions.
- Drain thoroughly, hiving off a cupful of cooking water to set aside.
- Meanwhile heat the oil in a pan and cook the sausages until starting to turn golden.
- Add the peppers and courgettes and stir until softened and golden. Add the thyme.
- Add a little cooking water to emulsify and form a sauce then toss in the pasta and mix well.
- Serve hot.

PREPARATION TIME 10 MINUTES

COOKING TIME 15 MINUTES

INGREDIENTS

320g / 11 oz / 1 ¼ cups farfalle pasta
2 tbsp olive oil
4 Italian-style sausages, cut into chunks
2 red peppers, deseeded and finely sliced
1 courgette (zucchini), finely diced
Few sprigs thyme
Salt and pepper

197

SERVES 4

Macaroni with Olives & Tomatoes

PREPARATION TIME 10 MINUTES

COOKING TIME 12 MINUTES

INGREDIENTS

500g / 1 lb / 2 cups macaroni pasta
300g / 10 oz / 1 ¼ cups cherry tomatoes, halved
Handful black olives, stoned and halved
½ bunch parsley, chopped
½ bunch thyme leaves
1 tsp dried oregano or fresh marjoram
Salt and pepper
Extra virgin olive oil

- Cook the pasta in boiling salted water according to packet instructions.
- Heat 4 tbsp olive oil in a pan and cook the cherry tomatoes until softened and collapsing.
- Add the olives and herbs.
- Drain the pasta, hiving off a cupful of cooking water.
- Toss with the tomato sauce, adding a little cooking water to loosen. Season and drizzle with extra virgin olive oil to serve.

198

SERVES 4

Tortellini in Brodo

PREPARATION TIME 5 MINUTES

COOKING TIME 5 MINUTES

INGREDIENTS

400g / 14 oz / 1 ½ cups ready-made tortellini, such as spinach and ricotta or wild mushroom
750ml / 1 ⅓ pints / 3 cups strong chicken or beef stock
½ bunch parsley
½ lemon, grated zest
Parmesan, grated
Extra virgin olive oil

- Cook the pasta in the stock until it rises to the surface and is cooked – about 3-5 minutes.
- Ladle into bowls and scatter with parsley and lemon zest, then grate over Parmesan and drizzle with oil.

Spaghetti with Red Pesto

Spaghetti with Green Pesto

200

- Make the green pesto sauce as on page 23 and use as above.

Spaghetti with Red Pesto Mascarpone Sauce

201

- Stir 3 tbsp mascarpone into the sauce for a creamy result.

Spaghetti Tricolore

202

- For a real shot of colour, stir wilted spinach through the spaghetti before topping with the pesto.

PREPARATION TIME 5 MINUTES

COOKING TIME 10 MINUTES

....

INGREDIENTS

500g / 1 lb / 2 cups spaghetti
Parmesan, grated to serve

FOR THE PESTO SAUCE

Small handful pine nuts
1 clove garlic, peeled and chopped
250g / 9 oz / 1 cup sun-dried or demi-sec tomatoes, drained
½ red chilli, deseeded and finely chopped
2 tbsp parsley, chopped
2 tbsp Parmesan, grated
Extra virgin olive oil

- Cook the pasta in boiling salted water according to packet instructions. Drain, reserving a little of the cooking water.
- Make the pesto sauce: Whiz all of the ingredients in a food processor until you have a rough paste or pound in a pestle and mortar. Drizzle in enough oil to make a loose sauce.
- Toss the pasta in the pesto, loosening with a little cooking water.
- Serve with extra Parmesan.

203
SERVES 4 Farfalle with Summer Vegetables

- Cook the pasta in boiling salted water according to packet instructions.
- 4 minutes before the end of cooking, add the peas. When cooked, drain, reserving a cupful of cooking water and toss with a little oil.
- Meanwhile drizzle the tomatoes with oil, toss with the garlic and seasoning and leave to macerate.
- Heat the oil in a pan and quickly cook the courgette until golden and tender.
- Toss the hot pasta with the peas, macerated tomatoes and courgette and a little reserved cooking water and top with pesto to serve.

PREPARATION TIME 10 MINUTES

COOKING TIME 12-15 MINUTES

INGREDIENTS

500g / 1lb/ 2 cups farfalle pasta
100g / 3 ½ oz / ½ cup peas
16 ripe cherry tomatoes, halved
½ clove garlic, crushed
Extra virgin olive oil
Salt and pepper
2 tbsp olive oil
1 courgette (zucchini), finely diced
4 tbsp pesto

Farfalle with Winter Vegetables 204

- Use shredded savoy cabbage or cavolo nero in place of the peas and courgette.

205
SERVES 4 Gnocchi in Tomato Sauce with Basil

- Boil the potatoes whole and unpeeled in boiling salted water for at least 25 minutes until completely tender.
- Drain and mash thoroughly.
- Heat the oil in a pan and fry the garlic gently, then add the tomatoes with a splash of water. Simmer for 10 minutes, then season and stir in the basil.
- Tip the cooled potatoes into a bowl and work in the flour, egg, a pinch of salt and nutmeg until you have a smooth dough. Cut the dough in half and roll out to make 2 fat sausages.
- Cut into pieces about 3cm long and press down gently with the tines of a fork to make the traditional indentations. Place on a floured baking sheet to cook when ready.
- To cook the gnocchi, bring a large pan of salted water to the boil then add the gnocchi. When they float to the top, they are ready. Remove and drain and toss with the tomato sauce and serve.

PREPARATION TIME 1 HOUR

COOKING TIME 5 MINUTES

INGREDIENTS

700g floury potatoes, such as Maris Piper
250g plain (all-purpose) flour
1 egg, beaten
Salt
Nutmeg

FOR THE TOMATO SAUCE

2 tbsp olive oil
1 clove garlic, finely chopped
1 x 400g can tomatoes
½ bunch basil, chopped
Salt and pepper

Baked Gnocchi with Tomato Sauce 206

- Tip into a gratin dish, top with slices of mozzarella and bake until melted and oozing.

207 SERVES 4

Fresh Gnocchi

PREPARATION TIME 45 MINUTES

COOKING TIME 5 MINUTES

INGREDIENTS

700g floury potatoes, such as Maris Piper
250g plain (all-purpose) flour
1 egg, beaten
Salt
Nutmeg

- Boil the potatoes whole and unpeeled in boiling salted water for at least 25 minutes until completely tender.
- Drain and mash thoroughly – or use a potato ricer – until completely smooth. Leave to cool.
- Tip the cooled potatoes into a bowl and work in the flour, egg, a pinch of salt and nutmeg until you have a smooth dough.
- Cut the dough in half and roll out to make 2 fat sausages.
- Cut into pieces about 3cm long and press down gently with the tines of a fork to make the traditional indentations. Place on a floured baking sheet to cook when ready.
- To cook the gnocchi, bring a large pan of salted water to the boil then add the gnocchi. When they float to the top, they are ready, so remove and drain on kitchen paper.

Spinach Gnocchi   208

- wilt 200g spinach and squeeze as dry as possible before stirring into the potato mixture. Proceed as above.

209 SERVES 4

Rigatoni with Aubergine & Goats' Cheese

PREPARATION TIME 1 HOUR

COOKING TIME 15 MINUTES

INGREDIENTS

500g / 1 lb / 2 cups rigatoni pasta
200ml / 7 fl oz / ¾ cup chicken or vegetable stock
Parmesan

FOR THE STUFFING

Olive oil
1 aubergine (eggplant), halved
1 tsp dried oregano
100g / 3 ½ oz / ½ cup ricotta
50g / 1 ¾ oz / ¼ cup goats' cheese
Small handful mint leaves
Salt and pepper

- Preheat the oven to 200°C (180° fan) / 400F / gas 6.
- Lay the halved aubergine in a roasting tin and toss generously with olive oil and oregano. Roast for at least 30 minutes until golden and collapsed.
- Remove from the tin and leave to cool for 10 minutes.
- Place in a food processor with the ricotta, goats' cheese and mint and process until smooth.
- Taste and season carefully.
- Cook the pasta in boiling salted water according to packet instructions. Drain.
- Using the handle of a teaspoon or a very fine piping nozzle and bag, stuff the rigatoni with the aubergine mixture.
- Lay in a baking dish, cover with the chicken stock and a little Parmesan and bake for 15 minutes until golden on top and bubbling.

Rigatoni Stuffed with   210
Courgettes and Goats Cheese

- Substitute chopped roasted courgettes for the aubergines.

211

SERVES 4

Vegetable Conchiglie with Pesto

Conchiglie with Peas and Broad Beans

 212

- cook broad beans and peas with the pasta and toss with pesto.

Conchiglie with a Creamy Pesto Sauce

213

- Stir 2 tbsp mascarpone into the pesto before serving.

Conchiglie with Mixed Mushrooms

214

- Omit the butternut squash and substitute different kinds of mushrooms for a meaty fungal feast.

PREPARATION TIME 15 MINUTES

COOKING TIME 20 MINUTES

INGREDIENTS

500g / 1 lb / 2 cups conchiglie pasta
50g / 1 ¾ oz / ¼ cup butter
½ butternut squash, diced
2 sticks celery, finely chopped
100g / 3 ½ oz / ½ cup chestnut mushrooms sliced
1 clove garlic, finely sliced
4 tbsp pesto
Salt and pepper

- Cook the pasta in boiling salted water according to packet instructions. Drain, reserving a cupful of the cooking water.
- Meanwhile heat the butter in a pan and cook the butternut squash gently for 10 minutes.
- Add the celery and mushrooms with the garlic and cook for another 5 minutes until tender.
- Toss the pasta with the vegetables, pesto and a little cooking water to loosen.
- Season and serve.

215

SERVES 4

Ratatouille Pasta

Caponata Pasta **216**

- Using the same method, substitute the courgettes for chopped celery, omit the mushrooms and peppers and serve with a handful of sultanas stirred in.

Deconstructed Ratatouille Pasta **217**

- Roast the chopped vegetables in olive oil in a hot oven with 2 halved tomatoes until golden and tender – omit the canned tomatoes. Toss with the pasta.

Ratatouille Pasta with Pesto **218**

- Top with home made pesto for deeper flavour (see page 23).

PREPARATION TIME 10 MINUTES

COOKING TIME 50 MINUTES

....

INGREDIENTS

4-6 tbsp olive oil
2 onions, peeled and finely sliced
2 aubergines (eggplants), cut in half lengthways and finely sliced
3 courgettes (zucchini), cut in half lengthways and finely sliced
2 cloves garlic, finely chopped
3 red peppers, seeded and cut into strips
Handful chestnut mushrooms, thickly sliced
1 x 400g can chopped tomatoes
1 tsp coriander seeds, crushed
Salt and pepper
Handful fresh basil leaves
500g / 1 lb / 2 cups spirali pasta

- Heat the oil in a pan and cook the onions until deep gold and sweet.
- Add the aubergines and cook for 2 minutes, then add the courgettes and garlic and cook for 2 minutes, then add the peppers and cook for 5 minutes.
- Add the mushrooms and cook for 5 minutes, then tomatoes and coriander seeds and leave to simmer for at least 30 minutes over a very low heat, stirring occasionally, until the vegetables are very soft.
- Cook the pasta in boiling salted water according to packet instructions. Drain, reserving a cupful of cooking water.
- Toss the pasta with the ratatouille, season and loosen with a little cooking water. Sprinkle over the basil before serving.

219

SERVES 4

Pasta with Tuna and Vegetables

- Preheat the oven to 200°C / 400F / gas 6.
- Roast the peppers in oil and seasoning for about 20 minutes or until soft and sweet.
- Cook the pasta in boiling salted water according to packet instructions. Drain, reserving a little of the cooking water and tip into a bowl.
- Toss with the roasted peppers, a little of the roasting juices and a tbsp of cooking water.
- Flake in the tuna and basil, stir through the sweetcorn and season then serve

PREPARATION TIME 5 MINUTES

COOKING TIME 25 MINUTES

INGREDIENTS

500g / 1 lb / 2 cups conchiglie pasta
3 tbsp olive oil
3-4 red peppers, 'cheeks' cut off and roughly chopped
Salt and pepper
2 x 185g cans tuna in olive oil, drained
50g / 1 ¾ oz / ¼ cup sweetcorn kernels, drained
½ bunch basil, chopped

Pasta with Salmon

220

- Substitute canned salmon for the tuna.

221

SERVES 4

Lasagne Tricolore

- Prepare the filling ingredients: tear the mozzarella into pieces.
- Roughly chop the tomatoes.
- Wilt the spinach, then squeeze dry and season. Toss with a little olive oil.
- Cook the lasagne sheets in boiling salted water according to the packet instructions. Drain.
- Lay a sheet of lasagne on each plate. Working quickly, top with some of the ingredients, then place another sheet on top and repeat, finishing with a layer of pasta.
- Finish with extra virgin olive oil, Parmesan and chives.
- Place under a hot grill for a few minutes to melt the cheese, then serve.

PREPARATION TIME 15 MINUTES

COOKING TIME 3 MINUTES

INGREDIENTS

12 sheets fresh lasagne
2 balls buffalo mozzarella
250g / 9 oz / 1 cup semi-dried tomatoes
1 kg / 2 ¼ lb / 4 ¼ cups spinach leaves, washed
Salt and pepper
Extra virgin olive oil
Parmesan, grated
½ bunch chives, chopped

Lasagne with Rocket and Watercress

222

- Substitute mixed rocket and watercress for the spinach for a peppery kick.

RICE AND NOODLES

223

SERVES 4

Paella

- Heat the olive oil in a large shallow pan and cook the onion, garlic and celery with the chorizo until the orange fat runs.
- Add the pepper, cook for a further 5 minutes, then stir in the chicken and paella rice and coat thoroughly in the oil.
- Stir the saffron into the stock then pour it over the rice. Add the paprika. Bring to a simmer and leave uncovered for 10 minutes.
- Add the tomatoes, peas and seafood and cook for a further 8-10 minutes until everything is just cooked through and the mussels have opened.
- Stir through the lemon juice, season well and serve.

PREPARATION TIME 20 MINUTES

COOKING TIME 30 MINUTES

INGREDIENTS

5 tbsp olive oil
1 onion, peeled and finely sliced
75g / 2 ½ oz / ⅓ cup chorizo, diced
2 cloves garlic, finely chopped
1 celery stick, finely chopped
1 red pepper, seeded and sliced
300g / 10 oz / 1 ¼ cups paella rice
2 chicken thighs, cubed
1L / 2 ¼ pints / 4 ¼ cups chicken stock
Pinch saffron threads
1 tsp paprika
4 ripe tomatoes, chopped
50g / 1 ¾ oz / ¼ cup frozen peas
12 raw prawns (shrimp), shell on
24 mussels, cleaned
2 fillets chunky white fish, skinned, boned and cubed
1 lemon, juiced
Salt and pepper

224

SERVES 4

Pilau Rice

PREPARATION TIME 30 MINUTES

COOKING TIME 15 MINUTES

INGREDIENTS

500g / 1lb/ 2 cups basmati rice
30g / 1 oz butter
1 onion, peeled and finely chopped

5 cardamom pods, lightly crushed
1 cinnamon stick
6 cloves
Pinch saffron soaked in 500ml /
1 pint / 2 cups vegetable stock
Salt

- Wash the rice in a sieve under cold running water, then leave to soak for 30 minutes.
- Heat the butter in a pan and when foaming add the onion. Cook until golden and sweet.
- Add the spices and toast lightly, then tip in the rice and stir well to coat in the butter.
- Pour over the stock and a little salt, bring to the boil and cover with a lid. Turn the heat down and leave to cook for 9-10 minutes.
- Turn off the heat and leave to stand for 5 minutes. Remove the lid and stir with a fork to separate the grains.

225

SERVES 2

Vermicelli Chive Paillasson

PREPARATION TIME 5 MINUTES

COOKING TIME 6 MINUTES

Salt and pepper
1 tsp sesame oil
1 tbsp groundnut oil

INGREDIENTS

150g / 5 oz / ⅔ cup rice vermicelli
1 bunch chives, chopped
1 egg

- Soak the vermicelli in boiling water to soften.
- After 30-60 seconds, drain thoroughly and snip into pieces.
- Mix with the chives and egg and season. Form into rough patties.
- Heat the oil in a pan and when hot, fry the patties on both sides for a couple of minute until golden.
- Drain briefly on kitchen paper and serve.

226

SERVES 4

Cep risotto

Cep and Red Wine Risotto
227

- Use red wine instead of white for a dramatic colour variation.

Cep and Parsley Risotto
228

- Stir in ½ bunch chopped parsley at the end of cooking.

Cep and Ham Risotto
229

- Some finely chopped ham will add depth of flavour.

PREPARATION TIME 10 MINUTES

COOKING TIME 25 MINUTES

INGREDIENTS

2 tbsp olive oil
40g / 1 oz butter
1 onion, peeled and finely chopped
2 cloves garlic, finely chopped
200g / 7 oz / ¾ cup ceps or other wild mushrooms
1 tbsp thyme leaves
320g / 11 oz / 1 ⅓ cups risotto rice
100ml / 3 ½ fl oz / ½ cup dry white wine
1L / 2 ¼ pints / 4 ¼ cups chicken or vegetable stock
Salt and pepper
3 tbsp butter
120g / 4 oz / ½ cup Parmesan, grated

- Heat the oil and butter in a large pan and add the onion and garlic. Cook until soft and translucent.
- Stir in the torn mushrooms and thyme and cook for a few minutes.
- Add the rice and stir to coat in the butter. Pour in the wine and stir the rice while the wine is absorbed.
- Once the wine has cooked in, reduce the heat a little and add the hot stock, a ladleful at a time, stirring fairly continuously. This will give the risotto its creamy texture.
- Keep stirring in the stock and tasting the rice. After about 15-20 minutes the rice should be soft but with a slight bite. If you've run out of stock before the rice is cooked, simply use water.
- Season and remove from the heat. Add the butter and Parmesan (mantecatura) and leave to melt into the risotto. Serve immediately.

230

SERVES 4

Asparagus Risotto

- Heat the oil and butter in a large pan and add the onion and garlic. Cook until soft and translucent.
- Chop the asparagus into short lengths and add to the pan. Cook for a few minutes.
- Add the rice and stir to coat in the butter. Pour in the wine and stir the rice while the wine is absorbed.
- Once the wine has cooked in, reduce the heat a little and add the hot stock, a ladleful at a time, stirring fairly continuously. This will give the risotto its creamy texture.
- Keep stirring in the stock and tasting the rice. After about 15-20 minutes the rice should be soft but with a slight bite. If you've run out of stock before the rice is cooked, simply use water.
- Season and remove from the heat. Add the butter and Parmesan (mantecatura) and leave to melt into the risotto. Stir in the lemon zest and juice.

Asparagus and Pea Risotto   231

- A handful of peas cooked in the risotto add sweetness.

PREPARATION TIME 10 MINUTES

COOKING TIME 25 MINUTES

INGREDIENTS

2 tbsp olive oil
40g / 1 oz butter
1 onion, peeled and finely chopped
1 bunch asparagus, woody ends snapped off
320g / 11 oz / 1 ⅓ cups risotto rice
100ml / 3 ½ fl oz / ½ cup dry white wine
1L / 2 ¼ pints / 4 ¼ cups chicken or vegetable stock
Salt and pepper
3 tbsp butter
120g / 4 oz / ½ cup Parmesan, grated
1 lemon, juiced and grated zest

232

SERVES 4

Pancetta & Parmesan Risotto

- Heat the oil and butter in a large pan and add the onion and garlic. Cook until soft and translucent.
- Add the pancetta and cook until golden.
- Add the rice and stir to coat in the butter. Pour in the wine and stir the rice while the wine is absorbed.
- Once the wine has cooked in, reduce the heat a little and add the hot stock, a ladleful at a time, stirring fairly continuously. This will give the risotto its creamy texture.
- Keep stirring in the stock and tasting the rice. After about 15-20 minutes the rice should be soft but with a slight bite. If you've run out of stock before the rice is cooked, simply use water.
- Season and remove from the heat. Add the butter and Parmesan (mantecatura) and leave to melt into the risotto. Serve immediately.

Pancetta Vegetable Risotto   233

- Peas, spinach and asparagus, all cooked in the risotto would complement the smoky pancetta.

PREPARATION TIME 10 MINUTES

COOKING TIME 25 MINUTES

INGREDIENTS

2 tbsp olive oil
40g /1 oz butter
1 onion, peeled and finely chopped
2 cloves garlic, finely chopped
150g pancetta, cubed
320g / 11 oz / 1 ⅓ cups risotto rice
100ml / 3 ½ fl oz / ½ cup dry white wine
1L / 2 ¼ pints / 4 ¼ cups chicken or vegetable stock
Salt and pepper
3 tbsp butter
120g / 4 oz / ½ cup Parmesan, grated

234

SERVES 4

Cantonese Rice

PREPARATION TIME 15 MINUTES

COOKING TIME 10 MINUTES

....

INGREDIENTS

2 tbsp vegetable oil
1 onion, peeled and finely chopped
1 clove garlic, finely chopped
3 eggs, beaten
200g / 7 oz / ¾ cup cooked meat or
prawns (shrimp), finely chopped
500g / 1lb / 2 cups cooked white rice
3-4 spring onions (scallions), sliced
Soy sauce
Handful bean sprouts
Handful cooked peas

- Heat the oil in a wok until nearly smoking then add the onion and garlic and stir fry briskly for 1 minute.
- Push to one side and add the eggs and cook for a couple of minutes until starting to set.
- Add the rice and meat and combine thoroughly.
- Stir in some soy sauce and the bean sprouts and peas and combine until everything is heated through.

Cantonese Rice with Duck
235

- Shredded duck meat, from a roast or pancakes, makes an excellent addition.

236

SERVES 4

Rice Pudding with Caramel Sauce

PREPARATION TIME 10 MINUTES

COOKING TIME 2 HOURS 10
MINUTES

....

INGREDIENTS

3 tbsp butter, melted
60g / 2 oz / ¼ cup pudding rice
30g / 1 oz caster (superfine) sugar
1 tsp vanilla extract
500ml / 1 pint / 2 cups full fat milk
Fresh nutmeg
250g / 9 oz / 1 cup caster (superfine)
sugar
Water

- Preheat the oven to 150°C (130° fan) / 300F / gas 2. Use half the butter to grease a baking dish.
- Add the rice, sugar and vanilla extract, then pour over the milk. Top with the remaining melted butter and grate over a little nutmeg.
- Bake very gently for about 2 hours, stirring every 30 minutes until the milk is absorbed and the rice creamy.
- Once cooked, make a caramel by melting the sugar and a little water in a pan. Once the sugar has dissolved, do not stir, but swirl the pan until a golden brown caramel appears.
- Pour the hot caramel into the bottom of ramekins, then top with the rice pudding.
- Grill until the pudding turns golden on top and serve.

Rice Pudding with
Caramel Nut Sauce
237

- Tip a few crushed hazelnuts into the caramel in the ramekins.

238
SERVES 4

Risotto Milanese

Risotto with Osso Bucco

239

- serve very traditionally Italian with veal osso bucco or indeed lamb shanks.

Risotto Milanese with Pancetta

240

- Stir 100g / 3 ½ oz cubed pancetta in with the onion for smokiness.

Milanese Risotto with Prawns

241

- Top with cooked king prawns for sweetness.

PREPARATION TIME 5 MINUTES

COOKING TIME 25 MINUTES

INGREDIENTS

2 tbsp olive oil
40g / 1 oz butter
1 onion, peeled and finely chopped
2 cloves garlic, finely chopped
320g / 11 oz / 1 ⅓ cups risotto rice
100ml / 3 ½ fl oz / ½ cup dry white wine
1 L / 2 ¼ pints / 4 ¼ cups chicken or vegetable stock with pinch saffron threads soaking
Salt and pepper
3 tbsp butter
120g / 4 oz / ½ cup Parmesan, grated

- Heat the oil and butter in a large pan and add the onion and garlic. Cook until soft and translucent.
- Add the rice and stir to coat in the butter. Pour in the wine and stir the rice while the wine is absorbed.
- Once the wine has cooked in, reduce the heat a little and add the hot stock, a ladleful at a time, stirring fairly continuously. This will give the risotto its creamy texture.
- Keep stirring in the stock and tasting the rice. After about 15-20 minutes the rice should be soft but with a slight bite. If you've run out of stock before the rice is cooked, simply use water.
- Season and remove from the heat. Add the butter and Parmesan (mantecatura) and leave to melt into the risotto. Serve immediately.

242

SERVES 4

Rice pudding

PREPARATION TIME 10 MINUTES

COOKING TIME 2 HOURS 10 MINUTES

....

INGREDIENTS

3 tbsp butter, melted
60g / 2 oz / ¼ cup pudding rice
30g / 1 oz caster (superfine) sugar
1 tsp vanilla extract
500ml / 1 pint / 2 cups full fat milk
Fresh nutmeg

- Preheat the oven to 150°C (130° fan) / 300F / gas 2.
- Use half the butter to grease a baking dish.
- Add the rice, sugar and vanilla extract, then pour over the milk.
- Top with the remaining melted butter and grate over a little nutmeg.
- Bake very gently for about 2 hours, stirring every 30 minutes until the milk is absorbed and the rice creamy.

Rice Pudding with Caramelised Apples

243

- Fry peeled apple slices in butter and sugar until golden then serve with the rice pudding.

244

SERVES 2

Noodles with Prawn & Vegetables

PREPARATION TIME 10 MINUTES

COOKING TIME 10 MINUTES

....

INGREDIENTS

2 tbsp vegetable oil
½ onion, peeled and finely sliced
1 clove garlic, finely sliced
1cm piece fresh ginger, finely sliced
1 red pepper, deseeded and finely sliced
1 yellow pepper, deseeded and finely sliced
½ courgette (zucchini), cut into matchsticks
½ aubergine (eggplant), cut into matchsticks
200g / 7 oz / ¾ cup raw prawns (shrimp)
3-4 tbsp soy sauce
2 tbsp oyster sauce
1 tbsp chilli sauce
2 nests noodles
1 tbsp sesame oil
1 tbsp Szechuan peppercorns, crushed

- Heat the oil in a wok until nearly smoking then stir fry the onion, ginger and garlic until golden.
- Add the vegetables and stir fry until just tender, then add the prawns and cook through.
- Meanwhile cook the noodles in boiling salted water according to packet instructions, then drain.
- Add the sauces to the pan and bubble up, then add the noodles and sesame oil.
- Serve topped with the crushed peppercorns.

Sautéed Noodles with Squid

245

- Substitute thawed squid rings for the prawns.

Chocolate Rice Pudding with Dried Fruit

246

SERVES 4

- Preheat the oven to 150°C (130° fan) / 300F / gas 2.
- Grease a baking dish. Add the rice, sugar, spices and dried fruit then stir in the milk.
- Bake the rice pudding for 90 minutes, stirring every 30 minutes.
- Stir the chocolate in and bake for another 15-20 minutes until all the milk has been absorbed and the rice is creamy.
- Garnish with the candies oranges and hazelnuts before serving.

PREPARATION TIME 15 MINUTES

COOKING TIME 2 HOURS

INGREDIENTS

1 tbsp butter softened
60g / 2 oz / ¼ cup pudding rice
30g / 1 oz caster (superfine) sugar
1 tsp vanilla extract
½ tsp cinnamon
50g / 1 ¾ oz / ¼ cup dried figs, chopped
50g / 1 ¾ oz / ¼ cup dried apricots, chopped
600ml / 1 pint / 2 ½ cups full fat milk
60g / 2 oz / ¼ cup dark chocolate

TO DECORATE

2 tbsp hazelnuts (cob nuts), crushed and toasted
Candied orange segments

Chocolate Rice Pudding with Sour Fruits

247

- Substitute sour dried fruit such as cranberries and cherries for a more adult version.

Fruit Sushi

248

SERVES 4

- Rinse the rice in a sieve under cold running water. Leave to dry for 30 minutes spread out on a plate.
- Place in a pan with 2 cups water and bring to the boil. Reduce the heat, cover with a lid and cook for 15 minutes.
- Remove from the heat and leave to stand for 5 minutes.
- Meanwhile, heat the vinegar, sugar and salt in a small pan until the sugar and salt have dissolved.
- Spoon the rice onto a baking sheet and spread across the tray in a thin even layer. Pour the dressing over and fold in until all the grains are coated and glossy.
- Allow to cool then form into thin fingers of rice, using your hands.
- Top with slices of fruit, tie with liquorice laces and serve.

PREPARATION TIME 1 HOUR

COOKING TIME 20 MINUTES

INGREDIENTS

500g / 1 lb / 2 cups Japanese sushi short-grain rice
150ml / 5 fl oz / ⅔ cup Japanese rice vinegar (mirin)
3 tbsp caster (superfine) sugar
1 tsp salt
1 small packet of liquorice laces

SLICES OF

Kiwi fruit
Strawberry
Melon
Orange

Winter Fruit Sushi

249

- Use finely sliced persimmon, pineapple and mango.

250
SERVES 4

Rice Parcels

PREPARATION TIME I HOUR

COOKING TIME 20 MINUTES

....

INGREDIENTS

500g / 1 lb / 2 cups Japanese sushi
short-grain rice
150ml / 5 fl oz / ⅔ cup Japanese rice
vinegar (mirin)
3 tbsp caster (superfine) sugar
1 tsp salt
Pieces of banana leaf
Soy sauce for dipping

- Rinse the rice in a sieve under cold running water. Leave to dry for 30 minutes spread out on a plate.
- Place in a pan with 2 cups water and bring to the boil. Reduce the heat, cover with a lid and cook for 15 minutes.
- Remove from the heat and leave to stand for 5 minutes.
- Meanwhile, heat the vinegar, sugar and salt in a small pan until the sugar and salt have dissolved.
- Spoon the rice onto a baking sheet and spread across the tray in a thin even layer. Pour the dressing over and fold in until all the grains are coated and glossy.
- Allow to cool then form into thin fingers of rice, using your hands.
- Place into strips of banana leaf and use soy sauce for dipping.

Rice Parcels with Thai Dipping Sauce
251

- Mix together 2 tbsp fish sauce, ½ tbsp lime juice, ½ finely chopped red chilli and a pinch of sugar for a Thai influence

252
SERVES 4

Basmati Rice with Peas

PREPARATION TIME 30 MINUTES

COOKING TIME 15 MINUTES

....

INGREDIENTS

500g / 1lb / 2 cups basmati rice
30g / 1 oz butter
1 onion, peeled and finely chopped
6 cardamom pods
1 tsp ground cumin
100g / 3 ½ oz / ½ cup frozen peas
500ml / 1 pint / 2 cups chicken or
vegetable stock
Salt

- Wash the rice in a sieve under cold running water, then leave to soak for 30 minutes.
- Heat the butter in a pan and when foaming add the onion. Cook until golden and sweet.
- Add the spices and toast lightly, then tip in the rice and peas and stir well to coat in the butter.
- Pour over the stock and a little salt, bring to the boil and cover with a lid. Turn the heat down and leave to cook for 9-10 minutes.
- Turn off the heat and leave to stand for 5 minutes. Remove the lid and stir with a fork to separate the grains.

Basmati Rice with Sweetcorn
253

- Substitute tinned drained sweetcorn.

254

SERVES 6

Vermicelli with Garlic and Parsley

- Soak the noodles according to packet instructions.
- Heat the oil in a pan and cook the garlic gently for a few seconds.
- Tip into a food processor, add the parsley, lemon zest, sesame oil and soy sauce and blitz until nearly smooth.
- Drain the noodles and toss with the sauce.

PREPARATION TIME 5 MINUTES

COOKING TIME 2 MINUTES

INGREDIENTS

250g / 9 oz / 1 cup vermicelli noodles
1 tbsp groundnut oil
2 cloves garlic, crushed
1 bunch parsley, chopped
1 lemon, grated zest
1 tsp sesame oil
4 tbsp soy sauce

Rice Pudding Gateau

255

SERVES 4

PREPARATION TIME 2 HOURS

COOKING TIME 35 MINUTES

1 tsp vanilla extract
Grated nutmeg

INGREDIENTS

100g / 3 ½ oz / ½ cup pudding rice
1 L / 2 ¼ pints / 4 ¼ cups milk
100g / 3 ½ oz / ½ cup caster (superfine) sugar

- Rinse the rice in cold running water in a sieve, then tip into a pan.
- Cover with boiling water and cook for 5 minutes, then drain.
- Measure out ¾ of the milk, add the sugar and vanilla and add the rice to the milk. Cook over a low heat for 30 minutes without stirring.
- Remove from the heat and add the remaining cold milk then leave the rice to cool completely.
- Spoon into a mold and refrigerate for at least 2 hours.
- Turn out and serve with a little grated nutmeg, jam or honey.

Chinese Noodles with Spring Onions

256

SERVES 2

PREPARATION TIME 5 MINUTES

COOKING TIME 10 MINUTES

1cm piece ginger, grated
2 cloves garlic, finely sliced
4 tbsp soy sauce

INGREDIENTS

2 nests noodles
1 tbsp sesame oil
1 bunch spring onions (scallions), finely chopped

- Cook the noodles according to packet instructions and drain.
- Meanwhile heat the oil in a wok.
- Sauté the spring onions, ginger and garlic over a high heat, then add the noodles and soy sauce.
- Toss well to heat through and serve.

SERVES 4

Noodles with Salmon, Peas & Broccoli

257

Noodles with Fresh Tuna
258

- Substitute fresh tuna steaks for the salmon.

Noodles with Salmon and Mustard Sauce
259

- Mix together 1 tsp English mustard powder with the soy and toss with the noodles for an anglo-oriental take.

Noodles with Salmon, Peas and Broccoli
260

- Use asparagus lengths rather than broccoli.

PREPARATION TIME 10 MINUTES

COOKING TIME 10 MINUTES

....

INGREDIENTS

4 nests dried noodles
1 head broccoli, cut into florets
100g / 3 ½ oz / ½ cup frozen peas
1 tbsp groundnut oil
4 spring onions (scallions), finely chopped
1cm piece ginger, finely sliced
2 salmon fillets, boned and cut into strips
2 tbsp soy sauce
2 tbsp chilli sauce
1 tsp sesame oil

- Cook the noodles in boiling salted water according to packet instructions.
- After 1 minute add the broccoli and peas.
- Drain well.
- Meanwhile heat the oil in a wok and add the spring onions and ginger. Sauté for a few minutes, then add the salmon and cook until just pink.
- Add the noodles and vegetables and pour in the sauces.
- Toss well to coat, then serve drizzled with sesame oil.

Arancini with Tomato and Mozzarella

261

SERVES: 4

- Leave the leftover risotto to get completely cold – preferably refrigerated overnight.
- Stir the tomato and Parmesan through the risotto.
- Shape into equal balls, pushing a small cube of mozzarella into the centre of each one and shaping the rice around it. If you prefer, you could make finger shapes instead.
- Lay out the flour, egg and breadcrumbs on separate plates.
- Dip the risotto balls into the flour, then the egg, then the breadcrumbs. Use one hand and keep the other clean for ease.
- Heat the oil to 180°C or until a cube of bread sizzles when dunked in. Fry the risotto balls until golden and crisp all over. Drain on kitchen paper and serve hot or warm.

PREPARATION TIME 20 MINUTES

COOKING TIME 10 MINUTES

INGREDIENTS

60g / 2 oz / ¼ cup leftover risotto rice, cooked
1 tbsp Parmesan, grated
1 tomato, seeded and finely diced
1 ball mozzarella, cut into small cubes
½ bunch basil leaves
1 tbsp plain (all purpose) flour
1 egg, beaten
40g / 1 ½ oz breadcrumbs
Vegetable oil, for deep frying

Blue Cheese Arancini

262

- Omit the tomato and use gorgonzola instead of the mozzarella.

Saffron Risotto

263

SERVES 4

- Heat the oil and butter in a large pan and add the onion and garlic. Cook until soft and translucent.
- Add the rice and stir to coat in the butter. Pour in the wine and stir the rice while the wine is absorbed.
- Once the wine has cooked in, reduce the heat a little and add the hot stock, a ladleful at a time, stirring fairly continuously. This will give the risotto its creamy texture.
- Keep stirring in the stock and tasting the rice. After about 15-20 minutes the rice should be soft but with a slight bite. If you've run out of stock before the rice is cooked, simply use water.
- Season and remove from the heat. Add the butter and Parmesan (mantecatura) and leave to melt into the risotto. Serve immediately.

PREPARATION TIME 5 MINUTES

COOKING TIME 25 MINUTES

INGREDIENTS

2 tbsp olive oil
40g / 1 oz butter
1 onion, peeled and finely chopped
2 cloves garlic, finely chopped
320g / 11 oz / 1 ⅓ cups risotto rice
100ml / 3 ½ fl oz / ½ cup dry white wine
1 L / 2 ¼ pints / 4 ¼ cups chicken or vegetable stock with pinch saffron threads soaking
Salt and pepper
3 tbsp butter
120g / 4 oz / ½ cup Parmesan, grated

Saffron Risotto with Mushrooms

264

- Add 100g / 3 ½ oz chopped mushrooms with the onion for earthy flavour.

265

SERVES 2

Noodles with Chorizo & Peas

PREPARATION TIME 5 MINUTES

COOKING TIME 10 MINUTES

....

INGREDIENTS

2 nests dried noodles
100g / 3 ½ oz / ½ cup frozen peas
1 tbsp groundnut oil
100g / 3 ½ oz / ½ cup chorizo
sausage, sliced
½ red onion, peeled and finely sliced
1 red chilli, finely sliced

- Cook the noodles according to packet instructions along with the peas.
- Drain and set aside.
- Meanwhile heat the oil in a pan and fry the chorizo and onion until the fat runs and the onion is soft.
- Toss in the noodles and peas then add the chilli.
- Serve.

Noodles with Chicken and Peas | 266

- Use leftover shredded roast chicken if you don't have chorizo.

267

SERVES 4

Tomato, Pepper and Mushroom Risotto

PREPARATION TIME 15 MINUTES

COOKING TIME 25 MINUTES

....

INGREDIENTS

2 tbsp olive oil
40g / 1 oz butter
1 onion, peeled and finely chopped
2 cloves garlic, finely chopped
100g / 3 ½ oz / ½ cup button
mushrooms, sliced
1 red pepper, deseeded and finely
chopped
150g cherry tomatoes, halved
320g / 11 oz / 1 ⅓ cups risotto rice
100ml / 3 ½ fl oz / ½ cup dry white
wine
1 L / 2 ¼ pints / 4 ¼ cups chicken or
vegetable stock
Salt and pepper
3 tbsp butter
120g / 4 oz / ½ cup Parmesan, grated

- Heat the oil and butter in a large pan and add the onion and garlic. Cook until soft and translucent.
- Add the mushrooms and cook until lightly golden then add the pepper and cook for a few minutes.
- Add the rice and stir to coat in the butter. Pour in the wine and stir the rice while the wine is absorbed.
- Once the wine has cooked in, reduce the heat a little and add the hot stock, a ladleful at a time, stirring fairly continuously. This will give the risotto its creamy texture.
- Keep stirring in the stock and tasting the rice. After about 15-20 minutes the rice should be soft but with a slight bite. If you've run out of stock before the rice is cooked, simply use water.
- Season and remove from the heat. Add the butter and Parmesan and leave to melt into the risotto. Serve immediately.

Tomato Red Pepper | 268
Courgette Risotto

- Omit the mushrooms and use 1 diced courgette.

269

SERVES 4

Noodles with Pork & Lemongrass

With Caramelised Chicken · 270

- Use chicken instead of pork.

With Caramelised Tofu · 271

- Use cubed tofu instead of pork.

Noodle Broth with Pork · 272

- Cook the noodles in 500ml/1 pint strong chicken stock, then pour the stock into bowls and serve the noodles and pork on top.

PREPARATION TIME 15 MINUTES

COOKING TIME 10 MINUTES

INGREDIENTS

4 nests dried noodles
1 small red onion, finely sliced
2 tbsp groundnut oil
2 cloves garlic, finely sliced
1cm piece ginger, finely sliced
1 red chilli, deseeded and finely chopped
2 stalks lemongrass, inner stalks only, finely chopped
300g / 10 oz / pork fillet, cubed
2 tbsp sugar
1 tbsp soy sauce

- Cook the noodles according to packet instructions. Drain.
- Heat the oil in a wok and sauté the garlic, onion, ginger and chilli with the lemongrass for a few minutes until golden.
- Add the pork and colour over a high heat, then add the sugar and soy and allow to caramelize.
- Add the noodles and toss well to heat through.

POTATOES

273

SERVES 2

Potato Omelette

- Cut the potatoes into dice and cook in boiling salted water until tender. Drain thoroughly and set aside.
- Meanwhile crack the eggs into a bowl and beat lightly. Tip into the pan and swirl gently to cover the base of the pan and help it set.
- When the omelette is nearly set, sprinkle over the potatoes, parsley and seasoning and flash under a hot grill to set it completely.
- Remove from the pan and serve.

PREPARATION TIME 15 MINUTES

COOKING TIME 5 MINUTES

INGREDIENTS

250g / 9 oz / 1 cup potatoes, peeled
1 tbsp butter
2 eggs
Salt and pepper
2 tbsp parsley, chopped

Potato Dauphinoise

274

SERVES 4-6

PREPARATION TIME 20 MINUTES

COOKING TIME 1 ½ - 2 HOURS

INGREDIENTS

50g / 1 ¾ oz butter, softened
1 kg / 2 ¼ lb / 4 ¼ cups floury potatoes, peeled
2 cloves garlic, crushed
Salt and pepper
½ bunch thyme
500ml / 1 pint / 2 cups double cream
Milk

- Preheat oven to 160°C (140° fan) / 300F / gas 2.
- Use the softened butter to generously grease a large baking dish.
- Slice the potatoes as thinly as possible – about as thin as a coin, using either a sharp knife or, preferably a mandoline.
- Layer the potatoes in the baking dish, seasoning and sprinkling with thyme leaves and garlic as you go.
- Pour the cream over the potatoes – it should come just to the top of the potatoes. If you don't have enough, just add some milk.
- Push the potatoes down into the cream, place on a baking sheet and bake for 1 ½ - 2 hours until the potatoes are completely tender all the way through and the gratin is golden and bubbling.
- Leave for 5 minutes to settle before serving.

Sweet Potato Mash

275

SERVES 4

PREPARATION TIME 5 MINUTES

COOKING TIME 15 MINUTES

INGREDIENTS

4 large sweet potatoes, peeled
Salt
50g / 1 ¾ oz butter
Pepper

- Cut the potatoes into large chunks and cook in boiling salted water until tender – about 10-12 minutes.
- Drain thoroughly, then set the pan over a low heat and shake the pan to drive off any excess moisture.
- Mash thoroughly with the butter until smooth then season generously and serve.

276

SERVES 4

Ultimate Mashed Potato

Cheese Mash   277

- Stir in 2-3 good handfuls, depending on taste, of grated cheddar.

Blue Cheese Mash   278

- Stir in 100g / 3 ½ oz gorgonzola.

Mushroom Mash   279

- Pan fry chopped wild mushrooms in butter with garlic, then stir into the mashed potato.

PREPARATION TIME 2 MINUTES

COOKING TIME 40 MINUTES

INGREDIENTS

1 kg / 2 ¼ lb / 4 ¼ cups floury potatoes such as King Edward or Desiree
100g / 3 ½ oz / ½ cup butter
75-100ml / 2 ½ - 3 ½ oz / ⅓ – ½ cup milk, warmed
Salt and pepper

- Cook the potatoes whole in their skins in boiling salted water until tender all the way through – about 30 minutes, but keep checking.
- Drain thoroughly and leave to cool for 5 minutes, then peel off the skins while still hot.
- Return the flesh to the pan, mash finely and stir in the butter and enough milk with a wooden spoon to make a light, creamy, smooth mash.
- Season generously and serve hot.

280

SERVES 4 # Stuffed Baked Potatoes

- Preheat the oven to 200°C / 400F / gas 7.
- Rub the potatoes all over with olive oil, prick the skins a few times with a fork and sprinkle generously with salt. Bake in the oven for at least 1 hour until completely cooked.
- For the filling: once the potatoes are cooked, heat the butter in a pan and cook the bacon until the fat starts to run.
- Add the diced courgette and cook until golden.
- Remove the top third of the potatoes, pack the insides down with the back of a teaspoon and spoon the bacon/courgette mix inside.
- Add the cheese and return to the oven until the filling is hot and the cheese melting. Serve immediately.

PREPARATION TIME 5 MINUTES

COOKING TIME 1 HOUR 10
MINUTES – 1 HOUR 40 MINUTES

INGREDIENTS

4 large baking potatoes, such as King
Edward or Maris Piper, scrubbed
2 tbsp olive oil
Salt

FOR THE FILLING
30g / 1 oz butter
4 rashers smoked streaky bacon
1 courgette (zucchini), finely diced
150g / 5 oz / ⅔ cup Tete-de-Moine
cheese or similar melting cheese
Pepper

Meaty Stuffed Baked Potatoes 281

- Try scooping out the baked potato and mixing with pork or game terrine, before piling back into the skins and baking until bubbling hot.

282

SERVES 4 # Baked Sweet Potatoes

- Preheat the oven to 200°C / 400F / gas 7.
- Rub the potatoes all over with oil, prick a few times with a fork, place on a baking sheet and bake in the oven for 30-40 minutes until completely soft.
- Split the potatoes and mash the flesh with butter, salt and pepper.

PREPARATION TIME 2 MINUTES

COOKING TIME 30-40 MINUTES

INGREDIENTS

4 large sweet potatoes, scrubbed
Olive oil
4 tbsp butter
Salt and pepper

Chilli Baked Potatoes 283

- Sprinkle halved sweet potatoes with dried chilli and salt before baking.

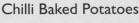

284

SERVES 4

Griddled Sweet Potato

PREPARATION TIME 10 MINUTES

COOKING TIME 8-10 MINUTES

INGREDIENTS

2 large sweet potatoes, scrubbed
4 tbsp olive oil
Pinch dried chilli flakes (optional)
2 sprigs thyme leaves
Salt and pepper

- Cut the potatoes across into thick rounds about 2cm thick.
- Rub with oil, chilli, thyme and season and score a cross-hatch into each side to help them cook quickly.
- Heat a griddle pan or barbecue until very hot then cook the potato slices until golden on both sides and tender all the way through – about 8-10 minutes per side, turning them regularly to prevent burning.

Griddled Potatoes

285

- You can sue this method with ordinary white potatoes as well.

286

SERVES 4

Baked Potatoes with Cottage Cheese

PREPARATION TIME 10 MINUTES

COOKING TIME 1 HOUR 10
MINUTES – 1 HOUR 40 MINUTES

INGREDIENTS

4 large baking potatoes, such as King Edward or Maris Piper, scrubbed
2 tbsp olive oil
Salt

FOR THE FILLING
250g / 9 oz / 1 cup cottage cheese
1 tbsp thyme leaves
1 tbsp parsley, chopped
2 tbsp chives, chopped
Salt and pepper
Squeeze of lemon juice
3 tbsp extra virgin olive oil

- Preheat the oven to 200°C / 400F / gas 7.
- Rub the potatoes all over with olive oil, prick the skins a few times with a fork and sprinkle generously with salt. Bake in the oven for at least 1 hour until completely cooked.
- Meanwhile mix together the ingredients for the filling and chill.
- Once the potatoes are cooked, split them in half and spoon the cold filling into the hot potatoes.

Stuffed with Herby Sour Cream

287

- Sour cream is a surprisingly delicious accompaniment, worth revisiting with the same mixture of herbs.

288

SERVES 4

Sautéed New Potatoes

New Potatoes with Rosemary

289

- Use finely chopped rosemary rather than thyme.

New Potatoes with Smoky Bacon

290

- Use 4 rashers chopped smoked streaky bacon for a punch.

New Potatoes with Wild Mushrooms

291

- Saute wild mushrooms with the potatoes.

PREPARATION TIME 10 MINUTES

COOKING TIME 10-15 MINUTES

INGREDIENTS

750g / 1 ⅓ lb / 3 cups new or salad potatoes such as Charlotte or Anya
5 tbsp olive oil
Salt and pepper
½ bunch thyme leaves
2 cloves garlic

- Parboil the potatoes in salted water for 6 minutes or so, until they begin to soften.
- Drain thoroughly, set back over a low heat to drive off any excess moisture.
- Use the end of a rolling pin to lightly crack or crush the potatoes to create crisp edges in the pan.
- Heat the oil in a pan large enough to hold them in one layer, then add the potatoes.
- Season well, toss in the thyme and garlic and sauté until golden and crisp – 10-15 minutes.

292

SERVES 4

Fried Potato Wedges

PREPARATION TIME 15 MINUTES

COOKING TIME 10-15 MINUTES

....

INGREDIENTS

4 large floury potatoes, scrubbed
5 tbsp olive oil
Salt and pepper
1 tsp paprika (optional)

- Cut the potatoes into wedges lengthways, about 6-8 per potato.
- Parboil in boiling water for 3-4 minutes.
- Drain thoroughly, then set back over a low heat to drive off any excess moisture.
- Heat the oil in a large pan, then add the potatoes and season well.
- Sauté on all sides until golden and crisp.

Fried Potato Wedges with Rosemary and Garlic **293**

- Toss with finely chopped rosemary and crushed garlic, then serve with sour cream.

294

SERVES 4

Roast Potato Slices with Béchamel Sauce

PREPARATION TIME 10 MINUTES

COOKING TIME 30 MINUTES

....

INGREDIENTS

2 large floury potatoes, peeled and cut into thick slices
Salt and pepper
4 tbsp olive oil

FOR THE BÉCHAMEL
1 tbsp butter
1 tbsp plain (all purpose) flour
300ml / 10 fl oz / 1 ¼ cups milk
1 bay leaf
Grated nutmeg
Salt and pepper

- Preheat the oven to 200°C / 400F / gas 7.
- Parboil the potatoes in salted water for 3-4 minutes until starting to soften.
- Drain thoroughly, then tip onto a baking sheet. Toss with olive oil and seasoning and bake in the oven until crisp and golden, turning once – about 20-30 minutes.
- For the béchamel: melt the butter in a pan, stir in the flour to make a paste.
- Whisk in the milk a bit at a time, stirring until the sauce is smooth and thick. Add the bay leaf and leave to cook for 10 minutes, stirring occasionally.
- Season, add the grated nutmeg and remove the bay leaf.
- Pour the sauce over the roasted potato slices.

Roast Potato Slices with Cheese Sauce **295**

- Stir 100g / 3 ½ oz gorgonzola into the sauce before serving.

296

SERVES 4

Herby Boiled New Potatoes

- Cook the potatoes in boiling salted water, lid on, for 20 minutes or until tender to the point of a knife.
- Drain thoroughly, then return to the pan.
- Add the butter, seasoning and herbs and swirl to coat the potatoes.
- Serve hot.

PREPARATION TIME 5 MINUTES

COOKING TIME 25 MINUTES

....

INGREDIENTS

750g / 1 ⅓ lb / 3 cups new potatoes, scrubbed
Salt
50g / 1 ¾ oz butter
Pepper
1 tbsp parsley, chopped
1 tbsp chives, chopped

Boiled New Potatoes with Spiced Butter

297

- Melt the butter with 1 tsp mustard seeds and when popping pour over the potatoes.

298

SERVES 4

Curried Potatoes, Turnips and Spinach

- Cook the potatoes and turnips in boiling salted water for 5 minutes.
- Drain thoroughly.
- Heat the oil in a large lidded pan and cook the mustard seeds for 30 seconds until they pop.
- Add the potatoes and turnips, coat in the spices, add a glass of water and cook with the lid on, turning regularly, for 10 minutes or until golden and starting to crisp.
- Add the spinach and a little more water if the pan looks too dry, put the lid back on and cook until the spinach has wilted.
- Season and serve hot.

PREPARATION TIME 15 MINUTES

COOKING TIME 20 MINUTES

....

INGREDIENTS

500g / 1 lb / 2 cups floury potatoes, peeled and cut into chunks
1 turnip, peeled and cut into chunks
3 tbsp groundnut oil
1 tsp mustard seeds
½ tbsp ground cumin
½ tbsp ground coriander
1 tsp turmeric
300g / 10 oz / 1 ¼ cups spinach leaves, washed
Salt and pepper

Curried Potatoes with Broccoli

299

- Stir in 1 broccoli head, cut into florets and cooked with the potatoes and omit the spinach.

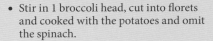

300
SERVES 6-8
Potato Crisps with Lemon Mustard Dip

Potatoe Crisps with Herby Sour Cream Dip | 301

- Stir chopped dill and mint into a small pot of sour cream.

Potato Crisps with Spicy Mayonnaise | 302

- Stir 1-2 tsp harissa or chilli paste into good quality mayonnaise or home made aioli.

Vegetable Crisps | 303

- Finely slice parsnips or peeled beetroot and cook in the same way.

PREPARATION TIME 10 MINUTES

COOKING TIME 10 MINUTES

INGREDIENTS

450g / 1 lb/ 2 cups floury potatoes, peeled
1 L / 2 ¼ pints / 4 ¼ cups vegetable oil
Salt or celery salt

FOR THE DIP
50g / 1 ¾ oz / ¼ cup Dijon mustard
1 tbsp grain mustard
1 tbsp crème fraîche
1 tsp honey
Squeeze of lemon juice

- Slice the potatoes into very thin slices either using a mandoline or a very sharp knife – as thin as you can.
- Wash in cold water to get rid of the starch.
- Heat the oil until a cube of bread sizzles immediately when dropped in, then fry the crisps in batches until golden.
- Remove to kitchen paper to drain and sprinkle liberally with salt or a little celery salt.
- To make the dip, mix the ingredients together and serve with the potato crisps.

304

SERVES 4

Roast New Potatoes

- Preheat the oven to 200°C / 400F / gas 7.
- Parboil the potatoes in salted water for 6 minutes until starting to soften.
- Drain thoroughly, then set back over a low heat to drive off any excess moisture.
- Tip into a roasting tin and coat with oil and salt and pepper.
- Roast in the oven for 20-30 minutes until golden and crisp, tossing once.

PREPARATION TIME 10 MINUTES

COOKING TIME 20-30 MINUTES

INGREDIENTS

750g / 1 ⅓ lb/ 3 cups new potatoes, scrubbed
4 tbsp olive oil
Salt and pepper

Roast New Paprika Potatoes

305

- Roll in paprika and ground cumin before baking.

306

SERVES 4

Potatoes with Cumin and Coriander

- Heat the oil in a large pan and add the mustard seeds. Cook for 30 seconds until they start to pop.
- Tip in the potatoes and the spices and a glass of water or vegetable stock, cover with a lid and cook gently for 10-15 minutes until the potatoes are tender. Stir every now and then to prevent sticking.
- To serve, season, sprinkle over the coriander and lemon juice.

PREPARATION TIME 10 MINUTES

COOKING TIME 15 MINUTES

INGREDIENTS

2 tbsp groundnut oil
1 tbsp mustard seeds
500g / 1 lb / 2 cups potatoes, peeled and diced
½ tsp turmeric
½ red chilli, deseeded and finely diced
½ tbsp ground cumin
½ tbsp ground coriander
1 glass water or vegetable stock
½ bunch fresh coriander (cilantro), chopped
Salt and pepper
½ lemon, juiced

Sag Aloo

307

- Stir a small bag of spinach leaves into the potatoes at the end of cooking for an easy take on this Indian classic.

SERVES 4

Potato & Red Pepper Cakes

PREPARATION TIME 20 MINUTES

COOKING TIME 15-20 MINUTES

....

INGREDIENTS

1 tbsp butter
1 red pepper, deseeded and finely diced
1 kg / 2 ¼ lb / 4 ¼ cups cooked potatoes
2 tbsp butter
Salt and pepper
½ bunch parsley or coriander (cilantro), chopped
2 tbsp plain (all purpose) flour, seasoned
Groundnut oil

- Heat the butter in a pan and cook the pepper gently until completely softened.
- Mash the potatoes thoroughly with the butter and salt and pepper until completely smooth. Mix with the peppers and herbs and shape into patties.
- Dust both sides with seasoned flour.
- Heat a thin film of oil in a pan and cook the potato cakes 2 at a time until golden and crisp on both sides.

Potato Mixed Pepper Cakes

309

- Use a mixture of ½ yellow, ½ red for colour.

310

SERVES 4

Oven-Baked Wedges

PREPARATION TIME 15 MINUTES

COOKING TIME 30 MINUTES

....

INGREDIENTS

4 large floury potatoes, scrubbed
5 tbsp olive oil
Salt
1 tsp paprika
Pinch Cayenne pepper
½ tsp celery salt
1 tsp dried oregano
Tomato relish or chutney, to serve

- Preheat the oven to 220°C / 450F / gas 7.
- Cut the potatoes into wedges lengthways, about 6-8 per potato. Parboil in salted water for 3-4 minutes.
- Drain thoroughly, then set back over a low heat to drive off any excess moisture.
- Place on a baking sheet and toss with the oil and seasonings until thoroughly coated.
- Bake in the oven for about 30 minutes until deep gold and crisp.
- Drain briefly on kitchen paper and serve with chutney or relish for dipping.

Wedges with Crispy Bacon Shards

311

- Grill streaky bacon until very crisp and blitz in a food processor to crumbs. Scatter over the potato wedges.

SERVES 4

Potato Salad

Potato Salad with Dill Mayonnaise

313

- Stir chopped dill through the mayo rather than parsley.

Potato Salad with Horseradish

314

- Stir 1 tbsp creamed horseradish into the mayonnaise for a fiery version.

Potato Salad with Capers

315

- Add 2 tbsp capers to the mayonnaise.

PREPARATION TIME 5 MINUTES

COOKING TIME 20 MINUTES

INGREDIENTS

1 kg / 2 ¼ lb / 4 ¼ cups new or salad potatoes such as Anya or Charlotte
2 sprigs mint
Salt
200g / 7 oz / ¾ cup mayonnaise
½ bunch chives, chopped
2 spring onions (scallions), chopped
½ bunch parsley, chopped
Salt and pepper

- Cook the potatoes whole in boiling salted water with the mint sprigs, covered with a lid, for about 20 minutes or until tender.
- Drain thoroughly.
- Leave to cool slightly then slice thickly.
- Mix the mayonnaise with the herbs and seasoning and toss with the potatoes while still warm.

316

SERVES 4

Sweet Potato Fritters

PREPARATION TIME 15 MINUTES

COOKING TIME 15-20 MINUTES

....

INGREDIENTS

2 large sweet potatoes, peeled
1 onion, peeled and very finely chopped
Salt and pepper
3 tbsp olive oil

- Grate the sweet potatoes then tip into a tea towel and squeeze out any excess moisture.
- Tip into a bowl and mix with the onion and seasoning.
- Form the mixture into equally shaped thin patties.
- Heat the oil in a pan and fry the patties for 8 minutes or until golden. Turn over and cook the other side.
- Drain on kitchen paper and serve.

Chilli Sweet Potato Fritters

317

- Add 1 finely chopped red chilli to the mix before cooking.

318

SERVES 4

Potato & Celeriac Paillasson

PREPARATION TIME 15 MINUTES

COOKING TIME 25 MINUTES

....

INGREDIENTS

250g / 9 oz / 1 cup floury potatoes, peeled
250g / 9 oz / 1 cup celeriac (celery root), peeled
2 tbsp butter, melted
2 tbsp vegetable oil
Salt and pepper

- Grate the potatoes and celeriac.
- Toss with the melted butter and seasoning, ensuring they are thoroughly coated.
- Heat the oil in a large frying pan, then add the mixture to the pan, pressing it down flat with a spatula.
- Cook over a medium heat for about 10 minutes until the base is brown.
- Run the spatula or a palette knife underneath to loosen, then invert the pan carefully onto a baking sheet and tip the cake onto it.
- Slide the cake back into the pan the other way up to cook the other side. Cook for a further 10 minutes until browned and crisp.

Potato Celeriac Paillasson with Thyme

319

- Add 2 tbsp thyme leaves to the mixture before cooking.

320

SERVES 4

Baked Potatoes with Bacon and Cheese

- Preheat the oven to 220°C (200° fan) / 430F / gas 7.
- Prick the potatoes and cook them in a microwave on high for 5 minutes.
- Meanwhile, fry the bacon in the oil for 4 minutes then stir in the crème fraîche and chives.
- Cut a slice off the top of the potatoes and scoop out the centres with a teaspoon.
- Mix 4 tablespoons of the scooped out potato with the bacon mixture, then stuff it back into the potato shells.
- Lay a slice of Raclette over each potato then bake in the oven for 20 minutes or until golden brown.

PREPARATION TIME 10 MINUTES

COOKING TIME 25 MINUTES

INGREDIENTS

4 medium baking potatoes
150 g / 5 ½ oz streaky bacon, chopped
1 tbsp olive oil
2 tbsp crème fraîche
2 tbsp chives, chopped
4 slices Raclette cheese

Potato Gratin with Munster

321

SERVES 4-6

PREPARATION TIME 20 MINUTES

COOKING TIME 1 ½ - 2 HOURS

INGREDIENTS

50g / 1 ¾ oz butter, softened
1 kg / 2 ¼ lb / 4 ¼ cups floury potatoes, peeled
2 cloves garlic, crushed

Salt and pepper
½ bunch thyme
500ml / 1 pint / 2 cups double cream
Milk
100g / 3 ½ oz / ½ cup Munster cheese

- Preheat oven to 160°C / 300F / gas 2.
- Use the softened butter to generously grease a large baking dish.
- Slice the potatoes as thinly as possible – about as thin as a coin, using either a sharp knife or, preferably a mandoline.
- Layer the potatoes in the baking dish, seasoning and sprinkling with thyme leaves and garlic as you go.
- Pour the cream over the potatoes – it should come just to the top of the potatoes. If you don't have enough, just add some milk.
- Push the potatoes down into the cream, place on a baking sheet and bake for 1 ½ - 2 hours.
- 30 minutes before the end of cooking, dot the top with the cheese, then continue to cook until golden and bubbling. Leave for 5 minutes to settle before serving.

Potato Boulangère

322

SERVES 4-6

PREPARATION TIME 20 MINUTES

COOKING TIME 1 HOUR

INGREDIENTS

50g / 1 ¾ oz butter, softened + butter for dotting
1.5 kg / 3 lb / 6 ⅓ cups potatoes, peeled and very thinly sliced

1 large onion, peeled and finely sliced
4 bay leaves
Small bunch thyme
Salt and pepper
300ml / 10 fl oz / 1 ½ cups chicken, lamb or vegetable stock

- Preheat the oven to 200°C / 400F / gas 6.
- Grease a large baking dish with the butter.
- Layer the potatoes, onions, herbs and seasoning in the dish.
- Pour over the stock and push the potatoes down with the back of a spatula. Dot with a little butter.
- Place in the oven and bake for about 1 hour or until the potatoes are completely tender and the top is crisp and golden.

323

SERVES 4

Patatas Bravas

Patatas Bravas with Peppers

324

- Add 1 red pepper, sliced, to the pan with the garlic and tomato.

Celeriac Bravas

325

- Use diced peeled celeriac in place of the potatoes.

Patatas Bravas Tortilla

326

- Stir beaten eggs into the leftover patatas bravas in a pan and cook for a few minutes until set.

PREPARATION TIME 25 MINUTES

COOKING TIME 20 MINUTES

INGREDIENTS

750g / 1 ⅓ lb / 3 cups floury potatoes, cut into small cubes
1 tsp salt
10 tbsp olive oil
2-3 cloves garlic, finely sliced
2 large tomatoes, skinned, deseeded and finely chopped
1 red chilli, deseeded and chopped or ½ tsp dried chilli flakes
1 tbsp paprika
Salt and pepper

- Sprinkle the potatoes with salt and leave in a sieve for 10 minutes. Do not rinse afterwards.
- Heat the olive oil in a deep-sided frying pan until quite hot, then carefully add the potatoes, in batches, and fry gently until soft but not coloured.
- Remove the potatoes from the pan, bring the oil back up to hot, then fry the potatoes again until crisp and deep gold.
- Drain on kitchen paper and keep warm.
- Pour most of the oil out of the pan, then add the garlic and fry for 1 minute until softened.
- Add the tomatoes, chilli and paprika and cook down until reduced and sticky.
- Adjust the seasoning and serve alongside the hot potatoes.

SERVES 4

Homemade Chips

- To make the chips, soak well in cold water to remove the starch then dry thoroughly.
- Bring a pan a third full of oil to 140°C / 275F and plunge in the chips, in batches if necessary and cook for 10 minutes until pale but starting to look 'cooked'.
- Remove, drain on kitchen paper.
- Heat the oil to 180°C / 350F and plunge the chips back in until golden and crisp. Remove to kitchen paper, season well and serve hot.

PREPARATION TIME 10 MINUTES

COOKING TIME 10-15 MINUTES

INGREDIENTS

4 large baking potatoes, peeled and cut into 1cm thick batons
Vegetable oil
Salt

Chips with Béarnaise Sauce

 328

- Serve the hot chips alongside béarnaise sauce (see page 24).

329

SERVES 4

Potatoes with Aioli

- Cook the potatoes in boiling salted water, lid on, for 20 minutes or until tender to the point of a knife.
- Drain thoroughly, then return to the pan. Add the butter and seasoning and swirl to coat the potatoes.
- Place the egg yolks in a bowl with the garlic, mustard powder, salt and pepper. Whisk well.
- Using an electric whisk or hand whisk, pour in the oils one drop at a time, whisking each one in thoroughly.
- Once the mixture begins to thicken, then add the oil a little faster, whisking well.
- After half the oil has been added, stir in 1 tsp of vinegar. Add the remaining oil in a thin trickle, constantly whisking. Season and add the mint.
- Serve hot with the aioli.

PREPARATION TIME 5 MINUTES

COOKING TIME 30 MINUTES

INGREDIENTS

750g / 1 ⅓ lb / 3 cups new potatoes, scrubbed

FOR THE AIOLI
2 egg yolks
4 cloves garlic, crushed
1 tsp mustard powder
1 tsp salt
Pepper
130ml / 4 ½ fl oz / ½ cup groundnut oil
130ml / 4 ½ fl oz / ½ cup olive oil
White wine vinegar
½ bunch mint leaves, finely chopped

Potatoes with Tomato Aioli

 330

- Stir 1 tbsp tomato puree into the aioli.

VEGETABLES

331 SERVES 4 Vegetable Cous Cous

- Place the cous cous in a bowl, cover with the hot stock and clingfilm the bowl. Leave for 10 minutes or so until tender, then fork through the grains and add the lemon.
- Meanwhile heat the oil in a pan and sauté the garlic, carrots and diced peppers and toss to coat and cook for 3 minutes.
- Add the beans and cover with vegetable stock and leave to simmer for 5-8 minutes until all is tender.
- Add the tomatoes and heat through.
- Tip the sautéed vegetables into the cous cous.
- Season generously then add the parsley and pine nuts and serve.

PREPARATION TIME 15 MINUTES

COOKING TIME 12 MINUTES

INGREDIENTS

250g / 9 oz / 1 cup cous cous
2 tbsp sultanas
250ml / 9 fl oz / 1 cup stock
Squeeze of lemon juice
2 tbsp olive oil
1 clove garlic, crushed
2 carrots, peeled and thickly sliced
1 red pepper, finely chopped
1 yellow pepper, finely chopped
Handful green beans
150ml / 5 fl oz / ⅔ cup vegetable stock
4 tomatoes, chopped
Salt and pepper
½ bunch parsley, roughly chopped
2 tbsp pine nuts, toasted

Cauliflower Gratin

332 SERVES 4-6

PREPARATION TIME 20 MINUTES

COOKING TIME 20 MINUTES

INGREDIENTS

1 head cauliflower
100g / 3 ½ oz / ½ cup butter
2 tbsp plain (all purpose) flour
1 tsp mustard powder
2 bay leaves
Grated nutmeg
¼ tsp mace
500ml / 1 pint / 2 cups milk
275g / 10 oz / 1 ¼ cups Cheddar, grated

- Cut the cauliflower into florets and cook in boiling salted water for 5 minutes. Drain well and set aside.
- Preheat the oven to 200°C / 400F / gas 6.
- Heat the butter in a pan and whisk in the flour and mustard powder to make a paste. Gradually whisk in the milk and stir until thick and smooth. Add the bay leaves, nutmeg and mace and leave to simmer gently, stirring occasionally, for 10 minutes.
- Stir in most of the cheese until melted.
- Tip the cauliflower into a baking dish and spoon over the sauce. sprinkle with the remaining cheese and bake for 20 minutes.

Chestnut and Bacon Srouts

333 SERVES 4

PREPARATION TIME 5 MINUTES

COOKING TIME 10 MINUTES

INGREDIENTS

400g / 14 oz / 1 ½ cups Brussels sprouts
30g / 1 oz butter
250g / 9 oz / 1 cup smoked streaky bacon, chopped
400g / 14 oz / 1 ½ cups vacuum-packed peeled chestnuts
100ml / 3 ½ fl oz / ½ cup dry white wine
Salt and pepper

- Remove any tough outer leaves from the sprouts.
- Bring a pan of salted water to the boil and cook the sprouts until just tender – 3-4 minutes.
- Drain and set aside to cool. Cut the sprouts in half.
- Heat the butter in a pan and add the bacon, frying until crisp and golden.
- Remove the bacon with a slotted spoon, then add the halved sprouts and chestnuts and the wine.
- Cook at a fast simmer until the wine has reduced to a syrupy consistency, then return the bacon to the pan and adjust the seasoning.

334

SERVES 4

Aubergine alla Parmigiana

PREPARATION TIME 30 MINUTES

COOKING TIME 20 MINUTES

INGREDIENTS

6 tbsp olive oil
1 tbsp dried oregano
3 aubergines (eggplants), thinly sliced lengthways
1 onion, peeled and chopped
2 cloves garlic, finely sliced
1 cinnamon stick
2 x 400g can chopped tomatoes
1 bunch basil
2 balls mozzarella
60g / 2 oz / ¼ cup Parmesan, grated

- Preheat the oven to 200°C / 400F / gas 6.
- Pour the oil and oregano onto a baking sheet and 'smoosh' the aubergine slices around in it on both sides. Bake for 15 minutes or until tender and golden. Drain on kitchen paper.
- Meanwhile heat a little oil in a pan and gently fry the onion and garlic until completely soft.
- Add the cinnamon stick and basil stalks, add the tomatoes and simmer for 20 minutes, season.
- Spoon a little sauce into the bottom of a gratin dish then layer aubergines, sauce and mozzarella to the top of the dish, seasoning as you go, finishing with a layer of sauce.
- Sprinkle over the Parmesan and bake for 15-20 minutes until golden and bubbling.

Aubergine Parmigiana with Courgettes

335

- Add 2 thinly sliced courgettes, layering them with the aubergines, for a summer version.

336

SERVES 4

Confit Carrots

PREPARATION TIME 5 MINUTES

COOKING TIME 2 HOURS

INGREDIENTS

350g / 12 oz / 1 ½ cups Chantenay or baby carrots, scrubbed
250g / 9 oz / 1 cup melted duck fat
2 cloves garlic, finely sliced
4 sprigs thyme

- Preheat oven to 140°C / 275F / gas 1.
- Lay the carrots in a baking dish and cover with duck fat, garlic and thyme, adding more fat if necessary to completely submerge the carrots.
- Bake in the oven for 2 hours until completely tender.
- Remove from the fat. For a crisp brown exterior, fry them off in a pan before serving.

Confit Carrots with Orange

337

- A strip of orange peel in the duck fat – no pith – will add to the French feel.

338

SERVES 4

Mushy Peas

- Heat the olive oil gently in a pan and add the peas and spring onions. Cook until they turn bright vivid green, then add the mint, seasoning and a little sugar.
- Crush with a potato masher and add the butter.
- Serve hot.

PREPARATION TIME 5 MINUTES

COOKING TIME 10 MINUTES

INGREDIENTS

4 tbsp olive oil
500g / 1 lb / 2 cups frozen peas
3 spring onions, (scallions), finely chopped
1 bunch mint leaves, chopped
Salt and pepper
1 tsp sugar
30g / 1 oz butter

Mashed Broad Beans

339

- Use double podded broad beans in the same way.

340

SERVES 4

Roasted Rosemary Tomatoes

- Preheat the oven to 150C/310F/Gas 2.
- Place the tomato halves in a single layer in a baking dish and drizzle generously with oil. Season and tuck the rosemary in between the tomatoes.
- Bake for 2-3 hours or even longer until the tomatoes have collapsed but retain their shape.

PREPARATION TIME 5 MINUTES

COOKING TIME 2-3 HOURS

INGREDIENTS

500g / 1 lb / 2 cups ripe tomatoes, halved
4 tbsp olive oil
2 branches rosemary
Salt and pepper

Roasted Tomatoes with Sherry Vinegar

341

- Sprinkle with 1 tbsp sherry vinegar before roasting.

342

SERVES 4

Grilled Red Peppers

PREPARATION TIME 5 MINUTES

COOKING TIME 40-50 MINUTES

INGREDIENTS

4 red peppers
Olive oil
Salt and pepper

- Preheat the oven to 200°C / 400F / gas 6.
- Halve and deseed the peppers and place in a roasting tin.
- Drizzle with oil and season and roast in the oven for at least 40 minutes until blackened and collapsed.
- To remove the skins, place in a freezer bag and leave to steam for 10 minutes before removing the skins.

Grilled Mixed Peppers   343

- You can grill yellow and orange peppers the same way. Store under olive oil in the fridge.

344

SERVES 4

Italian-style Courgettes

PREPARATION TIME 15 MINUTES

COOKING TIME 20 MINUTES

INGREDIENTS

4 courgettes (zucchini)
200g / 6 ½ oz / ¾ cup ricotta
1 tbsp parsley, finely chopped
1 tbsp basil, finely chopped
1 tbsp mint, finely chopped
Salt and pepper
Extra virgin olive oil
4 tbsp Parmesan, grated

- Preheat the oven to 200°C / 400F / gas 6.
- Slice the courgettes in half lengthways and scoop out the flesh, leaving the sides intact.
- Finely dice the flesh. Heat 2 tbsp oil in a pan and cook the courgette flesh until tender. Tip into a bowl and leave to cool.
- Once cool, stir into the ricotta, herbs and season well.
- Use a spoon to stuff the interiors of the courgettes, drizzle with oil and sprinkle over the Parmesan.
- Bake in the oven for about 20 minutes or until the courgettes are tender and bubbling.

Italian Style Courgettes with   345
Ricotta and Anchovies

- Add 4 chopped anchovies to the oil and cook until 'melted', then add the courgette flesh and proceed as

346
SERVES 4

Ratatouille

Crisp Ratatouille
347
- Cook the vegetables for less time so they remain crisp tender for a different salad-style texture.

Asian Style Ratatouille
348
- Omit the coriander seeds and basil and use finely chopped ginger and a touch of 5 spice.

Ratatouille with Risotto
349
- Stir into rice or risotto for a filling vegetarian supper.

PREPARATION TIME 10 MINUTES

COOKING TIME 50 MINUTES

INGREDIENTS

4-6 tbsp olive oil
2 onions, peeled and finely sliced
2 aubergines (eggplants), cut in half lengthways and finely sliced
3 courgettes (zucchini), cut in half lengthways and finely sliced
2 cloves garlic, finely chopped
3 red peppers, seeded and cut into strips
1 x 400g can chopped tomatoes
1 tsp coriander seeds, crushed
Salt and pepper
Handful fresh basil leaves

- Heat the oil in a pan and cook the onions until deep gold and sweet.
- Add the aubergines and cook for 2 minutes, then add the courgettes and garlic and cook for 2 minutes, then add the peppers and cook for 5 minutes.
- Add the tomatoes and coriander seeds and leave to simmer for at least 30 minutes over a very low heat, stirring occasionally, until the vegetables are very soft.
- Season and sprinkle over the basil before serving.

350

SERVES 4

Provencal Stuffed Tomatoes

Bacon Stuffed Tomatoes 351

- Stir in 2 rashers of bacon, finely chopped and fried, into the mixture.

Tuna Stuffed Tomatoes 352

- Omit the rosemary, but stir canned tuna into the mixture.

Taleggio Stuffed Tomatoes 353

- Stir cubes of taleggio into the breadcrumbs and bake until oozing.

PREPARATION TIME 40 MINUTES

COOKING TIME 30 MINUTES

INGREDIENTS

8 ripe beef tomatoes
Salt
1 tbsp olive oil
1 onion, peeled and finely chopped
2 cloves garlic, finely chopped
300g / 10 oz / 1 ¼ cups breadcrumbs
1 tbsp rosemary leaves, finely chopped
½ bunch parsley, finely chopped
2 tbsp Parmesan, grated

- Using a teaspoon, hollow out the tomatoes, discarding the seeds.
- Sprinkle the insides with a little salt and leave to drain upside down for 30 minutes.
- Meanwhile fry the onion and garlic in the oil until translucent.
- Add the breadcrumbs, rosemary and parsley and season.
- Stir in the Parmesan and leave to cool a little.
- Preheat the oven to 200°C / 400F / gas 6.
- Fill the tomatoes with the mixture and place in a roasting tin.
- Drizzle with olive oil and bake in the oven for about 30 minutes or until the tomatoes are soft but retaining their shape.

354

SERVES 4

Vegetable & Bean Estouffade

- Heat the butter in a shallow pan and gently cook the onions without colouring.
- Add the carrots and leeks and cook until softened.
- Add the mushrooms and cannellini beans, then pour in the stock.
- Add the dulse and thyme and simmer very gently until the liquid has nearly evaporated and the vegetables are very tender.
- Season and serve.

PREPARATION TIME 15 MINUTES

COOKING TIME 30 MINUTES

INGREDIENTS

30g / 1 oz butter
1 onion, peeled and finely sliced
2 carrots, peeled and finely sliced
2 leeks, white part only, finely sliced
200g / 7 oz / ¾ cup button mushrooms, sliced
2 x 400g can cannellini beans, drained
200ml / 7 fl oz / ¾ cup vegetable stock
2 tbsp dulse (sea lettuce), finely chopped
2 sprigs thyme
Salt and pepper

Vegetable Estouffade with Butter Beans

355

- Try using meatier butter beans instead of cannellini.

356

SERVES 4

Pan-fried Carrots and Parsnips

- Cut the carrots and parsnips lengthways into thin slices.
- Parboil the vegetables for 2 minutes to soften, then drain and dry thoroughly.
- Heat the oil in a pan and fry the carrot and parsnip slices in batches until crisp and browned with the thyme.
- At the end of cooking toss with the vinegar and season well.

PREPARATION TIME 10 MINUTES

COOKING TIME 20 MINUTES

INGREDIENTS

4 large carrots, peeled
2 parsnips, peeled
4 tbsp olive oil
4 sprigs thyme
1 tbsp red wine vinegar
Salt and pepper

Carrots and Parsnips with Balsamic Vinegar

357

- For a sweeter note, use balsamic in place of the red wine vinegar.

358

SERVES 4

Green Bean, Broccoli & Radish Salad

PREPARATION TIME 10 MINUTES

COOKING TIME 4 MINUTES

....

INGREDIENTS

1 head broccoli, broken into florets
100g / 3 ½ oz / ½ cup green beans,
topped and tailed
1 bunch radishes, trimmed and
thinly sliced
4 tbsp extra virgin olive oil
1-2 tbsp red wine vinegar
Salt and pepper

- Cook the broccoli and beans separately in boiling salted water for 4 minutes, then plunge immediately into iced water to stop the cooking.
- Tip into a bowl with the radishes.
- Whisk the oil and vinegar to make an emulsion and season.
- Toss the vegetables in the dressing and serve.

Green Bean Salad with Baby Courgettes   359

- Thinly slice baby courgettes with a vegetable peeler and toss raw with the salad.

360

SERVES 4

Spinach & Feta Flans

PREPARATION TIME 15 MINUTES

COOKING TIME 20 MINUTES

....

INGREDIENTS

1 tbsp butter
500g / 1 lb / 2 cups spinach leaves,
washed
2 eggs
80g / 2 ½ oz / ⅓ cup feta, crumbled
2 tbsp Parmesan, grated
2 tbsp double cream
Salt and pepper

- Preheat the oven to 180°C / 350F / gas 5.
- Wilt the spinach in the butter, then squeeze out any excess moisture. Season.
- Whisk the eggs in a bowl with the cream and stir in the spinach, feta and Parmesan. Season.
- Pour into 4 individual greased ramekins and bake for about 20 minutes or until just set.
- Serve immediately.

Watercress Feta Flan   361

- Use the same amount of watercress, finely chopped instead of the spinach.

362

SERVES 4

Cauliflower Fritters

- Mix together the spices with the flour and a pinch of salt. Pour in the beer a little at a time and whisk gently until it reaches the consistency of double cream.
- Heat the oil to 180°C / 350F.
- Dip the florets into the batter then into the fryer, a few at a time, cooking until golden brown and crisp all over.
- Remove to drain on kitchen paper and serve immediately with salt and lemon.

PREPARATION TIME 15 MINUTES

COOKING TIME 10 MINUTES

INGREDIENTS

1 cauliflower, separated into florets
1 tbsp curry powder
Pinch turmeric
200g / 7 oz / ¾ cup self raising flour
350ml / 12 fl oz / 1 ½ cups lager
Salt
Vegetable oil for deep frying
Salt and lemon wedges, to serve

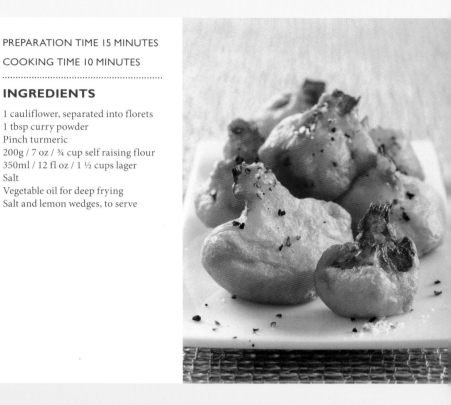

Caulifower Fritters with Tomato Chilli Jam
363

- Cook a sliced red onion until sticky, then stir in 2 chopped tomatoes and a sliced red chilli and cook until collapsed. Stir in red wine vinegar and serve.

364

SERVES 4

Breaded Mushrooms

- Lay the flour, eggs and breadcrumbs out in separate dishes, adding the mustard powder to the flour and Parmesan to the breadcrumbs.
- Dip the mushrooms one by one into each dish, coating thoroughly.
- Heat the oil to 180°C / 350F and deep fry the mushrooms a few at a time until golden brown all over.
- Drain on kitchen paper and serve.

PREPARATION TIME 15 MINUTES

COOKING TIME 20 MINUTES

INGREDIENTS

100g / 3 ½ oz / ½ cup button mushrooms, cleaned
100g / 3 ½ oz / ½ cup plain (all purpose) flour, seasoned
1 tsp mustard powder
2 eggs, beaten
100g / 3 ½ oz / ½ cup fine breadcrumbs
2 tbsp Parmesan, finely grated
Vegetable oil for deep frying

Spicy Breaded Mushrooms
365

- Try adding a pinch of dried chilli flakes to the breadcrumbs.

366

SERVES 4

Mixed Bean Salad

PREPARATION TIME 10 MINUTES

COOKING TIME 4 MINUTES

....

INGREDIENTS

300g / 10 oz / 1 ¼ cups mixed fine
beans, such as green and yellow
1 x 400g can butter beans, drained
1 shallot, finely chopped
2 tbsp extra virgin olive oil
½ lemon, juiced
Salt and pepper
2 tbsp breadcrumbs, lightly toasted

- Top and tail the beans.
- Blanch the fine beans in boiling salted water for 4 minutes, then drain and refresh in iced water to keep the colour.
- Whisk together the shallot, oil, lemon juice and seasoning and toss with the butter beans.
- Stir in the fine beans and spoon onto a plate.
- Top with the toasted breadcrumbs and serve.

Every Bean Salad   367

- Try adding broad beans and sliced runner beans to the salad as well.

368

SERVES 4

Sauteed Savoy Cabbage with Bacon

PREPARATION TIME 10 MINUTES

COOKING TIME 10 MINUTES

....

INGREDIENTS

260g / 2 oz / ¼ cup butter
2 juniper berries, lightly crushed
1 clove garlic, finely sliced
4 rashers smoked streaky bacon,
diced
1 Savoy cabbage, outer leaves and
core removed, leaves finely shredded
Salt and pepper

- Heat the butter in a large pan with the juniper berries and garlic, then add the diced bacon. Cook until the fat starts to render.
- Add the shredded cabbage and a glass of water and cover with a lid. Shake the pan for 4-5 minutes, then check to see if the cabbage has wilted. Give it another 2 minutes if necessary.
- Season well and serve.

Sautéed Greens, Chinese Style   369

- This works with any leafy greens, but try omitting the bacon and juniper and adding soy sauce instead.

370

SERVES 4

Celeriac, Turnip, Tomato & Parsley Salad

Grated Root Vegetable Salad

371

- Try shaving or grating other root vegetables such as beetroot or carrot; leave out the tomato.

Celeriac Salad with Sherry Vinegar Dressing

372

- Use sherry vinegar instead of red wine vinegar.

Celeriac Salad with Remoulade

373

- Stir finely chopped parsley into good quality mayonnaise, along with a little lemon juice and toss with the vegetables.

PREPARATION TIME 20 MINUTES

INGREDIENTS

½ celeriac (celery root), peeled
2 turnips, peeled
4 ripe tomatoes, diced
1 bunch parsley, finely chopped
4 tbsp hijiki seaweed

FOR THE DRESSING
2 tbsp red wine vinegar
1 tbsp Dijon mustard
Pinch salt
Pinch sugar
100ml / 3 ½ fl oz / ½ cup extra virgin olive oil

- Grate the celeriac and turnip in a food processor or box grater and tip into a bowl.
- Add the tomatoes parsley and seaweed and combine well.
- Whisk together the first 4 ingredients for the dressing then whisk in the oil a little at a time until emulsified.
- Stir the dressing into the vegetables, coating thoroughly and serve.

374

SERVES 4

French-Style Peas

PREPARATION TIME 10 MINUTES

COOKING TIME 10-15 MINUTES

INGREDIENTS

30g / 1 oz butter
1 bunch spring onions (scallions), sliced
100g / 3 ½ oz / ½ cup peas
2 heads Little Gem lettuce, quartered
Vegetable stock
Mint sprigs
Salt and pepper

- Heat the butter in a frying pan until foaming, then add the spring onions and cook until softened.
- Add the peas and lettuces and move everything around, then just cover with vegetable stock. Season and cook until everything is tender and the lettuce has wilted – 5-10 minutes.
- Serve with the mint sprigs.

French Style Peas with Beans and Artichokes

375

- Stir in cooked broad beans and artichoke hearts.

376

SERVES 4

Barbecued Sweetcorn

PREPARATION TIME 10 MINUTES

COOKING TIME 30 MINUTES

INGREDIENTS

4 sweetcorn in their husks
Salt and pepper

FOR THE BUTTER
1 red chilli, deseeded and finely chopped
½ bunch coriander (cilantro), chopped
1 lime, juiced
60g / 2 oz / ¼ cup butter, softened

- Mash the ingredients for the butter together and refrigerate.
- Peel the husks back off the corn, then lay them back again and twist the top together to seal in.
- Wrap the corn in foil and barbecue for about 30 minutes until the kernels are tender.
- Slather with the flavoured butter, season generously and eat.

Sweetcorn with Cheese and Mayonnaise

377

- Stir lime juice and Tabasco into mayonnaise, roll the sweetcorn in the mayo and coat with grated cheese – a Mexican version.

378

SERVES 2

Stuffed Aubergines

- Preheat the oven to 200°C / 400F / gas 6.
- Cut the aubergines in half lengthways, drizzle with 2 tbsp oil and bake in the oven for about 30 minutes until tender.
- Remove the flesh with a spoon, leaving the skin intact and with a margin of flesh to support the structure.
- Heat the olive oil in the pan and cook the onion with oregano, garlic and peppers until softened.
- Add the aubergine flesh and the rest of the ingredients and simmer for around 15 minutes.
- Season and spoon into the aubergine skins, sprinkle over the Parmesan and pop back into the oven until the cheese is bubbling.
- Serve immediately.

PREPARATION TIME 20 MINUTES

COOKING TIME 45 MINUTES

INGREDIENTS

2 aubergines (eggplants)
4 tbsp olive oil
1 tsp dried oregano
1 onion, peeled and finely chopped
2 cloves garlic
1 green pepper, finely chopped
1 yellow pepper, finely chopped
2 tomatoes, finely diced
Bunch flat leaf parsley, chopped
Handful green olives, stoned
Salt and pepper
4 tbsp Parmesan, grated

Mange Tout with Toasted Peanuts

379

SERVES 4

PREPARATION TIME 5 MINUTES

COOKING TIME 4 MINUTES

INGREDIENTS

200g / 7 oz / ¾ cup mange tout (snow peas)
2 tbsp peanuts
Salt and pepper
Extra virgin olive oil

- Cook the mange tout in boiling salted water until crisp-tender – about 4 minutes.
- Drain and plunge into iced water to keep the colour.
- Tip the peanuts on a baking sheet and grill for a few seconds until toasted – watch them carefully.
- Toss the mange tout with seasoning and 2 tbsp extra virgin olive oil and top with toasted peanuts.

Broad Beans with Pepper

380

SERVES 4

PREPARATION TIME 15 MINUTES

COOKING TIME 4 MINUTES

INGREDIENTS

300g / 10 oz / 1 ¼ cups broad beans (fava beans) in the pod
Salt and coarsely ground black pepper
50g / 1 ¾ oz / ¼ cup butter

- Remove the broad beans from their pods.
- Cook in boiling salted water for about 4 minutes until tender, then drain and plunge into iced water.
- Using the tips of your fingers, pinch the bright green beans from the grey casings.
- Tip into a pan and toss with butter and seasoning and serve.

SALADS

381

SERVES 4

Crunchy Asian Salad

- Peel the carrots and cut into matchsticks. Place in a bowl.
- Thinly slice the radishes and add to the carrots.
- Add the pepper, beans and cabbage.
- Whisk together the salt, vinegar and sugar and pour over the vegetables, coating thoroughly. Leave for 20 minutes, then serve.

PREPARATION TIME 30 MINUTES

INGREDIENTS

2 carrots
1 bunch radishes, washed
2 green peppers, deseeded and finely sliced
Handful green beans, lightly cooked
1/8 white cabbage, cored and finely shredded
1 tsp salt
5 tbsp rice vinegar
6 tbsp sugar

Fennel, Radish & Orange Salad

382

SERVES 4

PREPARATION TIME 10 MINUTES

INGREDIENTS

1 fennel (finocchio) bulb
1 orange
½ bunch radishes
1 tbsp red wine vinegar
4 tbsp extra virgin olive oil
Salt and pepper

- Halve and core the fennel bulb, remove the outer leaves. Slice very finely and tip into a bowl.
- Peel the orange and remove any pith. Holding it over the fennel bowl, cut out the orange segments and add to the fennel.
- Finely slice the radishes.
- Whisk together the vinegar and oil with a little seasoning, toss thoroughly with the salad and serve.

Tomato Salad

383

SERVES 4

PREPARATION TIME 20 MINUTES

INGREDIENTS

500g / 1 lb / 2 cups mixed heritage tomatoes
½ clove garlic, crushed
1 tbsp red wine or balsamic vinegar
6 tbsp extra virgin olive oil
½ red onion, finely sliced

4 radishes, thinly sliced
½ bunch basil
Salt and pepper

- Roughly chop the tomatoes any which way and tip into a bowl.
- Sprinkle over a little salt and leave for 10 minutes.
- Whisk together the garlic, vinegar and oil until thickened.
- Add the onion and radishes to the tomatoes, tip in the dressing and toss thoroughly to coat.
- Decorate with torn basil leaves and serve.

384

SERVES 4

Greek Salad

PREPARATION TIME 40 MINUTES

INGREDIENTS

150g / 5 oz / ⅔ cup cherry tomatoes
1 cucumber
1 red onion, halved and finely sliced
150g / 5 oz / ⅔ cup black olives, stoned
200g/ 7 oz / ¾ cup feta cheese
2-3 tbsp red wine vinegar
Salt and pepper
1 tsp dried oregano or small handful fresh oregano leaves
6-8 tbsp extra virgin olive oil

- Halve the cherry tomatoes and place in a bowl with a little salt and a drizzle of olive oil. Leave for up to 30 minutes.
- Halve the cucumber lengthways, then scrape out the seeds with a teaspoon. Slice the halves into half-moons, then place in a colander, sprinkle with a little salt and leave to drain for 30 minutes.
- When the tomatoes and cucumber are ready, combine them in a large salad bowl with the olives and crumble in the feta cheese.
- In a separate bowl, whisk together the vinegar and a little seasoning and the oregano. Then whisk in enough extra virgin olive oil to make a thickened emulsion.
- Drizzle the dressing over the salad vegetables and toss thoroughly before serving.

Greek Salad with Fresh Tuna   385

- Griddle fresh tuna steaks for 1-2 minutes per side, then slice thickly and arrange over the salad.

386

SERVES 4

Caesar Salad

PREPARATION TIME 15 MINUTES

INGREDIENTS

4 Little Gem lettuces
100g / 3 ½ oz / ½ cup ready-made croutons

FOR THE DRESSING

2 anchovy fillets
½ clove garlic, crushed
150ml / 5 fl oz / ⅔ cup crème fraîche
Squeeze of lemon juice
2 tbsp Parmesan, grated
Salt and pepper
Parmesan shavings

- Tip the salad leaves into a large bowl and add the croutons.
- For the dressing, mash the anchovy fillets with the garlic to a pulp, then stir in the crème fraîche, lemon juice and Parmesan and season carefully. You may want more lemon juice.
- Add 2 tbsp of the dressing to the salad leaves and coat thoroughly.
- Place the salad on a platter then spoon over the remaining dressing, scattering over the Parmesan shavings.

Chicken Caesar Salad   387

- Add slices of cooked chicken.

388

SERVES 4

Cherry Tomato Salad with Feta

- Place the tomatoes, feta and olives in a large bowl.
- Whisk together the remaining ingredients.
- Mix the dressing with the ingredients and serve.

PREPARATION TIME 5 MINUTES

INGREDIENTS

300g / 10 oz / 1 ¼ cups cherry tomatoes
100g / 3 ½ oz / feta, crumbled
Handful black olives
1 tsp dried oregano
1 tbsp red wine vinegar or balsamic vinegar
4 tbsp extra virgin olive oil
Salt and pepper

Cherry Tomato Salad with Goats Cheese   389

- A mild (or strong) goats cheese works well with sweet tomatoes in place of the feta.

390

SERVES 4

Tomato Mozzarella Salad

- Slice the tomatoes thickly and lay on a serving platter.
- Pour over the oil. Tear up the basil and scatter over then season generously and leave for 15 minutes or so for the tomato juices to release and create a dressing.
- Tear or slice the mozzarella and scatter over the tomatoes before serving.

PREPARATION TIME 20 MINUTES

INGREDIENTS

6 ripe tomatoes
4 tbsp extra virgin olive oil
1 bunch basil leaves
Salt and pepper
2 balls buffalo or cow's milk mozzarella

Tomato Mozzarella Salad with Baby Spinach   391

- Baby spinach leaves tossed with the tomatoes and cheese make this a more substantial salad

SERVES 4

Carrot and Green Olive Salad

392

PREPARATION TIME 5 MINUTES

COOKING TIME 7-9 MINUTES

....

INGREDIENTS

4 large carrots, peeled and sliced
1 lemon, juiced
1 tsp mustard seeds
4 tbsp extra virgin olive oil
Salt and pepper
Handful green olives, stoned and
halved

- Steam cook the carrots for 7-9 minutes until tender but firm, then allow to cool.
- Stir in the lemon juice, mustard seeds and oil and season.
- Spoon onto a plate and scatter over the olives.

Celeriac and Green Olive Salad

393

- Try adding grated celeriac instead of the carrots.

SERVES 4

Waldorf Salad

394

PREPARATION TIME 15 MINUTES

....

INGREDIENTS

225g / 8 oz / 1 cup celery sticks, finely
chopped
225g / 8 oz / 1 cup walnuts, toasted
under a hot grill
225g / 8 oz / 1 cup seedless grapes,
halved
2 eating apples, cored and thinly
sliced
4 tbsp mayonnaise
½ lemon, juiced
Salt and pepper
Letttuce leaves, to serve

- Place the celery, walnuts, grapes and apple in a bowl.
- Mix together the mayonnaise, a little lemon juice and seasoning.
- Stir into the salad ingredients and serve on the lettuce leaves.

Waldorf Salad with Herby Mayonnaise

395

- Try stirring ¼ bunch finely chopped parsley or tarragon into the mayonnaise before dressing the salad.

396

SERVES 4

Fennel, Pear and Rocket Salad

Fennel, Apple Rocket Salad

397

- Add batons of crisp green apples instead of the pear.

Fennel Pear and Watercress Salad

398

- If rocket is too strong use watercress or even baby spinach leaves for a milder salad.

Fennel Pear Rocket Salad with Mackerel

399

- Fresh mackerel fillets make an excellent accompaniment to this salad.

PREPARATION TIME 15 MINUTES

INGREDIENTS

1 fennel (finocchio) bulb, cored and finely sliced
2 ripe pears, cored
250g / 9 oz / 1 cup rocket (arugula) leaves
2 tbsp capers
3 tbsp extra virgin olive oil
2 tbsp lemon juice
Salt and pepper

- Place the fennel in a bowl. Thinly slice the pears and toss with half the lemon juice to prevent browning.
- Scatter the rocket on a platter with the capers.
- Whisk together the oil, lemon juice and seasoning and toss with the fennel and pears.
- Tip onto the leaves and serve.

400

SERVES 4

Salad Niçoise

Salad Niçoise with Canned Tuna   **401**

- Traditionally this salad was made with canned tuna, so feel free to use as a more economical substitute.

Salad Niçoise with Anchovies   **402**

- Fresh anchovies add punch to this salad.

Salad Niçoise with Chicken   **403**

- Hot or cold chicken would add substance to the salad.

PREPARATION TIME 30 MINUTES

COOKING TIME 10 MINUTES

....

INGREDIENTS

4 eggs at room temperature
120g / 4 oz / ½ cup fine green beans, topped and tailed
4 tuna steaks, 2.5cm thick
8-10 small new potatoes, cooked whole and quartered
8 plum tomatoes, quartered
4 Little Gem lettuces, quartered lengthways
8 anchovy fillets
Handful black olives
½ bunch parsley, roughly chopped

FOR THE DRESSING
3 tbsp red wine vinegar
½ clove garlic, crushed
Salt and pepper
100ml / 3/12 fl oz / ½ cup extra virgin olive oil

- Whisk together the red wine vinegar and garlic, season and whisk in the oil until emulsified. Set aside.
- Cook the eggs for 5 minutes in boiling water, then cool and remove the shells.
- Cook the green beans in boiling salted water for 4 minutes, then drain and plunge into iced water. Set aside.
- Heat a griddle and cook the tuna steaks, oiled and seasoned, on each side for 90 seconds, then set aside to rest.
- On a large platter, arrange the lettuce leaves and cooked potatoes. Cut the eggs in half and arrange amongst the leaves. Slice the tuna thickly and add to the plate with the tomatoes, anchovies and olives.
- Drizzle with dressing and scatter with parsley before serving.

404

SERVES 4

Chinese Cabbage and Apple Salad

- Halve the cabbage, remove the core and very finely shred the leaves.
- Core the apple and cut into thin matchsticks.
- Deseed and finely slice the pepper. Place the salad ingredients in a bowl.
- Whisk together the soy, ginger and lime. Whisk in the oils until emulsified.
- Toss the salad in the dressing and leave for 10 minutes to soften slightly.
- Serve on a platter, decorated with coriander and sprinkle with black sesame seeds.

PREPARATION TIME 15 MINUTES

INGREDIENTS

1 Chinese cabbage
2 eating apples
1 red pepper
1 bunch coriander (cilantro), finely chopped
2 tbsp black sesame seeds

FOR THE DRESSING
2 tbsp soy sauce
1 tsp fresh ginger, grated
½ lime, juiced
1 tsp sesame oil
1 tbsp groundnut oil

White Cabbage and Apple Salad   405

- If you can't source Chinese cabbage, very finely shredded white cabbage would do.

406

SERVES 4

Smoked Salmon and Spinach Salad

- Cook the mange tout for 2 minutes in boiling salted water then drain and plunge into iced water.
- Arrange the salad leaves on a large platter and decorate with smoked salmon and mange tout.
- Toast the walnuts lightly under a hot grill for a few seconds, then add to the platter.
- Whisk together the dressing until emulsified, then drizzle over the salad. Decorate with the flowers and serve.

PREPARATION TIME 10 MINUTES

COOKING TIME 2 MINUTES

INGREDIENTS

100g / 3 ½ oz / ½ cup mange tout (snow peas)
120g / 4 oz / ½ cup baby spinach leaves
100g / 3 ½ oz / ½ cup mache (corn lettuce)
200g / 7 oz / ¾ cup smoked salmon slices
50g / 1 ¾ oz / ¼ cup walnuts
Handful edible flowers, washed

FOR THE DRESSING
2 tbsp lemon juice
½ red chilli, deseeded and very finely chopped
6 tbsp extra virgin olive oil
Salt and pepper

Fresh Salmon Spinach Salad   407

- Fresh salmon fillets would work well with these ingredients whilst giving a milder flavour.

408

SERVES 4

Spinach, Tomato and Egg Salad

PREPARATION TIME 10 MINUTES

COOKING TIME 5 MINUTES

··

INGREDIENTS

4 eggs at room temperature
200g / 7 oz / 6 ½ cups baby spinach leaves
8 plum tomatoes, quartered

FOR THE DRESSING
½ clove garlic, crushed
1 tbsp sherry vinegar
4 tbsp extra virgin olive oil
Salt and pepper
Edible flowers, to decorate

- Cook the eggs in boiling water for 5 minutes then set aside to cool. Peel carefully.
- Place the leaves and tomatoes in a serving bowl.
- Whisk together the ingredients for the dressing and pour into the bowl. Combine thoroughly to coat.
- Add the eggs, quartered and decorate with edible flowers.

Spinach, Tomato and Egg Salad with Heritage Tomatoes

409

- Try sourcing different colours of tomatoes in season to add even more colour.

410

SERVES 4

Rainbow Salad

PREPARATION TIME 15 MINUTES

··

INGREDIENTS

200g / 7 oz / 6 ½ cups watercress, washed
4 beetroot, ready-cooked and sliced
2 carrots, peeled
1 handful dulse or hijiki seaweed, cooked

FOR THE DRESSING
1-2 tbsp sherry vinegar
1 tsp Dijon mustard
Salt and pepper
6 tbsp extra virgin olive oil
1 tbsp sesame seeds

- Place the watercress and beetroot in a bowl with the seaweed.
- Coarsely grate or cut the carrots into fine matchsticks – it's up to you – and add to the bowl.
- Whisk together the ingredients for the dressing.
- Combine the salad with the dressing, coating thoroughly.
- Sprinkle over the sesame seeds and serve.

Rainbow Salad with Tomatoes

411

- Add finely sliced salad tomatoes and yellow beetroot for more colour.

412

SERVES 4

Rice Salad

- Measure the rice (in volume) into a saucepan and cover with the stock. Cover with a lid and cook for 10 minutes.
- Remove from the heat and leave to sit for 5 minutes with the lid on. Then remove the lid and leave to cool a little in a bowl while you prepare the remaining salad
- Meanwhile, halve and stone the avocados. Remove the flesh and dice into a bowl. Add the lemon juice to prevent browning. Add the peppers to the bowl.
- Lightly toast the almonds in a hot frying pan for a few seconds until lightly golden, then add to the bowl.
- Add the warm rice to the bowl and stir through the vinegar and oil. Season well and serve.

PREPARATION TIME 20 MINUTES

COOKING TIME 15 MINUTES

INGREDIENTS

240ml / 8 ½ oz / 1 cup rice
480ml / 1 pint / 2 cups weak chicken or vegetable stock
2 ripe avocados
1 tsp lemon juice
1 red pepper, deseeded and finely chopped
4 tbsp flaked (slivered) almonds
2 tbsp white wine vinegar
4 tbsp olive oil
Salt and pepper

Bulghur Wheat Salad   413

- Try using bulghur wheat as a substitute for the rice.

414

SERVES 4

Mixed Salad

- Separate the lettuce leaves, wash and dry thoroughly then place in a bowl, tearing them into manageable pieces.
- Quarter the tomatoes and add to the bowl.
- Slice the cucumber into thin half-moons and add to the bowl.
- Slice the red onion into thin rings or half-moons and add.
- Whisk together the first 4 ingredients until thickened then add the oil and pepper until emulsified.
- Coat the salad thoroughly in the dressing and serve.

PREPARATION TIME 15 MINUTES

INGREDIENTS

1 head lettuce, such as butter or another softer leaf
6 plum tomatoes
½ cucumber
½ red onion, peeled

FOR THE DRESSING
1 tbsp Dijon mustard
2 tbsp red wine vinegar
Pinch salt
Pinch sugar
6 tbsp extra virgin olive oil
Pepper

Mixed Salad with Olives   415

- Add a handful of pitted, mixed olives.

416
SERVES 4

Mexican Tuna Salad

PREPARATION TIME 20 MINUTES

INGREDIENTS

1 x 185g can tuna, drained
200g / 7 oz / ¾ cup sweetcorn kernels
1 red pepper, deseeded and diced
1 green pepper, deseeded and diced
4 plum tomatoes, chopped
1 avocado
1 x 400g can kidney beans, drained

FOR THE DRESSING
½ red chilli, deseeded and finely chopped
1 shallot, finely chopped
1 lime, juiced
2 tbsp tomato juice
4 tbsp extra virgin olive oil
Salt and pepper

- Flake the tuna into a bowl and add the sweetcorn, peppers and tomatoes.
- Halve the avocado, take out the stone, scoop the flesh out of the skins and dice, then add to the tuna.
- Tip in the kidney beans and mix gently.
- Whisk together the ingredients for the dressing until emulsified, then carefully mix with the salad ingredients.

Tuna Salad with Hard Boiled Eggs 417
- A couple of quartered hard or soft boiled eggs will make this salad go further.

418
SERVES 4

Mushroom, Beansprout & Celery Salad

PREPARATION TIME 10 MINUTES

INGREDIENTS

200g / 7 oz / ¾ cup button mushrooms
1 stick celery
2 handfuls beansprouts
1 grapefruit
3 tbsp extra virgin olive oil
Salt and pepper

- Finely slice the mushrooms and add to a bowl.
- Finely chop the celery and add to the mushrooms with the beansprouts.
- Peel the grapefruit and remove any pith. Holding the flesh over a bowl, cut the segments into the bowl.
- Drizzle with olive oil and a little seasoning and serve.

Mixed Microshoot Salad 419
- Microshoots are very 'in' right now – try adding peashoots for sweetness.

420

SERVES 4

Crayfish Salad

- Cook the eggs in boiling water for 6 minutes then leave to cool. Peel and quarter.
- Arrange a layer of shredded lettuce in the base of 4 bowls.
- Halve and core the fennel, remove the outer leaves, then finely slice and add to the lettuce with the tomatoes.
- Flake over the tuna and tip in the crayfish. Add the quartered eggs.
- Whisk together the ingredients for the dressing and drizzle over the top of the salad. Serve.

PREPARATION TIME 15 MINUTES

COOKING TIME 6 MINUTES

INGREDIENTS

4 eggs at room temperature
2 Little Gem lettuces, shredded
1 fennel (finocchio) bulb
4 plum tomatoes, quartered
1 x 185g can tuna, drained
500g / 1 lb / 2 cups crayfish tails, ready-cooked
4 plum tomatoes, quartered

FOR THE DRESSING
1 orange, juiced
½ lemon, juiced
1 red chilli, deseeded and finely sliced
1 shallot, very finely chopped
7 tbsp extra virgin olive oil
Salt and pepper

421

SERVES 4-6

Coleslaw

PREPARATION TIME 40 MINUTES

INGREDIENTS

¼ white cabbage, finely shredded
¼ red cabbage, finely shredded
Salt
½ red onion, finely sliced
2 carrots, peeled and grated

1 apple, peeled and cut into fine matchsticks

FOR THE DRESSING
6 tbsp mayonnaise
2 tbsp sour cream
2 tbsp grain mustard
1 tbsp lemon juice
Pepper

- Salt the shredded cabbage in a bowl and set aside for 30 minutes.
- Drain off any excess liquid, then tip into a large bowl.
- Add the onion, carrots and apple.
- Mix together the ingredients for the dressing with a pinch of salt and toss the salad thoroughly in it.
- Serve within 2 hours.

422

SERVES 2

Quinoa and Pumpkin Salad

PREPARATION TIME 5 MINUTES

COOKING TIME 40 MINUTES

INGREDIENTS

1 butternut squash, deseeded and cut into chunks
2 tbsp oil
140g quinoa

280ml water
2 tbsp sultanas
½ bunch coriander (cilantro), finely chopped
1-2 tbsp white wine vinegar
2 tbsp olive oil
1 red chilli, deseeded and finely chopped
Salt and pepper

- Preheat the oven to 200°C / 400F / gas 6.
- Roast the butternut squash, drizzled with oil and seasoning, for 30 minutes until completely tender and caramelised.
- Place the quinoa in the pan with the water and bring to the boil – do not add salt.
- Once boiling, turn the heat down and simmer for 10 minutes until the germ separates.
- Remove from the heat, cover with a lid and leave to absorb the remaining water.
- Add the butternut squash to a bowl with the sultanas.
- Add the coriander, oil, vinegar, chilli and seasoning.
- Once the quinoa is ready, stir into the squash mixture. Adjust the seasoning if necessary.

423

SERVES 4

Prawns, Mushrooms and Caper Salad

PREPARATION TIME 10 MINUTES

COOKING TIME 10 MINUTES

INGREDIENTS

320g / 11 oz / 1 ½ cups fusilli pasta
200g / 7 oz / ¾ cup cooked king prawns (shrimp)
100g / 3 ½ oz / ½ cup button mushrooms
2 tbsp capers, drained
8 cherry tomatoes
1-2 tbsp red wine vinegar
6 tbsp extra virgin olive oil
Salt and pepper

- Cook the pasta in boiling salted water according to packet instructions.
- Drain and tip into a bowl.
- Add the prawns. Finely slice the mushrooms and add with the capers.
- Halve the tomatoes and add to the pasta.
- Whisk together the vinegar and oil and toss the salad in the dressing. Season and serve.

Pasta Salad with Basil Dressing   424

- Peppery basil complements all the ingredients. Try whizzing a handful of leaves in a little oil and trickling over.

425

SERVES 4

Apple & Goats' Cheese Salad

PREPARATION TIME 15 MINUTES

INGREDIENTS

2 crisp green eating apples
Lemon juice
200g / 7 oz / ¾ cup log goats' cheese
100g / 3 ½ oz / ½ cup button mushrooms
½ pomegranate
1 small romaine lettuce, cut into ribbons

- Halve the apples and core, then slice into thin half moons. Tip into a bowl and stir in a little lemon juice to prevent browning.
- Cut the cheese into thick slices and arrange on a plate with the apple slices and lettuce ribbons.
- Finely slice the mushrooms and scatter around the cheese.
- Holding the pomegranate half skin side up, bash with a wooden spoon to release the seeds.

Apple & Goats' Cheese Salad   426
with a Honey Mustard Dressing

- Whisk 1 tbsp wholegrain mustard with ½ tbsp honey, a little seasoning and extra virgin oil then drizzle over for extra tang.

427

SERVES 4

Pasta, Ham and Artichoke Salad

- Cook the pasta in boiling salted water until al dente. Drain thoroughly, then toss with a little olive oil and leave to cool.
- Mix together the artichokes, chopped ham, tomatoes and rocket in a bowl.
- For the dressing: whisk together the vinegar, mustard, salt, pepper and sugar. Whisk in the oil until thickened and amalgamated. Check the seasoning and adjust if necessary.
- Add the pasta to the other ingredients, pour over the dressing then, using large spoons, toss everything until coated.

PREPARATION TIME 20 MINUTES

COOKING TIME 10 MINUTES

INGREDIENTS

300g / 10 oz / 1 ¼ cups pasta
1 jar artichoke hearts, drained
200g / 7 oz / ¾ cup ham, trimmed and cut into cubes
300g / 10 oz / 1 ¼ cups cherry tomatoes, halved
60g rocket (arugula) leaves

FOR THE DRESSING
2-3 tsp red wine vinegar
½ - 1 tsp grain mustard
½ tsp salt
Pepper
Pinch sugar
6 tbsp extra virgin olive oil

Pasta Prawn Artichoke Salad   428

- Try adding cooked prawns instead of ham if you want a lighter option.

429

SERVES 4

Chicken, Grape and Walnut Salad

- Preheat the oven to 200°C / 400F / gas 6.
- Roast the chicken breasts, drizzled with oil and a little lemon juice and seasoned for 25 minutes, until just cooked through. Leave to rest.
- Toss the grapes, walnuts and lettuce leaves together.
- Grate the carrot and toss with the salad.
- Thickly slice the chicken, removing the skin if desired and add to the leaves.
- Squeeze a little more lemon juice and the extra virgin olive oil into the roasting tin and whisk in. Spoon the juices over the salad sparingly and serve.

PREPARATION TIME 10 MINUTES

COOKING TIME 25 MINUTES

INGREDIENTS

4 chicken breasts, skin on
Olive oil
Salt and pepper
Juice of ½ lemon
80g / 2 ½ oz / ⅓ cup green grapes
80g / 2 ½ oz / ⅓ cup walnuts
3 Little Gem lettuces
1 carrot, peeled
2 tbsp extra virgin olive oil

Chicken, Grape and Walnut Salad with a Creamy Dressing   430

- Mix 4-5 tbsp crème fraîche with a little lemon juice and 1 tbsp wholegrain mustard for a creamy dressing.

BEEF

431

SERVES 4

Home-Made Burgers

- Season the meat well, mix well with the mustard if using and form into patties around 2 cm thick. Refrigerate until needed.
- Heat a griddle to very hot, then brush the burgers on each side with a little oil. Cook for 3-4 minutes each side, then leave to rest for 5-8 minutes wrapped in foil, the slices of cheese melting on top. Serve in buns topped with tomatoes, red onion and salad.

PREPARATION TIME 10 MINUTES

COOKING TIME 25 MINUTES

INGREDIENTS

4 sirloin steaks, minced until coarsely ground but not mush (ask your butcher)
1 tsp salt
1 tbsp grain mustard (optional)
Black pepper
Olive oil
4 slices Jarlsberg cheese
1 large tomato, thickly sliced
4 burger buns

Beef Meatballs in Tomato Sauce

432

SERVES 4-6

PREPARATION TIME 20 MINUTES
+ CHILLING TIME

COOKING TIME 30 MINUTES

INGREDIENTS

400g / 14 oz / 1 ½ cups minced beef
1 egg
2 tbsp parsley, chopped
1 clove garlic, crushed
½ lemon, grated zest
Salt and pepper
1 thick slice of white bread, crusts removed soaked in 2 tbsp milk
3 tbsp olive oil
1 x 400g can chopped tomatoes
400ml / 14 fl oz / 1 ½ cups beef stock
1 tsp sugar

- Place the meat in a large bowl with the egg, garlic, lemon zest and 1 tbsp parsley and season.
- Mulch the bread in your fingers and crumble into the mix. Mix everything together with your hands to become smooth and sticky.
- Roll into small walnut-sized balls with cold wet hands, place on a tray and chill for 30 minutes.
- Heat the oil in a pan and fry the meatballs in batches until brown.
- Add the tomatoes and stock, then add the sugar and season and bring to the boil. Lower the heat and simmer for about 20 minutes.
- Serve with pasta or cous cous.

Beef Wellington

433

SERVES 6

PREPARATION TIME 45 MINUTES

COOKING TIME 20 MINUTES

INGREDIENTS

1 beef fillet, weighing 1 kg / 2 ¼ lb
3 tbsp olive oil
3 tbsp butter
250g / 9 oz / 1 cup mushrooms
1 shallot, finely chopped
2 sprigs thyme leaves
75ml / 2 ½ oz / ⅓ cup dry white wine
1 sheet ready rolled puff pastry
1 tbsp flour
2 egg yolks, beaten

TO SERVE
750g / 1 ⅓ lb / 3 cups new potatoes, roasted

- Preheat oven to 220°C (200° fan)/ 450F / gas 7.
- Place the beef in a roasting tin, drizzle with oil and roast for 15 minutes.
- Meanwhile, place the mushrooms in a food processor with the shallot and process as finely as possible.
- Heat the butter in a pan and dry the mushroom mixture with thyme leaves and a little seasoning until softened. Add the wine and cook until the wine has been absorbed. Set aside to cool.
- Roll the pastry out a little more on a floured surface. Spoon the cooled mushrooms over the pastry, leaving a small margin around the edges.
- Place the beef in the centre and roll the pastry up like sausage, fully encasing the beef. Seal the edges with egg yolk, then brush the pastry with the remaining egg.
- Reduce the oven to 200°C (180° fan)/ 400F / gas 6 and roast for 20 minutes until puffed and golden.

434

SERVES 6

Beef with Apricot and Almond Crust

PREPARATION TIME 10 MINUTES

COOKING TIME 20-25 MINUTES

INGREDIENTS

1 beef fillet, weighing 1 kg / 2 ¼ lb
Salt and pepper
50g / 1 ¾ oz / ¼ cup dried apricots
60g / 2 oz / ¼ cup flaked (slivered) almonds
½ tbsp rosemary leaves
2 tbsp Dijon mustard
Olive oil

- Preheat the oven to 200°C (180° fan) / 400F / gas 6.
- Season the beef fillet and place it in a roasting tin.
- Whiz the apricots, almonds and rosemary leaves in a food processor to fine crumbs.
- Spread the mustard over the top of the beef fillet to act as a glue. Pat the crust onto the beef then drizzle with oil.
- Bake in the oven for about 20 minutes for rare beef, 25 minutes for medium-rare.
- Allow to rest for 10 minutes before serving.

Beef with Apricot Pistachio Crust 435

- The same quantity of peeled crushed pistachio nuts goes well with the beef.

436

SERVES 4

Beef Hot Pot

PREPARATION TIME 25 MINUTES

COOKING TIME 2 HOURS 45 MINUTES

INGREDIENTS

2 tbsp vegetable oil or dripping
1 kg / 2 ¼ lb / 4 ¼ cups stewing beef
4 onions, peeled and chopped
1 tbsp butter
1 tbsp flour
500ml / 1 pint / 2 cups beef stock
1 tbsp Worcestershire sauce
2 bay leaves
1 sprig rosemary
1 kg / 2 ¼ lb / 4 ¼ cups potatoes, peeled and cut into 2cm slices
Salt and pepper

- Preheat the oven to 170°C (150° fan) / 325F / gas 3.
- Heat the fat in a large casserole and fry the meat in batches until browned. Remove with a slotted spoon and set aside.
- Adding a little butter, cook the onions until translucent, then stir in the flour to make a paste.
- Whisk in the stock and Worcestershire sauce to make a smooth sauce and bring to a simmer. Return the meat to the sauce.
- Add the herbs then top with slices of potato, seasoning the layers, arranging in an overlapping pattern.
- Cover with a lid and bake for 2 hours, then remove the lid and cook for a further 45 minutes to crisp up the potatoes.

Beef Hot Pot with Celeriac 437

- Use the same quantity of celeriac and potatoes to layer over the top.

SERVES 2

Griddled Rump Steak with Mushrooms

Grilled Rump Steak with Béarnaise 439

- Bearnaise is a classic combination with steak – see page 24.

Marinated Rump Steaks 440

- An hour before serving, marinate the steaks with rosemary sprigs and a crushed clove garlic and a little oil to infuse them with flavour.

Rump Steak with Mushroom Sauce 441

- Add 4 tbsp double (heavy) cream or crème fraîche to the mushrooms after cooking to make a sauce.

PREPARATION TIME 30 MINUTES

COOKING TIME 10 MINUTES

INGREDIENTS

2 x rump steaks, about 3cm / 1 inch thick
Olive oil
Salt and pepper
50g / 1 ¾ oz / ¼ cup butter
400g / 14 oz / 1 ½ cups mixed wild mushrooms
2 sprigs thyme
1 clove garlic, finely sliced
½ bunch parsley, finely chopped
Squeeze of lemon juice

- Rub the steaks all over with olive oil and season. Preheat a griddle pan or the barbecue until searingly hot.
- Place the steaks in the pan, placing them away from you and leave for 2 minutes until char marks form.
- Turn the steaks over and leave for 3 minutes.
- At this point, for rare steak, you can remove them from the heat. If you prefer your beef more well cooked, turn the steaks once more and leave for another minute.
- Wrap the steaks securely in a large piece of foil and leave to rest for at least 5 minutes, but no longer than 8.
- Meanwhile heat the butter in a pan and when foaming add the mushrooms, thyme and garlic. Cook until the liquid has evaporated from the mushrooms then season. Toss with parsley and lemon juice.
- Just before serving, season the steaks again and pour the juices back over the steaks on the plate. Serve with the mushrooms.

442

SERVES 4 # Burritos

PREPARATION TIME 25 MINUTES

COOKING TIME 10 MINUTES

INGREDIENTS

2 tbsp vegetable oil
1 onion, peeled and finely sliced
350g / 12 oz / 1 ½ cups rump steak, finely sliced
1 clove garlic, finely chopped
½ green chilli, finely chopped
1 tsp paprika
1 tbsp Worcestershire sauce
Salt and pepper

TO SERVE

4 flour tortillas, warmed briefly
400g / 14 oz / 1 ½ cups refried beans, heated through
100g / 3 ½ oz / ½ cup Cheddar, grated
Guacamole
Tomato salsa
Sour cream

- Heat the oil in a pan and fry the onion until softened.
- Add the steak, increase the heat and fry quickly for 2 minutes, adding the garlic, chilli, paprika and Worcestershire sauce. Remove from the heat.
- Lay the tortillas out on a surface and spoon the steak mixture down the middle and top with a line of refried beans.
- Wrap the tortilla around the filling and place on a baking sheet, seam side down. Scatter with cheddar.
- Grill until cheese has melted and serve with accompanying sauces.

Chicken or Lamb Burritos

 443

- Try the burritos made with pinkly-cooked lamb or chicken strips.

444

SERVES 4 # Chilli con Carne

PREPARATION TIME 20 MINUTES

COOKING TIME 2 HOURS 10 MINUTES

INGREDIENTS

2 tbsp vegetable oil
500g / 1 lb / 2 full cups stewing beef, diced
1 onion, peeled and chopped
2 cloves garlic, finely chopped
1 tsp paprika
1 tsp ground cumin
1 tsp cinnamon
½ - 1 tsp Cayenne pepper or ½ tsp dried chilli flakes
1 x 400g can kidney beans
1 x 400g can chopped tomatoes
300ml / 10 fl oz / 1 ¼ cups beef stock
20g / ½ oz dark chocolate, finely chopped

TO SERVE

1 lime, juiced
Sour cream
Rice

- Heat the oil in a large casserole and cook the beef until browned. Remove with a slotted spoon.
- Add the onion and garlic and fry for a further 5 minutes until golden.
- Add the spices and mix well, then pour over the kidney beans, tomatoes and stock, add the beef back in and bring to the boil.
- Simmer over a low heat for at least 2 hours, stirring occasionally, until the chilli has thickened and reduced.
- When the meat is falling apart, stir in the chocolate and season.
- Serve with a squeeze of lime juice, sour cream and rice.

Baked Chilli with Crispy Crust

445

- Tip the chilli into a gratin dish, top with lightly crushed tortilla chips and blue cheese and bake for 20 minutes.

446
SERVES 4-6 Cottage Pie

- Preheat the oven to 180°C (160° fan) / 350F / gas 4.
- Heat the oil in a large pan and briskly fry the lamb mince. Add the vegetables and sweat until soft.
- Stir in the tomato puree and cook out for 2 minutes, before adding the herbs and pouring over the stock. Simmer until the stock has reduced and there is just a little liquid left in the bottom of the pan.
- Meanwhile cook the potatoes in boiling salted water until tender to the point of a knife.
- Drain thoroughly, then mash until completely smooth with the butter and season well.
- Pour the lamb base into a baking dish, then spoon over the mashed potato. Run a fork down the length of the potato to create edges that will crisp in the oven.
- Bake for 30 minutes until bubbling and golden.

Cottage Pie with
Horseradish Potato Crust   447
- Stir 1-2 tbsp creamed horseradish into the mashed potatoes before spooning over.

PREPARATION TIME 25 MINUTES

COOKING TIME 35 MINUTES

INGREDIENTS

2 tbsp vegetable oil
450g / 1 lb / 2 cups minced beef
1 onion, peeled and finely chopped
2 carrots, peeled and finely chopped
2 sticks celery, finely chopped
100g / 3 ½ oz / ½ cup flat field mushrooms, finely chopped
1 tbsp tomato puree
1 bay leaf
1 sprig rosemary
350ml / 12 fl oz / 1 ½ cups beef stock
Salt and pepper

900g / 2 lb / 3 ½ cups floury potatoes, peeled and cut into chunks
100g / 3 ½ oz / ½ cup butter

448
SERVES 6 Beef Stew

- Heat the oil in a casserole. Dust the beef with flour and sear in the oil on all sides, in batches, removing as you go with a slotted spoon.
- Cook the carrots, onions and celery until softened, then stir in the tomato puree.
- Add the beef back to the pan with any resting juices and the bouquet garni, then pour in the red wine and stock and bring to a simmer.
- Reduce the heat, season, partially cover with a lid and cook very gently for 2-3 hours until the meat is tender.
- Serve with mashed potato.

PREPARATION TIME 45 MINUTES

COOKING TIME 3 ½ HOURS

INGREDIENTS

3 tbsp vegetable oil
600g / 1 ⅓ lb / 2 ½ cups stewing beef, cubed
1 tbsp seasoned flour
2 carrots, peeled and cut into short lengths
2 onions, peeled and sliced
2 sticks celery, finely chopped
1 tbsp tomato puree
1 bouquet garni
300ml / 10 fl oz / 1 ¼ cups red wine
500ml / 1 pint / 2 cups beef stock
Salt and pepper

Beef Stew with Port and Mustard   449
- Use port instead of the red wine for a sweeter flavour and balance with a good tbsp Dijon or wholegrain mustard.

450

SERVES 4

Spicy Beef with Chickpea Mash

Spicy Beef with Cannellini Bean Mash
451

- Use cannellini beans in the same way as the chickpeas.

Moroccan Beef with Chickpea Mash
452

- Rub the steaks with ras el-hanout spice mix before cooking.

Garam Masala Beef
453

- Rub the steaks with garam masala before cooking.

PREPARATION TIME 2 HOURS

COOKING TIME 20 MINUTES

....

INGREDIENTS

2 large rump steaks
1 tsp ground cumin
1 tbsp paprika
½ tsp Cayenne
1 tsp dried oregano
3 tbsp olive oil

FOR THE CHICKPEA MASH

1 x 400g can chickpeas (garbanzo beans), drained
200ml / 7 fl oz / ¾ cup vegetable stock
1 clove garlic, peeled
1 sprig thyme
2 tbsp plain yoghurt
Salt and pepper

- Rub the steaks all over with the mixed spices and oil and set aside in the refrigerator for at least 2 hours.
- Simmer the chickpeas in the vegetables tock with the garlic and thyme for 15 minutes. Drain, then mash with the yoghurt and season.
- Heat a griddle until very hot and cook the steaks for 2-3 minutes per side for rare.
- Wrap in foil and rest for 8 minutes, then slice thinly, season and serve with the chickpea mash and the resting juices poured over.

454

SERVES 4 Spicy Beef Kebabs

- Rub the cubes of beef with paprika and Cayenne and a little oil and season with salt.
- Thread alternately onto skewers with courgette and peppers.
- Cook on a griddle for 5-6 minutes until the beef is charred outside and pink inside.
- Serve.

PREPARATION TIME 10 MINUTES

COOKING TIME 6 MINUTES

INGREDIENTS

800g / 1 ¾ lb rump steak cubed
½ tsp Cayenne
1 tsp paprika
Salt
Olive oil
1 courgette (zucchini), cut into cubes
2 yellow peppers, deseeded and roughly chopped

Italian Beef Kebabs

455

- Marinate the beef for 1 hour in rosemary, garlic, lemon zest and olive oil before cooking.

456

SERVES 2 Beef Entrecôte with Roasted Tomatoes

- Preheat the oven to 200°C / 400F / gas 6.
- Place the tomatoes on the vine in a roasting tin and drizzle with 2 tbsp olive oil and the balsamic vinegar. Roast for 30 minutes until slightly blackened.
- Meanwhile, season the steaks and preheat the griddle to very hot. Cook for 3-4 minutes per side until cooked to your liking, then wrap in foil and rest for 5 minutes.
- Serve the steaks with the roasted tomatoes and resting juices poured over.

PREPARATION TIME 10 MINUTES

COOKING TIME 30 MINUTES

INGREDIENTS

2 branches vine cherry tomatoes
Olive oil
1 tbsp balsamic vinegar
2 entrecôte steaks, weighing 225g / 8 oz each
Salt and pepper

Beef Entrecôte with Roasted Mushrooms

457

- Field or portabella mushrooms can be treated in the same way as the tomatoes for a deeply meaty feast.

SERVES 6

Beef Bourguignon

PREPARATION TIME 15 MINUTES

COOKING TIME 3 HOURS

....

INGREDIENTS

1 kg / 2 ¼ lb / 4 ¼ cups stewing beef, cubed
225 g / 7 ½ oz / 1 ½ cups baby carrots, washed and scrubbed
3 tbsp vegetable oil
1 onion, peeled and sliced
1 tbsp flour
400ml / 14 fl oz / 1 ½ cups red wine, preferably Burgundy
2 cloves garlic, sliced
1 sprig thyme
1 bay leaf
12 pearl or button onions, peeled
225g / 8 oz / 1 cup smoked streaky bacon, diced
200g / 7 oz / ¾ cup chestnut mushrooms
Salt and pepper

- Preheat the oven to 140°C / 275F / gas 1.
- Sear the beef in 1 tbsp oil in a casserole until brown all over. Remove with a slotted spoon.
- Add the onion and cook until beginning to brown, then return the meat to the pan.
- Stir in the flour and soak up the juices, then pour in the wine. Add the garlic and herbs, season, cover with a lid and cook for 2 hours.
- Meanwhile fry the onions and bacon in a little oil, then add, with the mushrooms and carrots to the casserole and cook for 1 more hour.
- Adjust the seasoning and serve.

Beef Bourguignon with Garlic Bread

459

- For the last 20 minutes of cooking, top with thin slices of toasted baguette spread with garlic butter.

460

SERVES 6

Thai Beef Green Curry

PREPARATION TIME 15 MINUTES

COOKING TIME 45 MINUTES

....

INGREDIENTS

500ml / 1 pint / 2 cups coconut milk
750g / 1 ⅓ lb / 3 cups rump steak, sliced
2 aubergines (eggplant), chopped
1-2 tbsp caster (superfine) sugar
1-2 tbsp fish sauce
2 limes, juiced
Thai basil

FOR THE CURRY PASTE

1 tbsp coriander seeds
1 tbsp cumin seeds
½ - 1 tbsp black peppercorns
2-4 green chillies
8 cloves garlic, peeled
2 stalks lemongrass
1 bunch coriander (cilantro)
2 tbsp fresh galangal or ginger
3 kaffir lime leaves
6 shallots, peeled
1 tbsp dried shrimp paste

- Pound the seeds in a pestle and mortar or in a freezer bag with a rolling pin until finely ground.
- Tip into a food processor and whiz with the rest of the ingredients until smooth. You will only need 4-5 tbsp for this recipe, so keep the rest in a sealed jar in the fridge.
- Heat a wok and add 4-5 tbsp curry paste and 2 tbsp of the cream off the top of the coconut milk and stir until sizzling.
- Add the beef and coat thoroughly in the paste, then pour in the coconut milk.
- Add the aubergines, sugar, fish sauce and juice of 1 lime and simmer gently for about 15-20 minutes or until the aubergine is cooked and tender.
- Adjust the flavours with more sugar, fish sauce and lime juice, then serve with Thai sticky rice, sprinkled with coriander and Thai basil leaves.

Thai Seafood Green Curry

461

- Make it with mixed seafood such as prawns, squid and chunky white fish.

462

Fried Chilli Beef with Noodles

- Whisk together the eggs, salt and cornflour and coat the beef strips.
- Heat the oil to 180°C / 350F and deep fry the beef in small batches. Cook for about 5 minutes until brown and crisp. Remove and drain on kitchen paper.
- Heat a little oil in a wok and stir fry the carrots, spring onion and chilli. Add the remaining ingredients and toss together, adding the beef at the last minute.
- Cook the noodles according to packet instructions and serve topped with the chilli beef.

PREPARATION TIME 10 MINUTES

COOKING TIME 15 MINUTES

INGREDIENTS

2 eggs, beaten
½ tsp salt
1 ½ tbsp cornflour (cornstarch)
150g / 5 oz / ⅔ cup rump steak, sliced
Vegetable oil for deep frying
1 carrot, shredded
2 spring onions (scallions), chopped
1 red chilli, deseeded chopped
1 tsp sugar
2 tbsp rice vinegar
2 tbsp sweet chilli sauce
1 tbsp soy sauce
Noodles, to accompany

463

Beef Stroganoff

PREPARATION TIME 15 MINUTES

COOKING TIME 20 MINUTES

INGREDIENTS

2 tbsp butter
1 onion, peeled and sliced
2 cloves garlic, finely sliced
400g / 14 oz / 1 ½ cups mushrooms, sliced

500g / 1 lb/ 2 cups sirloin or rump steak, thinly sliced
Salt and pepper
275ml / 10 fl oz / 1 cup sour cream
1 tbsp smoked paprika

TO GARNISH

Chopped cornichons
Flat leaf parsley
Boiled rice

- Fry the onions and garlic in the butter until golden and sweet then add the mushrooms. Cook until all the liquid has evaporated and season. Remove from the pan with a slotted spoon.
- Increase the heat and fry the beef quickly for 2 minutes, then return the vegetables to the pan and pour in the sour cream and paprika.
- Bubble up, adjust the seasoning and serve with the garnishes.

464

Beef Choucroute

PREPARATION TIME 25 MINUTES

COOKING TIME 2 HOURS

INGREDIENTS

2 tbsp goose fat or vegetable oil
2 large onions, sliced
2 cloves garlic, finely sliced
2 large carrots, peeled and chopped
200g / 7 oz streaky bacon, diced
3 large floury potatoes, peeled and cut into chunks
300g / 10 oz / 1 ¼ cups sauerkraut
1 tsp caraway seeds
4 juniper berries, lightly crushed
2 bay leaves
150ml / 5 fl oz / ⅔ cup dry white wine
150ml / 5 fl oz / ⅔ cup chicken stock
2 apples, quartered
2 x sirloin steaks, weighing 225g / 8oz each

- Heat the fat in a large casserole and cook the onions and garlic until golden.
- Add the bacon and cook until the fat starts to render and they begin to crisp.
- Add the potatoes and sauerkraut, stir in the spices, then pour over the wine and stock.
- Cover tightly with a lid and cook gently for 1 hour, stirring occasionally and checking it's not too dry.
- Add the apples and cook for a further 30 minutes.
- Cook the steaks on a griddle for 4 minutes per side, then rest for 5 minutes. Slice thickly and place on top of the choucroute.
- Adjust the seasoning and serve.

465

SERVES 2

Honey-Cooked Rump Steak

PREPARATION TIME 10 MINUTES

COOKING TIME 30 MINUTES

INGREDIENTS

2 rump steaks
Salt and pepper
Olive oil
1 tbsp butter
1 tbsp heather honey
500g / 1 lb / 2 cups potatoes, peeled
and sliced
2 tbsp goose fat or olive oil
1 clove garlic
Salt and pepper
½ bunch parsley, chopped

- Heat the fat in a large frying pan and add the potato slices and garlic. Season and cook over a low heat until golden and crusty.
- Season the steaks and rub with oil. Heat a frying pan and sear the steaks on each side for 2 minutes.
- Add the butter to the pan and then the honey. Baste the steaks as they cook for 2 minutes more, then remove from the pan and rest for 5 minutes.
- Serve the steak with the potatoes alongside.

Honey Mustard Rump Steak

466

- 1 tbsp Dijon mustard added with the honey will lend warmth without spice.

467

SERVES 4-6

Bourguignon Hachis Parmentier

PREPARATION TIME 25 MINUTES

COOKING TIME 35 MINUTES

INGREDIENTS

2 tbsp vegetable oil
450g / 1 lb / 2 cups minced beef
1 onion, peeled and finely chopped
2 carrots, peeled and finely chopped
2 sticks celery, finely chopped
100g / 3 ½ oz / ½ cup flat field
mushrooms, finely chopped
1 tbsp tomato puree
1 bay leaf
1 sprig rosemary
200ml / 7 fl oz / ¾ cup red wine
350ml / 12 fl oz / 1 ½ cups beef stock
Salt and pepper
900g / 2 lb / 3 ½ cups floury potatoes,
peeled and cut into chunks
100g / 3 ½ oz / ½ cup butter
100g / 3 ½ oz / ½ cup Gruyere
cheese, grated

- Preheat the oven to 180°C (160° fan) / 350F / gas 4.
- Heat the oil in a large pan and briskly fry the beef mince. Add the vegetables and sweat until soft.
- Stir in the tomato puree and cook out for 2 minutes, before adding the herbs and pouring over the wine and stock. Simmer until the stock has reduced and there is just a little liquid left in the bottom of the pan.
- Meanwhile cook the potatoes in boiling salted water until tender to the point of a knife.
- Drain thoroughly, then mash until completely smooth with the butter and season well.
- Pour the beef base into a baking dish, then spoon over the mashed potato. Run a fork down the length of the potato to create edges that will crisp in the oven. Sprinkle over the cheese.
- Bake for 30 minutes until bubbling and golden.

Lamb Bourguignon Hachis Parmentier

468

- Make with minced lamb and 1 tsp ground cumin + ½ tsp ground cinnamon for a

469

SERVES 4

Steak Tartare

Steak Tartare with Hot Thin Chips

470

- See PXX for a classic accompaniment.

Steak Tartare with Tarragon

471

- Although to be used in moderation, finely chopped tarragon works well with beef instead of parsley.

Spicy Beef Tartare

472

- A few dried chilli flakes will pep up the tartare.

PREPARATION TIME 15 MINUTES

INGREDIENTS

300g / 10 oz / 1 ¼ cups fillet beef
1 shallot, very finely chopped
1 tbsp Worcestershire sauce
1 tsp Tabasco (optional)
1 tsp extra virgin olive oil
Salt and pepper
2 tbsp cornichons, chopped
1 tbsp capers
1 tbsp parsley, chopped
2 egg yolks

- Using a sharp knife finely chop the beef into tiny pieces and tip into a bowl.
- Mix loosely with the shallot, sauces, oil and seasoning.
- Spoon into rings and unmould on plate.
- Around the steak place small piles of the cornichons and capers.
- Make a small dent in the top of each tartare and slip the egg yolk in. Sprinkle with parsley and serve.

473

SERVES 4-6 # Beef Carpaccio

PREPARATION TIME 40 MINUTES

INGREDIENTS

250g centre cut beef fillet
Handful rocket (arugula) leaves
Parmesan shavings
1 tbsp capers, drained
Extra virgin olive oil
½ lemon, juiced
Salt and pepper

- Place the fillet in the freezer for 30 minutes to firm it up and make it easier to slice.
- Slice the fillet as thinly as you possibly can with a razor-sharp knife. Place clingfilm over each slice to prevent colouring and use it to stop the slices sticking together. You can keep them this way in the refrigerator until serving.
- 30 minutes before serving remove the beef from the refrigerator and bring up to room temperature.
- Decorate with the rocket, Parmesan and capers and drizzle over the oil and lemon. Season and serve.

Tuna Carpaccio 474

- You can achieve the same effect with fresh tuna steaks for fish lovers.

475

SERVES 4 # Stuffed Peppers

PREPARATION TIME 30 MINUTES

COOKING TIME 30 MINUTES

INGREDIENTS

4 ripe red peppers
1 tbsp olive oil
1 onion, peeled and finely chopped
2 cloves garlic, finely chopped
300g / 10 oz / 1 ¼ cups minced beef
1 tbsp rosemary leaves, finely chopped
2 tbsp tomato puree
200g / 7 oz / ¾ cup white rice, cooked
2 tbsp Parmesan, grated

- Cut the tops off the peppers, setting them aside, and hollow out the insides.
- Fry the onion and garlic in the oil until translucent.
- Add the beef and rosemary, turn up the heat and fry briskly, stirring, until the beef is cooked. Season.
- Stir in the tomato puree and a cup of water and leave to simmer until the water is absorbed.
- Stir in the Parmesan and rice and leave to cool a little.
- Preheat the oven to 200°C (180° fan) / 400F / gas 6.
- Fill the peppers with the beef mixture and place in a roasting tin.
- Drizzle with olive oil and bake in the oven for about 30 minutes or until they are soft but retaining their shape.

Stuffed Peppers with Gherkins 476

- Finely chopped gherkins lend a piquancy to the stuffing.

477

SERVES 6

Beef Daube

- Place the meat in a large bowl with the orange zest, bouquet garni. Pepper generously, add a little oil and the red wine. Cover with clingfilm and leave to marinate for 24 hours in the refrigerator.
- The same day, peel the remaining onion, cut in half and push the cloves into it.
- Remove the meat from the marinade, pat dry and add to a casserole in batches to colour on all sides.
- Add the vegetables and cook for 10 minutes until softened then return all the meat to the pan.
- Add the lardons and fry gently, then stir in the tomato puree. Season and cook gently for 10 minutes.
- Add the marinade and its ingredients. Cover and cook over the lowest heat for 3 hours.
- Fish the cloved onion and bouquet garni out of the stew and serve with mashed potato.

Beef Daube with Bulghur Wheat   478

- Serve with bulghur wheat to mop up the juices – lighter than pasta or mash.

PREPARATION TIME 45 MINUTES
+ OVERNIGHT MARINATING

COOKING TIME 3 ½ HOURS

INGREDIENTS

600g / 1 ⅓ lb / 2 ½ cups stewing beef, cubed or 1 large piece if preferred
3 tbsp olive oil
1 orange, grated zest
1 bouquet garni
500ml / 1 pint / 2 cups red wine
2 carrots, peeled and chopped
2 onions, peeled and chopped
3 cloves garlic, peeled and sliced
2 cloves
125g / 4 oz / ½ cup smoked bacon lardons
1 tbsp tomato puree
Salt and pepper

479

SERVES 4

Creole-style Braised Beef Cheeks

- Preheat the oven to 150°C (130° fan) / 300F / gas 2.
- Heat the oil and sear the beef on all sides until golden. Remove with a slotted spoon and set aside.
- Add the onion and peppers and cook until softened, then add the garlic and spices and cook for 2 minutes.
- Add the chillies, stock and tomatoes and bring to a simmer.
- Cover with a lid and cook in the oven for at least 3 hours until the meat is tender stirring occasionally and checking the liquid levels.
- Remove the chillies, adjust the seasoning and serve.

Shin of Beef, Creole Style   480

- If you can't get hold of beef cheeks, chunkily-cut shin of beef will give a similar effect.

PREPARATION TIME 20 MINUTES

COOKING TIME 3 HOURS

INGREDIENTS

1 tbsp vegetable oil
500g / 1 lb / 2 cups beef cheek, cubed
Salt and pepper
1 onion, peeled and chopped
2 green peppers, deseeded and chopped
3 cloves garlic, crushed
2 tbsp curry powder
6 sprigs thyme leaves
1 tsp ground allspice
½ tsp ground cinnamon
2 bay leaves
1-2 Scotch Bonnet chillies (depending on how hot you want it)
500ml / 1 pint / 2 cups beef stock
1 x 400g can chopped tomatoes

PORK

Loin of Pork with Apples and Crumble
481 SERVES 6

- Preheat the oven to 200°C (180° fan) / 400F / gas 6.
- Lay the onion slices in a roasting tin and place the pork on top, seasoning and tucking the bay leaves underneath. Drizzle with oil and roast for 1hr 40 minutes.
- Meanwhile, tip the flour into a bowl and rub in the butter using the tips of your fingers until the mixture resembles breadcrumbs. Stir in the hazelnuts and sugar.
- Tip the crumble in an even layer onto a baking sheet and bake until lightly browned – a few minutes.
- Remove the pork from the oven and remove from the tin. Place the tin on the hob and pour in equal quantities wine and water, scraping at the bottom to deglaze. Bubble up and reduce until syrupy.
- Heat the butter in a pan and cook the apple quarters until golden and slightly softened.
- Serve the pork in thick slices with the apple quarters and the crumble sprinkled on top.

PREPARATION TIME 20 MINUTES
COOKING TIME 2 HOURS

INGREDIENTS
1 onion, peeled and thickly sliced
2kg / 4 ½ lb pork loin, boned, derinded and rolled
Olive oil
Bay leaves
1 glass dry white wine

FOR THE CRUMBLE
120g / 4 oz / ½ cup plain (all purpose) flour
100g / 3 ½ oz / ½ cup butter
50g / 1 ¾ oz / ¼ cup crushed hazelnuts (cob nuts)
1 tbsp dark soft brown sugar
4 apples, cored and quartered
2 tbsp butter

Pork Chops & Herbed Potatoes
482 SERVES 4

PREPARATION TIME 10 MINUTES
COOKING TIME 30 MINUTES

INGREDIENTS
500g / 1 lb / 2 cups salad potatoes, such as Anya or Charlotte
Salt
2 tbsp olive oil
2 sprigs rosemary leaves, chopped
4 pork chops
4 tbsp olive oil
½ lemon, juiced
½ bunch parsley, chopped
1 glass dry white wine, water or chicken stock
½ cucumber, peeled into thin ribbons with a vegetable peeler

- Cook the potatoes in boiling salted water for 20 minutes or until tender.
- Drain thoroughly then set back over the heat to drive off any excess moisture.
- Heat the oil in a large pan. Roughly crush the potatoes with the end of a rolling pin, then tip into the hot oil with the rosemary. Cook until golden and crusty – about 10 minutes.
- Meanwhile heat a frying pan with a little oil. Season the pork chops and cook 2 at a time for 4 minutes per side. Once cooked, squeeze over a little lemon juice and keep warm in a low oven.
- Deglaze the pan with the wine and add in the parsley. Nap over the pork chops and serve with potatoes and cucumber ribbons.

Pork Chops & Sauteed Potatoes
483 SERVES 4

PREPARATION TIME 15 MINUTES
COOKING TIME 30 MINUTES

INGREDIENTS
500g / 1 lb / 2 cups potatoes, peeled and sliced
2 tbsp goose fat or olive oil
1 clove garlic
Salt and pepper
300g / 10 oz / 1 ¼ cups mushrooms, sliced
½ bunch parsley, chopped
4 pork chops
2 tbsp butter

- Heat the fat in a large frying pan and add the potato slices and garlic. Season and cook over a low heat until golden and crusty.
- Heat the butter in a frying pan and season the pork chops. When foaming add the pork and cook for 4 minutes per side, basting with the butter.
- Set aside to rest.
- Increase the heat under the potato pan and add the mushrooms. Cook until golden and tender then throw in the parsley.
- Serve the pork chops with the potatoes and mushrooms alongside.

484

SERVES 4-6

Roast Spare Ribs

PREPARATION TIME 20 MINUTES

COOKING TIME 3 HOURS 30 MINUTES

INGREDIENTS

2 racks pork spare ribs

FOR THE RUB

2 tbsp salt
1 tbsp freshly ground black pepper
4 tbsp soft dark brown sugar
2 tbsp smoked paprika
1-2 tbsp crushed dried chilli flakes (as desired)
2 tbsp ground cumin
1 tbsp ground ginger

FOR THE BASTING SAUCE

10 tbsp tomato ketchup
4 tbsp cider vinegar
3-4 tbsp maple syrup
4 tbsp orange or apple juice
2 tbsp grain mustard
Salt and pepper

- Preheat the oven to 100°C / 200F / gas ¼
- Combine all of the rub ingredients together in a bowl.
- Lay out the racks in a roasting tin then pat the rub into the meat, coating thoroughly on both sides. If you are preparing this ahead of time, you can leave them in the refrigerator for up to 24 hours at this stage.
- Make the basting sauce: Combine the ingredients in a bowl, tasting as you go to get a balance of sweet and savoury.
- Coat the ribs in the sauce and roast in the oven, covered with foil, for about three hours or until the meat pulls easily away from the bone, basting with the sauce every hour and turning them over.
- Serve the ribs with any remaining basting sauce.

Devilled Spare Ribs   485

- A mixture of Worcestershire sauce, English mustard, ketchup, garlic and a splash of red wine vinegar – mixed to your taste – makes a great marinade.

486

SERVES 4

Caramelised Spare Ribs

PREPARATION TIME 4 HOURS

COOKING TIME 3 HOURS

INGREDIENTS

2 racks baby back ribs
2 tbsp runny honey
3 tbsp tomato ketchup
1 tbsp black treacle or molasses
2 star anise, lightly crushed
2 tsp English mustard
Pinch chilli flakes
2 tbsp olive oil
Salt and pepper

- Mix together the marinade ingredients and taste. You may want it sweeter or spicier in which case add more of the chosen ingredients.
- Coat the ribs thoroughly in the marinade and refrigerate for at least 4 hours or overnight.
- The next day, preheat the oven to 150°C (130° fan) / 300F / gas 2.
- Remove the ribs from the marinade and place in a roasting tin, cover with foil and cook slowly for 2-3 hours until the meat falls from the bone. Baste with any leftover marinade every now and then.
- To serve, heat a griddle pan until hot and lay the ribs on to caramelise the outside. Season well and serve.

Chinese Style Ribs   487

- Adding Chinese 5 spice to the mix – about ½ tsp – will give it an authentic Chinese flavour.

488

SERVES 4-6

Gammon with Leek Mashed Potato

Gammon with Colcannon **489**

- Substitute finely chopped greens for the leeks and add plenty of butter.

Baked Ham with Leek Mash **490**

- Spread the ham with honey and mustard and bake in a 200C/450F oven for 20 minutes or so until golden.

Gammon with Leek Mash and Mustard Sauce **491**

- Spoon a little wholegrain mustard into a few tbsp of the cooking liquor for a thin but tasty gravy.

PREPARATION TIME 10 MINUTES

COOKING TIME 2 HOURS 30 MINUTES

INGREDIENTS

2kg / 4 ½ lb gammon (ham), soaked to get rid of excess salt
2 carrots, quartered
1 onion, studded with 2 cloves
2 leeks, chopped
10 peppercorns
2 sticks celery, chopped
Bouquet garni
1 L / 2 ¼ pints / 4 ¼ cups dry cider
1 kg / 2 ¼ lb / 4 ¼ cups floury potatoes such as King Edward or Desiree
100g / 3 ½ oz / ½ cup butter
2 leeks, white part only, finely sliced
75-100ml / 2 ½ - 3 ½ oz / ⅓ – ½ cup milk, warmed
Salt and pepper

- Bring the gammon to room temperature and place in a large pot with the vegetables, peppercorns, bouquet garni and cider. Add enough cold water to cover and bring to a boil.
- Lower the heat to a 'blip' for 30 minutes + 30 minutes per 500g / 1 lb.
- Meanwhile cook the potatoes whole in their skins in boiling salted water until tender all the way through – about 30 minutes, but keep checking.
- Drain thoroughly and leave to cool for 5 minutes, then peel off the skins while still hot.
- Melt half the butter in the pan and cook the leeks gently until soft.
- Return the potato to the pan and stir in the remaining butter and enough milk with a wooden spoon to make a light, creamy, smooth mash. Season generously and keep warm.
- When the ham is cooked, remove and leave to cool for a few minutes before carving thickly and serving with the mash.

492

SERVES 6

Pork Loin with Caramelised Vegetables

Pork Loin with Pan Juices

493

- Empty the roasting tin, place over a heat and deglaze with cider or white wine.

Roast Pork Loin with Fennel Seeds

494

- Lightly crush 2 tbsp fennel seeds and use to coat the pork before cooking.

Pork Loin with Root Vegetables

495

- Turnips, parsnips and swede would all make good accompaniments roasted around the pork in the same way.

PREPARATION TIME 20 MINUTES

COOKING TIME 1 HOUR 50 MINUTES

INGREDIENTS

1 onion, peeled and thickly sliced
2kg / 4 ½ lb pork loin, derinded
2 cloves of garlic, finely chopped
1 tbsp felled seeds, lightly crushed
Salt and pepper
Olive oil
Bay leaves
Rosemary sprigs (leaves plucked)
3 carrots, peeled and chopped into short lengths
2 leeks, chopped into short lengths
8 shallots, whole

- Preheat the oven to 200°C (180° fan) / 400F / gas 6.
- Sprinkle the pork loin with garlic, fennel seeds and plucked rosemary.
- Lay the onion slices in a small roasting tin and place the pork on top, seasoning and tucking the herbs underneath. Tuck the vegetables all around and pour a glass of water into the tin.
- Drizzle with oil and roast for about 1hr 40 minutes.
- Remove the pork from the oven and rest for 10 minutes before carving.
- Increase the oven heat to 220°C (200° fan)/ 450F / gas 7 and brown the vegetables in the tin.
- Squeeze the shallots from their skins. Carve the pork and serve the caramelized vegetables alongside.

SERVES 4

Gammon with Pears

- Bring the gammon to room temperature and place in a large pot with the vegetables, peppercorns, bouquet garni and cider. Add enough cold water to cover and bring to a boil.
- Lower the heat to a 'blip' for 30 minutes + 30 minutes per 500g / 1 lb.
- When the ham is cooked, remove from the pan and leave to rest for 10 minutes. Preheat the oven to 200°C (180° fan) / 400F / Gas 7.
- Mix together the oil, honey and mustard. Cover the ham with the mixture and roast in the oven for about 20-30 minutes until golden and caramelised.
- Heat the butter in a pan and when foaming, add the pears cut side down. Caramelise on each side, drizzling over the honey.
- Serve with thick slices of ham.

PREPARATION TIME 10 MINUTES

COOKING TIME 2 ½ HOURS

INGREDIENTS

2kg / 4 ½ lb gammon (ham), soaked
to get rid of excess salt
2 carrots, quartered
1 onions, studded with 2 cloves
2 leeks, chopped
10 peppercorns
2 sticks celery, chopped
Bouquet garni
1 L/ 2 ¼ pints / 4 ¼ cups dry cider

4 tbsp honey
4 tbsp grain mustard
2 tbsp olive oil

4 pears, halved and cored
2 tbsp butter
1 tbsp honey

Gammon with Apples

497

- Substitute apple slices for the pears.

SERVES 6

Roast Pork Loin with Confit Onions

- Preheat the oven to 200°C (180° fan) / 400F / gas 6.
- Lay the onion slices in a small roasting tin and place the pork on top, seasoning and tucking the bay leaves underneath. Drizzle with oil and roast for about 1hr 40 minutes.
- Meanwhile melt the butter in a pan and add the onions. Cook very slowly for about 20 minutes until golden.
- Add the sugar, vinegar and a little salt and simmer gently for about 30 minutes until dark and sticky, stirring occasionally.
- Remove the pork from the oven and rest for 10 minutes before carving. Serve with the onion confit.

PREPARATION TIME 20 MINUTES

COOKING TIME 1 HOUR 45 MINUTES

INGREDIENTS

1 onion, peeled and thickly sliced
2kg / 4 ½ lb pork loin, boned,
derinded and rolled
Salt and pepper
Olive oil
Bay leaves
1 kg / 2 ¼ lb/ 4 ¼ cups onions, peeled
and finely sliced
50g / 1 ¾ oz / ¼ cup butter
100g / 3 ½ oz / ½ cup soft dark
brown sugar
3 tbsp red wine vinegar or sherry
vinegar
Salt and pepper

Roast Pork with Garlic Onion Confit

499

- Add 3-4 whole cloves garlic to the onions for a sweet sticky garlicky flavour.

500

SERVES 4

Pork Fillet with Summer Vegetables

PREPARATION TIME 10 MINUTES

COOKING TIME 20 MINUTES

INGREDIENTS

1 pork fillet, weighing 750g / 1 ⅓ lb
Salt and pepper
Olive oil
2 tbsp butter
2 handfuls green beans, topped and tailed
1 large handful runner beans, cut into short diamond shapes
2 courgettes (zucchini), cut into matchsticks
½ bunch parsley, finely chopped.

- Preheat the oven to 200°C (180° fan) / 400F / gas 6.
- Place the pork in a roasting tin and season well. Drizzle with oil and roast for 20 minutes until just cooked through.
- Meanwhile heat the butter in a pan and add the vegetables. Pour in a glass of water, cover with a lid and stew gently for 10-15 minutes until all is tender. Season and add the parsley.
- Rest the pork for 5 minutes before carving and serving with the vegetables.

Pork Fillet with Mixed Greens **501**

- You can braise hearty winter greens such as kale or cavolo nero in the same way.

502

SERVES 4

Sweet and Sour Pork

PREPARATION TIME 15 MINUTES

COOKING TIME 20 MINUTES

INGREDIENTS

500g / 1 lb pork loin, cubed
1 egg white
2 tsp cornflour
Salt
1 tsp sesame oil
1 tbsp vegetable oil
1 carrot, peeled and cut into matchsticks
1 red pepper, deseeded and finely sliced
50g / 1 ¾ oz / ¼ cup pineapple chunks

FOR THE SAUCE

125ml / 4 fl oz / ½ cup pineapple juice
Splash dry sherry or rice wine
2 tbsp tomato ketchup
2 tbsp soy sauce
2 tbsp Chinese vinegar or red wine vinegar

- Slice the pork into strips. Combine the egg white, cornflour, a pinch of salt and sesame oil in a bowl then thoroughly coat the chicken strips in the mixture.
- Heat the vegetable oil in a wok until smoking, then add the coated pork and stir fry over a high heat until the chicken turns white.
- Remove the pork from the pan and set aside. Discard the oil.
- Heat the oil in the wok again and stir fry the vegetables over a high heat for 4 minutes.
- Mix together the sauce ingredients. Add the pork back to the pan with the sauce, bubble up and serve with white rice.

Sweet Sour Pork Buns **503**

- This makes a surprisingly delicious filling for baguette or soft white rolls if you're short of time.

504
SERVES 2

Sausage and Potato Gratin

- Cook the potatoes in boiling salted water until tender. Drain then roughly mash with the butter.
- Heat the oil in a pan and cook the onions until soft and sweet. Add the carrots and cook for a further 10 minutes until soft.
- Add the sausages and cook for another 10 minutes, then pour over the stock and thyme and bubble up.
- Spoon into a gratin dish and season. Top with the roughly mashed potato, then top with smashed potato crisps.
- Grill until golden and bubbling, watching the crisps don't burn.

PREPARATION TIME 15 MINUTES

COOKING TIME 30 MINUTES

INGREDIENTS

2 large floury potatoes, peeled and chopped
2 tbsp butter
2 tbsp vegetable oil
1 onion, thickly sliced
2 carrots, peeled and thickly sliced
4 Cumberland sausages, cut into chunks
200ml / 7 fl oz / ¾ cup chicken stock
1 sprig thyme
Salt and pepper
2 bags crisps (potato chips)

Sausage Celeriac Gratin
505
- Crushed celeriac can be treated in the same way as the potato.

506
SERVES 4

Sausages with Onion Gravy

- Preheat the oven to 200°C (180° fan) / 400F / gas 6.
- Prick the sausages all over with a fork.
- Drizzle the sausages with oil in a roasting tin and roast for 30 minutes until browned all over, turning occasionally.
- Meanwhile heat the butter in a pan and cook the onions with thyme for 15-20 minutes, until deep gold and sweet.
- Stir in the flour and cook out for 2 minutes, then stir in the wine and stock. Season and simmer for 20 minutes until thickened.
- Stir in the grain mustard, then serve with the cooked sausages and mashed potato.

PREPARATION TIME 10 MINUTES

COOKING TIME 35 MINUTES

INGREDIENTS

8 sausages
Vegetable oil
2 tbsp butter
2 large onions, peeled and thickly sliced
2 sprigs thyme
½ tbsp flour
150ml / 5 fl oz / ⅔ cup Marsala or red wine
400ml / 14 fl oz / 1 ½ cups beef stock
Salt and pepper
1 tbsp grain mustard

TO SERVE
Ultimate mashed potato (see page 82)

Sausages with Sweet Sticky Onion Gravy
507
- Add 1 tbsp redcurrant jelly or 1 tbsp honey to the onions, but keep the mustard to balance the sweetness.

508

SERVES 4

Pork chops in Cider

PREPARATION TIME 10 MINUTES

COOKING TIME 30 MINUTES

INGREDIENTS

2 tbsp butter
1 large onion, peeled and thinly sliced
2 apples, peeled, cored and sliced
2 sprigs thyme
1 clove garlic, finely sliced
4 pork chops
Salt and pepper
300ml / 10 fl oz / 1 ¼ cups dry cider
100ml / 3 ½ fl oz / ½ cup double cream (optional)
1 tbsp Dijon mustard

- Heat the butter in a pan and cook the onions and apple with thyme and garlic for 15-20 minutes until all is golden and sweet.
- Remove from the pan with a slotted spoon and increase the heat.
- Sear the pork chops on both sides, seasoning as you go, then lower the heat slightly.
- Return the onions and apples to the pan, pour in the cider, bubble up and cook for 10 minutes.
- Stir in the cream if using and the mustard, adjust the seasoning and serve.

Pork Chops in Beer   509

- A light beer would work the same way as the cider.

510

SERVES 4

Sauteed Pork with Curried Onions

PREPARATION TIME 15 MINUTES

COOKING TIME 30 MINUTES

INGREDIENTS

4 pork escalopes
2 tbsp vegetable oil
2 large onions, peeled and finely sliced
1 red onion, peeled and finely sliced
2 cloves garlic, finely sliced
½ tsp turmeric
1 tsp ground cumin
1 tsp fennel seeds, crushed
1 tsp ground coriander
2 tsp garam masala
200ml / 7 fl oz / ¾ cup chicken stock
Salt and pepper
1 lime, juiced

- Place the pork escalopes between 2 sheets of clingfilm and bat out very thin with a rolling pin. Cut into strips.
- Heat the oil in a pan and cook the onions until deep gold and sweet – about 15-20 minutes.
- Add the garlic and spices and cook for 3 minutes.
- Increase the heat, add the pork strips and sauté until golden.
- Pour in the stock, season and cook until reduced and slightly thickened.
- Serve with the lime squeezed over.

Thai Style Sautéed Pork   511

- Use a red chilli, fish sauce and lime juice in place of the spices to make this a Thai style dish.

512

SERVES 4-6

Hawaiian Skewers

Pork Skewers
with Mango   513

- Stoned peeled mango gives a sweet juicy result.

Hawaiian Luxe Skewers   514

- Alternate the pork cubes and pineapple with chunks of ham, mozzarella and cherry tomatoes for a full-on Hawaiian.

Chicken Kebabs   515

- Chicken or even rabbit would work well here with the fruit.

PREPARATION TIME 15 MINUTES

COOKING TIME 8-10 MINUTES

INGREDIENTS

800g pork fillet
1 pineapple, skinned and cored, flesh cut into chunks
½ red chilli, deseeded and very finely diced
Salt and pepper
Olive oil
Sweet chilli sauce, to serve

- Cut the pork into bite-size pieces.
- Toss the chunks of pineapple with the chilli.
- Thread the pork and pineapple alternately onto skewers.
- Brush with olive oil and season.
- Heat the barbecue until the coals are glowing and there are no flames.
- Cook the skewers on the grill for about 8 minutes, or until the pork is cooked through.
- Serve alongside sweet chilli sauce.

516

SERVES 4

Curried Pork Meatballs

PREPARATION TIME 15 MINUTES

COOKING TIME 20 MINUTES

....

INGREDIENTS

2 slices stale bread, crusts removed
1kg/2 ¼ lbs/4 ¼ cups minced pork
1 onion, peeled and grated
1 clove garlic, crushed
10 curry leaves, finely sliced
1 tsp ground cumin
1 tbsp garam masala
500ml / 1 pint / 2 cups chicken stock

- Soak the bread in warm water then squeeze it out. Mix thoroughly with the meat, onions, herbs and mustard and season.
- Form into small balls around 6cm in diameter.
- Bring the chicken stock to the boil in a pan, then reduce the heat and add the meatballs and poach for around 20 minutes, in batches if necessary.

Chinese Style Meatballs

517

- Combine the pork mince with a little fresh grated ginger and use star anise, Chinese 5 spice and a little chilli in place of the Indian spices.

518

SERVES 4

Braised Pork with Five Spices

PREPARATION TIME 40 MINUTES

COOKING TIME 3 HOURS 30 MINUTES

....

INGREDIENTS

1 piece pork belly, about 2 kg / 4 ½ lb
250ml / 9 fl oz / 1 cup dry sherry or Shaoxing rice wine
1 L / 2 ¼ pints / 4 ¼ cups chicken stock
8 tbsp soy sauce
100g / 3 ½ oz / ½ cup sugar
3cm piece fresh ginger, sliced
4 cloves garlic, sliced
1 tbsp Chinese 5 spice
2 star anise
1 stick cinnamon
1 red chilli, pricked with a knife
1 bunch spring onions (scallions), chopped
Salt and pepper

- Add the pork to a pan of boiling water, reduce the heat and simmer gently, skimming, for 30 minutes to remove excess fat. Drain well.
- Combine the rest of the ingredients in a large stockpot and bring to a simmer.
- Add the blanched pork, return to a gentle simmer and cook for 3 hours, covered with a lid, skimming occasionally until the pork is very tender.
- Remove from the liquid and take off the skin. Cut the meat into bite size pieces.
- Skim as much fat as possible from the braising liquid and reduce over a high heat by half.
- Serve the pork in small bowls with the braising liquid poured over, rice alongside.

Braised Pork with Greens

519

- Finely shredded Chinese cabbage or spinach would work well here to boost the vitamin content.

520
SERVES 4

Hot & Spicy Pork and Pepper Stew

- Heat the oil in a pan and cook the pork over a high heat until golden all over.
- Reduce the heat, add the onion and garlic and cook till translucent.
- Add the peppers and stir-fry until softened, then add the spices, stir well and add the tomatoes and stock.
- Season and simmer for 30 minutes until the pork is tender and the sauce has thickened.
- Adjust the seasoning and serve.

PREPARATION TIME 20 MINUTES

COOKING TIME 45 MINUTES

INGREDIENTS

1 tbsp vegetable oil
1 piece pork belly, about 1.5kg / 3 lb, boned and cubed
1 onion, peeled and finely sliced
2 cloves garlic, finely sliced
1 red pepper, deseeded and finely sliced
1 green pepper, deseeded and finely sliced
1 tbsp paprika
1 tsp ground cumin
1 tsp Cayenne pepper
1 x 400g can chopped tomatoes
400ml / 14 fl oz / 1 ½ cups chicken stock
Salt and pepper

Pork and Pepper Stew with Sour Cream

521

- A tbsp or so of sour cream either served alongside or stirred in makes a creamier stew.

522
SERVES 4

Pork and Paprika Brochettes

- Tip the pork into a bowl and mix well with the oil, garlic, zest, thyme and paprika.
- Chill for 30 minutes.
- Thread the marinated pork onto skewers and cook on the barbecue or griddle for 8-10 minutes until cooked through.
- Serve with the cold tomato salsa.

PREPARATION TIME 40 MINUTES

COOKING TIME 10 MINUTES

INGREDIENTS

800g / 1 ¾ lb / 3 ⅓ cups pork fillet, cubed
2 tbsp olive oil
1 clove garlic, finely sliced
½ lemon, grated zest
2 sprigs thyme
1 tsp paprika

Tomato salsa, to serve

Pork Pepper Paprika Brochettes

523

- Alternate the pork with chunks of red pepper and black olives for a more Spanish influence.

524

SERVES 4

Pork Colombo

Rabbit Colombo

525

- Rabbit or chicken for the faint hearted would suit this quick stew.

Mild Pork Colombo

526

- If scotch bonnet chillies are too hot, try a softer fruitier type such as jalapeno.

Pork Colombo
with Spinach

527

- Try stirring baby spinach leaves through the stew just before serving.

PREPARATION TIME 20 MINUTES

COOKING TIME 45 MINUTES

·······································

INGREDIENTS

1 tbsp vegetable oil
500g / 1 lb / 2 cups pork loin, cubed
Salt and pepper
1 onion, peeled and chopped
2 green peppers, deseeded and chopped
3 cloves garlic, crushed
2 tbsp curry powder
6 sprigs thyme leaves
1 tsp ground allspice
½ tsp ground cinnamon
2 bay leaves
1-2 Scotch Bonnet chillies (depending on how hot you want it)
750g / 1 ⅓ lb sweet potatoes, peeled and cubed
500ml / 1 pint / 2 cups chicken stock
1 x 400g can chopped tomatoes

- Heat the oil and sear the pork on all sides until golden. Remove with a slotted spoon and set aside.
- Add the onion and peppers and cook until softened, then add the garlic and spices and cook for 2 minutes.
- Add the chillies, sweet potatoes, stock and tomatoes and bring to a simmer.
- Reduce the heat, cover with a lid and cook for 20 minutes until the potatoes are tender.
- Add the pork back to the pan and simmer for 10 minutes until cooked.
- Remove the chillies, adjust the seasoning and serve.

528

SERVES 4

Breaded Pork Chops

- Trim the thick white fat from around the pork chops. Place between 2 pieces of clingfilm and bat out with a rolling pin until about half as thick.
- Lay the flour, egg, breadcrumbs with oregano and mustard powder and seasoning in separate bowls.
- Dip the pork chops into each bowl in turn, thoroughly coating each time.
- Heat a thin layer of oil in a pan and cook the chops 2 at a time for 5 minutes per side until golden. Keep warm in a low oven while you cook the remaining chops.
- Serve with lemon wedges.

PREPARATION TIME 15 MINUTES

COOKING TIME 20 MINUTES

INGREDIENTS

4 pork chops
1 egg, beaten
4 tbsp flour
100g / 3 ½ oz / ½ cup fine breadcrumbs
1 tsp dried oregano
1 tsp mustard powder
Salt and pepper
Vegetable oil
Lemon wedges

Herby Pork Chops 529

- Finely chop rosemary, parsley and thyme with the breadcrumbs.

530

SERVES 4

Pork Fillet with Creamy Munster Sauce

- Preheat the oven to 200°C (180° fan) / 400F / gas 6.
- Place the pork in a roasting tin, season, drizzle with oil and roast for 18 minutes, until just pink in the centre.
- Meanwhile heat the butter in a pan and sweat the shallots until translucent.
- Add the garlic and thyme and cook for 3 minutes.
- Add the wine, bubble up and reduce until about 1 tbsp is left in the bottom, then add the cream.
- Bubble up, then stir in the cheese until melted. Adjust the seasoning.
- Rest the pork for 5 minutes before slicing and serving with the creamy sauce.

PREPARATION TIME 10 MINUTES

COOKING TIME 20 MINUTES

INGREDIENTS

1 pork tenderloin, weighing 750g / 1 ⅓ lb
30g / 1 oz butter
1 tbsp oil
2 shallots, finely chopped
1 clove garlic, finely sliced
2 sprigs thyme
150ml / 5 fl oz / ⅔ cup dry white wine
300ml / 10 fl oz / 1 ¼ cup double cream
80g / 2 ½ oz / ⅓ cup Munster cheese, cubed
Salt and pepper

Pork Fillet with Creamy Blue Sauce 531

- If Munster is too strong, try a melting gorgonzola dolce.

532

SERVES 4

Roast Pork in Milk Sauce

PREPARATION TIME 5 MINUTES

COOKING TIME 3 ½ HOURS

....

INGREDIENTS

100g / 3 ½ oz / ½ cup butter
1 pork shoulder, boned and skin removed
1.5 L / 3 pints / 6 ⅓ cups full fat milk
1 lemon, juiced plus grated zest
4 cloves garlic
3 bay leaves
Salt and pepper

- Heat the butter in a casserole and sear the pork on all sides until golden brown. Remove from the pan and pour off the butter if it's dark brown.
- Pour the milk into the pan and add the lemon rind and juice, garlic and bay leaves and bring to a boil.
- Place the pork into the milk, then reduce the heat to as low as possible, partially cover with a lid and cook for 2 ½ hours.
- Carefully turn the pork over to submerge the other side in milk and cook for 1 hour.
- Remove the pork and leave to rest. The milk will have formed curds which make a 'sauce'.
- Serve the pork carved thickly with the milk curds.

Roast Pork with Polenta

533

- The only accompaniment to this in true Italian style is creamy polenta.

534

SERVES 4

Toad in the Hole

PREPARATION TIME 35 MINUTES

COOKING TIME 20 MINUTES

....

INGREDIENTS

300ml / 10 fl oz / 1 ¼ cups milk
4 eggs
250g / 9 oz / 1 cup plain (all purpose) flour
1 tbsp grain mustard
Salt
8 chipolata sausages
4 tbsp vegetable oil or beef dripping

- Preheat oven to 220°C (200° fan) / 425F / gas 7
- Make the batter: whisk together the eggs and milk and leave to stand for 15 minutes.
- Heat the oil in a roasting tin and brown the sausages on all sides to stop them looking anaemic.
- Whisk the flour into the milk and eggs then the mustard, then pour into the hot tin around the sausages.
- Cook in the oven for 20 minutes until golden and billowing. Serve with onion gravy.

Italian Sausage Toad in the Hole

535

- Different sausage varieties would all work well but a red wine, herby Italian-style sausage would be particularly good.

536

SERVES 4

Black Pudding and Bacon Choucroute

Black Pudding with Duck Legs

537

- Confit duck legs make an excellent addition to choucroute.

Black Pudding with Pork Belly

538

- Chunky pieces of pork belly would make a good substitute for the black pudding.

Black Pudding with Chicken Wings

539

- Add roasted chicken wings for enhanced flavour.

PREPARATION TIME 25 MINUTES

COOKING TIME 1 HOUR 30 MINUTES

....

INGREDIENTS

2 tbsp goose fat or vegetable oil
2 large onions, peeled and thickly sliced
2 cloves garlic, finely sliced
200g / 7 oz / ¾ cup smoked streaky bacon in the piece, cubed
250g / 9 oz / 1 cup black pudding, cut into big chunks
3 large floury potatoes, peeled and cut into chunks
300g / 10 oz / 1 ¼ cups ready-made sauerkraut
1 tsp caraway seeds
4 juniper berries, lightly crushed
2 bay leaves
150ml / 5 fl oz / ⅔ cup dry white wine
150ml / 5 fl oz / ⅔ cup chicken stock
Salt and pepper
2 apples, peeled, cored and quartered

- Heat the fat in a large casserole and cook the onions and garlic until golden.
- Add the bacon and black pudding and cook until the fat starts to render and they begin to crisp.
- Add the potatoes and sauerkraut, stir in the spices, then pour over the wine and stock.
- Cover tightly with a lid and cook gently for 1 hour, stirring occasionally and checking it's not too dry.
- Add the apples and cook for a further 30 minutes. Adjust the seasoning and serve.

LAMB

SERVES 4 # Lamb in Milk Sauce

- Preheat the oven to 180°C (160° fan) / 350F / gas 5.
- Place the lamb in a casserole and make small deep cuts all over.
- Mix the butter with the herbs, garlic and a pinch of salt and push into the cuts on the lamb.
- Cover with a lid and bake in the oven for about 30 minutes.
- Remove the lid and cook for a further 20 minutes, then pour over the milk and cook for 30 minutes. The milk will set into 'curds' and form a sauce.
- Leave to rest for 10 minutes before serving with steamed potatoes.

PREPARATION TIME 15 MINUTES

COOKING TIME 1 HOUR 20 MINUTES

INGREDIENTS

1 leg of lamb, weighing about
1.5 kg / 3 lb
50g / 1 ¾ oz / ¼ cup butter
½ bunch sage leaves, chopped
1 tbsp thyme leaves
3 cloves garlic, crushed
300ml / 10 fl. oz / 1 ¼ cups milk
Extra virgin olive oil

SERVES 4

Irish Stew

PREPARATION TIME 15 MINUTES

COOKING TIME 6 HOURS

INGREDIENTS

55 ml / 2 fl. oz / 1/4 cup sunflower oil
450 g / 1 lb / 3 cups lamb shoulder, diced
300 g / 10 ½ oz / 2 cups new potatoes, peeled and sliced

2 carrots, peeled and sliced
2 onions, chopped
1 tbsp juniper berries, lightly crushed
2-3 bay leaves
500 ml / 18 fl. oz / 2 cups lamb stock
salt and pepper

TO GARNISH

1 tbsp curly leaf parsley leaves, finely chopped

- Heat half of the oil in a large casserole dish set over a moderate heat until hot.
- Season the lamb generously and seal in batches until golden brown in colour all over.
- Transfer the sealed lamb to a slow cooker and reduce the heat under the casserole dish a little.
- Add the remaining oil and saute the onions and carrots for 4-5 minutes, stirring occasionally.
- Add the bay leaves, potatoes, juniper berries, stock and a little seasoning and stir well.
- Pour on top of the lamb in the slow cooker and stir thoroughly.
- Cover and cook on a medium setting for 6 hours.
- Adjust the seasoning to taste after 6 hours and ladle the stew into serving dishes.
- Garnish with the chopped parsley before serving.

SERVES 4

Lamb stuffed with Pancetta

PREPARATION TIME 20 MINUTES

COOKING TIME 2 HOURS

INGREDIENTS

1 leg of lamb, tunnel boned
(ask your butcher)
120ml / 4 fl. oz / ½ cup white wine
2 bay leaves
2 cloves garlic, whole

FOR THE STUFFING
2 tbsp olive oil
4 slices pancetta, diced
1 onion, peeled and finely chopped
1 cloves garlic, finely chopped
1 sprig rosemary, finely chopped
2 tbsp black olives, chopped
5 sage leaves, finely chopped

- Preheat the oven to 200°C (180° fan) / 400F / gas 6.
- Make the stuffing: heat the oil in a pan and cook the pancetta till the fat runs and it starts to turn crisp.
- Add the onion, garlic and rosemary and cook until soft and golden. Add the olives, sage and season carefully.
- Lay the lamb in a roasting tin and stuff the tunnelled-out section with the stuffing using a teaspoon. Seal the ends with toothpicks or skewers.
- Pour equal amounts wine and water into the roasting tin with the bay leaves and garlic. Season the lamb, tent with foil and cook for about 1 ½ - 2 hours until meltingly tender.
- Leave for 15 minutes before carving.

543

SERVES 4

Lamb Chops with Mint, Chilli & Lemon

PREPARATION TIME 40 MINUTES

COOKING TIME 10 MINUTES

·······························

INGREDIENTS

8 lamb chops
2 red chillies, deseeded and chopped
½ bunch mint leaves
½ lemon, juiced
Handful black olives, stoned
1 clove garlic, peeled
Olive oil
Salt and pepper

- Whiz the chilli, mint, lemon juice, olives, garlic and a little oil in a blender until a rough paste.
- Coat the lamb chops in the paste and set aside for at least 30 minutes.
- Cook on a hot griddle for 4 minutes per side or until rosy pink in the middle.

Lamb Chops with Garlic, Parsley and Orange
544

- Whiz 2 cloves garlic, parsley and the zest of 1 orange until smooth, then coat the lamb chops in the paste.

545

SERVES 4

Lamb Hotpot

PREPARATION TIME 25 MINUTES

COOKING TIME 2 HOURS 15 MINUTES

·······························

INGREDIENTS

2 tbsp vegetable oil or dripping
1 kg / 2 ¼ lb/ 4 ¼ cups neck of lamb, cut into chops
4 lambs' kidneys, cored and chopped small
4 onions, peeled and chopped
1 tbsp butter
1 tbsp flour
500ml / 1 pint / 2 cups lamb stock or water
1 tbsp Worcestershire sauce
2 bay leaves
1 kg / 2 ¼ lb/ 4 ¼ cups potatoes, peeled and cut into 2cm slices
Salt and pepper

Pickled red cabbage, to serve

- Preheat the oven to 170°C / 325F / gas 3.
- Heat the fat in a large casserole and dry the meat in batches until browned. Add the kidney and cook alongside. Remove with a slotted spoon and set aside.
- Adding a little butter, cook the onions until translucent, then stir in the flour to make a paste.
- Whisk in the stock and Worcestershire sauce to make a smooth sauce and bring to a simmer. Return the meat and kidneys to the sauce.
- Add the herbs then top with slices of potato, seasoning the layers, arranging in an overlapping pattern.
- Cover with a lid and bake for 1 ½ hours, then remove the lid and cook for a further 45 minutes to crisp up the potatoes.
- Serve with the pickled cabbage.

Lamb Hotpot with Turnips
546

- Add quartered turnips to the hot pot before cooking.

547

SERVES 4 # Lamb Navarin

- Preheat the oven to 180°C / 350F / gas 4.
- Heat the oil in a casserole and cook the lamb in batches.
- Add the chopped vegetables and cook until softening.
- Stir in the flour to make a paste, then add the tomato puree and red wine and bubble up, scraping at the bottom to deglaze.
- Pour in the stock and add the herbs. Season and cook in the oven for 1 ½ hours until the lamb is tender.
- Meanwhile heat a little butter in a pan and cook the vegetables individually in a little vegetable stock until tender. Keep warm in a low oven until needed, cooking the peas and beans at the end.
- When the lamb is ready, remove with a slotted spoon to a dish, strain the sauce, then pour back into the casserole and heat through. Add the lamb and vegetables back into the sauce and serve.

Lamb Navarin with Pesto   548

- Loosen pesto with a little more oil and drizzle over the navarin before serving.

PREPARATION TIME 30 MINUTES

COOKING TIME 1 HOUR 30 MINUTES

INGREDIENTS

2 tbsp vegetable oil
500g / 1 lb / 2 cups stewing lamb, cut into bite size pieces
1 carrot, roughly chopped
1 stick celery, chopped
1 onion, peeled and chopped
1 leek, white part only, chopped
1 tbsp flour
1 tbsp tomato puree
100ml / 3 ½ fl. oz / ½ cup red wine
500ml / 1 pint / 2 cups lamb stock
2 bay leaves
Sprig thyme and rosemary
Peas and green beans

549

SERVES 6 # Lamb Curry with Onions and Bananas

- Cut the lamb shoulder into cubes.
- Heat the oil in a pan and add the meat. Cook briskly until golden-brown all over, then remove to a plate with a slotted spoon.
- Add the chopped garlic and onions and cook for two minutes. Return the meat to the pan, add the curry powder, 150ml / 5 fl. oz / ⅔ cup hot water and the yoghurt and stir well. Cover and cook gently for about 30 minutes, stirring regularly.
- Heat the butter in a pan, add the banana. Season.
- Serve the curry in small bowls with the cooked fruit alongside. Decorate with coriander.

PREPARATION TIME 15 MINUTES

COOKING TIME 40 MINUTES

INGREDIENTS

3 tbsp oil
1kg / 2 ¼ lbs / 4 ¼ cups lamb shoulder, deboned
2 onions, peeled and chopped
2 cloves garlic, peeled and chopped
100g plain yoghurt
3 tbsp curry powder
50g / 1 ½ oz / ⅓ cup butter
2 bananas
Coriander (cilantro)
Salt and pepper

Lamb Curry with Onions and Plantains   550

- Plantains make a good substitute for bananas and aren't as sweet.

551

SERVES 4

Redcurrant-Glazed Lamb Cutlets

Mixed Currant Glazed Cutlets

552

- Use the same quantity of mixed red, white and blackcurrants, whizzed in a blender for the marinade along with the port.

Lamb Cutlets with Mustard Redcurrant Glaze

553

- Adding a tbsp wholegrain mustard adds heat without fire.

Lamb Cutlets with Flageolet Beans

554

- Instead of the usual potatoes, try serving with warm flageolet beans as a classic accompaniment.

PREPARATION TIME 10 MINUTES

COOKING TIME 12 MINUTES

....

INGREDIENTS

2 racks of lamb, trimmed

FOR THE GLAZE
230g / 8 oz / 1 cup redcurrant jelly
1 sprig thyme
100ml / 3 ½ fl. oz / ½ cup port or cassis
1 sprig rosemary

- Preheat the oven to 180°C / 350F / gas 5.
- Warm the jelly, port and thyme in a small pan and reduce until thickened and syrupy.
- Using the rosemary, brush the glaze onto the lamb racks in a roasting tin and season.
- Cook for about 12 minutes, glazing once again half way through, then remove from the oven and rest for 5 minutes before carving.
- Serve with the remaining sauce.

555

SERVES 4

Marinated Lamb Kebabs

- Toss the cubed lamb with the garlic, balsamic, rosemary, a little oil and salt and pepper and leave to marinate for up to 30 minutes.
- Thread the lamb onto skewers, alternating with the tomatoes, peppers and onion. Sprinkle a little seasoning over.
- Cook over hot embers for 8-10 minutes until the lamb is rose pink inside and charred outside

PREPARATION TIME 35 MINUTES

COOKING TIME 10 MINUTES

INGREDIENTS

500g lamb fillet or leg steak, cut into 2cm cubes
2 cloves garlic, crushed
2 tbsp balsamic vinegar
1 tbsp rosemary leaves, chopped
Olive oil
Salt and pepper
16 cherry tomatoes
8 mild red chilli peppers, whole
1 onion, cut into chunks

Spanish Style Kebabs

556

- Whizz together 1 tbsp smoked paprika, a handful bottled roasted peppers, 2 cloves garlic and a splash of dry sherry in a food blender until smooth for an alternative.

557

SERVES 4

Roast Shoulder of Lamb with Thyme

- Preheat the oven to 180°C / 350F / gas 5.
- Place the shoulder in a tin and rub in the herbs, oil, honey and seasoning, massaging them into the meat.
- Pour a glass of water or wine into the bottom of the tin, cover tightly with foil and bake for about 2-3 hours until the lamb is meltingly tender and falls from the bone.
- Allow to rest for a few minutes before 'carving.'

PREPARATION TIME 10 MINUTES

COOKING TIME 2-3 HOURS

INGREDIENTS

1 lamb shoulder weighing 1.5kg / 3 lb
1 bunch thyme leaves
1 tbsp oregano
4 tbsp olive oil
2 tbsp runny honey
Salt and pepper
Water or red wine

Shoulder of Lamb with Lavender

558

- In the summer use dried lavender heads in place of the thyme.

559
SERVES 4

Spicy Roasted Leg of Lamb

PREPARATION TIME 2 HOURS

COOKING TIME 1 HOUR

INGREDIENTS

1 leg of lamb, weighing 1.5kg / 3 lb
2 tbsp ground cumin
2 tbsp ground coriander
1 red chilli, deseeded and chopped
½ bunch coriander (cilantro), chopped
½ tsp turmeric
½ tbsp cinnamon
½ tsp ground cloves
Olive oil
Salt and pepper

- Whiz the spices together with the oil and herbs in a food processor to make a paste.
- Massage the paste into the lamb and marinate for at least 2 hours.
- Preheat the oven to 220°C (200° fan) / 450F / gas 7.
- Remove the lamb from the fridge 30 minutes before cooking to bring to room temperature. Roast for 20 minutes, then turn the heat down to 160°C (140° fan) / 325F gas 3 and cook for a further 45 minutes for pink lamb.
- Leave to rest for 15 minutes before carving.

Leg of Lamb with Orange 560

- The zest and juice of 1 orange adds a citrus twist.

561
SERVES 4

Rack of Lamb with Herb Pine Nut Crust

PREPARATION TIME 10 MINUTES

COOKING TIME 12 MINUTES

INGREDIENTS

2 racks of lamb, trimmed

FOR THE CRUST
1 bunch parsley, finely chopped
3 sprigs thyme leaves
2 tbsp pine nuts (kernels)
1 clove garlic, chopped
Olive oil
Salt and pepper
Dijon mustard

- Preheat the oven to 180°C (160° fan) / 350F / gas 5.
- Whiz the herbs, pine nuts and garlic in a food processor to a nubbly paste then add enough olive oil to loosen.
- Spread the fat on the racks with a tbsp mustard to act as glue. Press on the crust and season the lamb.
- Roast in the oven for 12 minutes for pink lamb.
- Rest for 5 minutes before carving.

Rack of Lamb with Herb Walnut Crust 562

- Use walnuts in place of the pine nuts in the autumn.

563

SERVES 4

Herby Lamb Shanks

Moroccan Style Lamb Shanks 564

- Use 1 tbsp of ras-el-hanout spice mix instead of the herbs and 4 preserved lemons and substitute white wine for the red wine for a Moroccan spin.

Indian Style Shanks 565

- Use 1 tbsp of garam masala and fennel seeds and omit the wine.

Herby Lamb Chops 566

- Replace the lamb shanks with lamb chops and cook in the same way.

PREPARATION TIME 15 MINUTES

COOKING TIME 3 HOURS

INGREDIENTS

4 tbsp olive oil
4 lamb shanks
1 onion, peeled and thickly sliced
1 carrot, peeled and chopped
2 sticks celery, chopped
4 cloves garlic, finely sliced
1 bay leaf
4 sprigs rosemary
2 sprigs thyme
300ml / 10 fl. oz / 1 ¼ cups red wine
500m / 1 pint / 2 cups chicken stock
2 tbsp runny honey
Salt and pepper
Cooked puy lentils, to serve
Coriander (cilantro), to garnish

- Preheat the oven to 150°C (130° fan) / 300F / gas 2.
- Heat the oil in a casserole and brown the shanks on all sides. Remove from the pan and set aside.
- Add the vegetables to the pan and cook until softened. Add the herbs and cook for 2 minutes.
- Add the lamb shanks back to the pan, pour over the wine, stock and honey and bubble up.
- Season, cover with a lid and cook for 3 hours in the oven or until the lamb is very tender.
- If necessary, remove the shanks from the pan and reduce the sauce on the hob to thicken before serving.
- Serve on a bed of puy lentils and garnish with the coriander.

567

SERVES 4

Griddled Lamb with Feta Salad

PREPARATION TIME 15 MINUTES

COOKING TIME 5-10 MINUTES

·····

INGREDIENTS

4 lamb leg steaks
2 tbsp Balsamic vinegar
1 tbsp marjoram leaves
Salt and pepper
Olive oil
150g / 5 oz / ⅔ cup feta, crumbled
4 ripe tomatoes, chopped
½ cucumber, diced
2 handfuls black olives
Salad leaves
Extra virgin olive oil
½ lemon, juiced

- Marinade the lamb in the balsamic, herbs, oil and a little seasoning.
- Heat a griddle until nearly smoking and cook 3 minutes per side for pink lamb.
- Place on foil and wrap up; leave to rest for 5 minutes.
- Meanwhile assemble the salad on a large platter, scattering the ingredients on.
- Toss with oil, lemon juice and a little seasoning and mix with your hands.
- Lay the lamb and its resting juices on the salad and serve.

Lamb with Middle Eastern Salad 568

- Mix a can of drained chickpeas with the salad ingredients and add thyme leaves and a little dried chilli.

569

SERVES 4

Moroccan Lamb Meatballs

PREPARATION TIME 50 MINUTES

COOKING TIME 15 MINUTES

·····

INGREDIENTS

500g / 1 lb / 2 cups minced lamb
1 onion, very finely chopped
2 cloves garlic, finely chopped
6 tbsp breadcrumbs
1 tbsp tomato puree
1 tsp ground cinnamon
1 tsp ground cumin
½ lemon, juiced
Salt and pepper
2 tbsp olive oil

- Place the minced lamb in a large bowl and bring to room temperature.
- Add the rest of the ingredients and mix well with your hands to ensure even distribution.
- Roll the mixture into small walnut-sized balls with your hands and place on a baking sheet. Cover with clingfilm and refrigerate for 30 minutes.
- Heat the olive oil in a large pan.
- Add the meatballs in batches, cooking on all sides until golden and just cooked through – about 6-8 minutes.

Meatballs in Broth 570

- Serve in hot strong chicken stock with rice alongside for a filling supper.

571

SERVES 4

Spicy Lamb Kebabs

- Pat the cubes of lamb dry with kitchen paper.
- Whiz the ingredients for the marinade in a food processor until smooth.
- Toss the lamb in the paste and leave to marinate in the refrigerator for at least 1 hour or overnight.
- Thread the lamb onto skewers and cook either on a barbecue or very hot griddle pan until charred on the outside and pink in the centre – about 5-6 minutes.

PREPARATION TIME 10 MINUTES
+ MARINADING TIME

COOKING TIME 5-6 MINUTES

INGREDIENTS

500g / 1 lb / 2 cups lamb, cut into cubes

FOR THE MARINADE
½ onion, peeled and chopped
2-3 green chillies, deseeded if preferred and chopped
3 cloves garlic, peeled
2 tsp fresh ginger, chopped
1 tsp ground cumin
1 tsp ground coriander
1 tbsp dried mint
4 tbsp plain yoghurt
Salt

Tikka Style Kebabs   572

- Add 1 tbsp tomato puree to the marinade.

573

SERVES 4

Lamb Cassoulet

- Rinse the beans and place in a pan covered with cold water. Bring to a simmer and cook for 2 hours or until soft.
- Preheat the oven to 160°C (140° fan) / 325F / gas 4.
- Add the oil to a casserole and render the fat from the bacon. Add the onions and garlic and cook until browned.
- Add the lamb and cook on all sides, then add the tomatoes and stock and herbs. Add the drained beans, cover with a lid and cook in the oven for 2 ½ hours, stirring the beans to disturb the crust every 30 minutes.
- Remove the lid for the last 30 minutes of cooking and scatter with the breadcrumbs to create a crust.
- Serve hot with a crisp salad.

PREPARATION TIME 30 MINUTES

COOKING TIME 2 HOURS 30 MINUTES

INGREDIENTS

350g / 12 oz / 1 ½ cups dried cannellini beans (or traditional Tarbais beans), soaked overnight
750g / 1 ⅓ lb / 3 cups boneless stewing lamb, cubed
2 rashers smoked streaky bacon, diced
1 tbsp oil
2 onions, peeled and chopped
3 cloves garlic, chopped
1 x 400g can chopped tomatoes
500ml / 1 pint / 2 cups chicken stock
Bouquet garni
Salt and pepper
3 handfuls breadcrumbs

Toulouse-Style Cassoulet   574

- Some good quality lamb and mint sausages make an excellent addition if you can find them.

575

SERVES 4

Moroccan Lamb Shanks

PREPARATION TIME 15 MINUTES

COOKING TIME 3 HOURS 10 MINUTES

....

INGREDIENTS

2 tbsp olive oil
4 lamb shanks
1 onion, peeled and sliced
2 cloves garlic, finely sliced
1 carrot, peeled and diced
1 tbsp ground cumin
1 tsp ground cinnamon
1 tbsp paprika
1 tbsp fresh ginger, grated
½ tbsp ras-el-hanout
2 preserved lemons
2 x 400g cans chickpeas (garbanzo beans), drained
500ml / 1 pint / 2 cups chicken stock
Salt and pepper
Handful dried apricots

- Preheat the oven to 160°C (140° fan) / 300F / gas 2.
- Heat the oil in a large casserole and colour the lamb on all sides. Remove to a bowl.
- Add the onion, garlic and carrot and cook until softened and golden. Add the spices and cook for 2 minutes
- Add the lamb back to the pan with the chickpeas, pour over the stock, season and bubble up.
- Cover with a lid and bake in the oven for 2 hours.
- Tip in the apricots and stir well. Top up with a little water if it looks dry. Place the lid back on and cook for a further hour.
- When the lamb is tender, adjust the seasoning and serve.

Lamb Shanks with Tomatoes

576

- A handful of cherry tomatoes will add a welcome acidity.

577

SERVES 4

Lamb Chops with Parmesan & Coriander

PREPARATION TIME 40 MINUTES

COOKING TIME 8 MINUTES

....

INGREDIENTS

100g / 3 ½ oz / 1 ¼ cups Parmesan, grated
1 bunch coriander (cilantro), chopped
2 tbsp pine nuts
75ml / 2 ½ fl. oz / ⅓ cup olive oil
½ lemon, juiced
Salt and pepper
8 lamb chops

- Whiz the ingredients for the marinade in a food processor until a fairly smooth paste, adding the oil a little at a time. You may not need all of it.
- Coat the lamb chops in the marinade thoroughly and set aside for at least 30 minutes.
- Heat a griddle pan and cook the lamb chops 3-4 minutes on each side until rosy pink in the middle.
- Rest for 5 minutes and serve.

Lamb Chops with Parmesan and Basil and Parsley

578

- Use ½ bunch each parsley and basil for non-lovers of coriander.

579

SERVES 4

Lamb Tagine

- Preheat the oven to 160°C (140° fan) / 300F / gas 2.
- Mix the spices together in a bowl and toss the cubed lamb in half of the spice mix. Marinade overnight or for at least 4 hours.
- The next day heat 2 tbsp oil in a large casserole or tagine and cook the onions and garlic gently for at least 15 minutes until softened and sweet. Add the spice mix and stir well.
- Add the lamb to the pan, then the preserved lemons and increase the heat a little to brown.
- Add the tomatoes, stock and dried fruit with the honey and season. Cover with a lid and bake in the oven for 3 hours until the meat is very tender.
- When the lamb is tender, adjust the seasoning and stir in the coriander. If liked, serve packed into timbales and remove the moulds before serving.

PREPARATION TIME 4 HOURS

COOKING TIME 3 HOURS

INGREDIENTS

Olive oil
2 onions, peeled and sliced
4 cloves garlic, finely sliced
3 preserved lemons
2 x 400g cans chopped tomatoes
500ml / 1 pint / 2 cups chicken stock
100g / 3 ½ oz / ½ cup dried apricots
50g / 1 ¾ oz / ¼ cup dates
2 tbsp sultanas, 2 tbsp honey
1 bunch coriander (cilantro)
chopped Cous cous to serve

FOR THE SPICE RUB

½ tsp Cayenne, 1 tbsp paprika
1 tsp turmeric, 2 tsp ground cinnamon
1 tbsp ground cumin, Salt and pepper
1 kg / 2 ¼ lb / 4 ¼ cups lamb shoulder, cubed

580

SERVES 4

Lamb Burger

PREPARATION TIME 45 MINUTES

COOKING TIME 8-10 MINUTES

INGREDIENTS

500g / 1 lb / 2 cups minced lamb
1 onion, peeled and chopped
2 cloves garlic, chopped
½ tsp cinnamon
½ tbsp dried oregano
½ tbsp dried mint
Salt and pepper
1 egg, beaten
4 burger buns, toasted
mixed salad, to serve

- Whiz the onion, garlic, cinnamon and dried herbs in a food processor until a mush.
- Place the lamb mince in a bowl and stir in the herbed mush with some of the egg and knead thoroughly to combine. Season the mix and form into 4 large lamb burgers. Refrigerate for 30 minutes.
- Heat a griddle pan to nearly smoking and cook the burgers for 3-4 minutes each side, leaving the middle slightly pink. Rest covered in foil.
- Place the burgers in the buns, topped with mixed salad.

581

SERVES 4

Lamb Sauté with Spring Vegetables

PREPARATION TIME 20 MINUTES

COOKING TIME 40 MINUTES

INGREDIENTS

3 tbsp olive oil
1 kg / 2 ¼ lbs / 4 ¼ cups cubed lamb fillet
1 onion, peeled and finely sliced
2 cloves garlic, finely sliced
1 sprig rosemary
2 red peppers, finely sliced
12 artichoke hearts
100g / 3 ½ oz / ½ cup frozen peas
150g / 5 oz / ⅔ cup double-podded broad beans
200ml / 7 fl. oz / ¾ cup chicken stock
Handful black olives
2 tbsp sultanas
Salt and pepper

- Heat the oil in a large pan and when smoking sear the lamb on all sides until golden. Remove with a slotted spoon.
- Add the onion and cook gently until softened, then add the garlic and rosemary.
- Stir in the peppers and cook for 10 minutes until softened and starting to colour, then add the artichokes, peas and beans.
- Pour in the stock, season and simmer over a medium-high heat until the liquid becomes syrupy and the vegetables are tender.
- Add the lamb back to the pan, toss well and stir in the olives and sultanas. Cook for 5 minutes, season and serve.

582

SERVES 3-4

Lamb Rogan Josh

PREPARATION TIME 5 MINUTES

COOKING TIME 50 MINUTES

....

INGREDIENTS

4 cloves garlic
2cm piece fresh ginger, sliced
4 tbsp vegetable oil
1 tbsp black peppercorns
6 cardamom pods
3 cloves
1 cinnamon stick
1 onion, peeled and finely chopped
750g / 1 ⅓ lb / 3 cups lamb leg, cubed
(preferably bone in)
1 tbsp ground coriander
1 tbsp ground cumin
½ tsp Cayenne
2 tsp fennel seeds, crushed
2 tsp garam masala
4 tomatoes, chopped
75ml / 2 ½ oz / ⅓ cup plain yoghurt
Salt and pepper

- Whiz the garlic and ginger to a paste in a food processor with a little water.
- Heat the oil in a large casserole and add the spices. Stir fry for 2 minutes until fragrant.
- Add the onion and fry until golden brown, then add the lamb and sear on all sides.
- Stir in the garlic paste and cook out for a few minutes, then add the ground spices, a little salt and tomatoes, reduce the heat and simmer for 15 minutes or until the sauce is nearly dry.
- Add enough water to come to nearly the top of the lamb and simmer for about 20 minutes or until the lamb is cooked through.
- Remove from the heat and stir in the yoghurt before serving.

Lamb Rogan Josh with Spiced Potatoes

583

- Toss sautéed cubed potatoes with a mixture of coriander and mustard seeds to serve alongside.

584

SERVES 4

Lamb in Filo Pastry with Honeyed Figs

PREPARATION TIME 20 MINUTES

COOKING TIME 15-20 MINUTES

....

INGREDIENTS

4 x lamb loin fillets, weighing 100g /
3 ½ oz each
Salt and pepper
1 tbsp honey
6 sheets filo pastry
60g / 2 oz / ¼ cup butter, melted
1 tbsp flaked (slivered) almonds
12 figs
2 tbsp honey
2 tbsp pistachios, crushed

- Preheat the oven to 200°C (180° fan) / 400F / gas 6.
- Sear the lamb fillets on all sides in a pan for 1-2 minutes. Season and set aside.
- Lay the filo sheets out and cut in half, to give 12 sheets.
- Place a layer of filo on the surface, brush with melted butter, then repeat with 2 more sheets. Place the lamb fillet on top, brush with a little honey and wrap in filo to enclose and make a parcel. Place on a baking sheet and repeat for the remaining lamb fillets.
- Brush with more melted butter, sprinkle with flaked almonds and bake in the oven for 15 minutes.
- Meanwhile, make a cross in the top of the figs and place snugly in a small baking dish. Drizzle with honey and sprinkle with pistachios and bake for 5-6 minutes until warmed through.
- Serve the lamb parcels with the honeyed figs alongside.

Spicy Fillet of Lamb

585

- Spread a thin layer of harissa along the lamb fillet to cut through the sweetness.

Lamb with Herb Crust & Mashed Potato

586

SERVES 4

- Preheat the oven to 180°C / 350F / gas 5.
- Cook the potatoes whole in their skins in boiling salted water until tender all the way through – about 30 minutes, but keep checking.
- Whiz the herbs, pine nuts and garlic in a food processor to a nubbly paste then add enough olive oil to loosen.
- Spread the fat on the racks with a tbsp mustard to act as glue. Press on the crust and season the lamb.
- Roast in the oven for 12 minutes for pink lamb.
- Drain the potatoes thoroughly and leave to cool for 5 minutes, then peel off the skins while still hot.
- Return the flesh to the pan and stir in the butter and enough milk with a wooden spoon to make a light, creamy, smooth mash.
- Rest the lamb for 5 minutes before carving and serving with the mash.

Lamb with Cannellini Bean Mash 587

- Mash drained cannellini beans with a little hot chicken stock and cream to make a lighter version.

PREPARATION TIME 30 MINUTES

COOKING TIME 12 MINUTES

INGREDIENTS

1 kg / 2 ¼ lb / 4 ¼ cups floury potatoes such as King Edward or Desiree
2 racks of lamb, trimmed
100g / 3 ½ oz / ½ cup butter
75-100ml / 2 ½ - 3 ½ oz / ⅓ – ½ cup milk, warmed
Salt and pepper

FOR THE CRUST
1 bunch parsley, finely chopped
3 sprigs thyme leaves
2 tbsp breadcrumbs
1 clove garlic, chopped
Olive oil
Salt and pepper
Dijon mustard

Moroccan Lamb Tagine with Couscous

588

SERVES 4

- Preheat the oven to 160°C / 310F / gas 3.
- Toss the cubed lamb in half of the ras el hanout. Marinate overnight or for at least 4 hours.
- The next day heat 2 tbsp oil in a tagine and cook the onions and garlic gently for at least 15 minutes until softened and sweet. Add the ras el hanout and stir well.
- Add the vegetables and cook until softening, then add the lamb to the pan. Tip in the preserved lemons and chickpeas and increase the heat a little to brown.
- Add the tomatoes, stock and dried fruit with the honey and season. Cover with a lid and bake in the oven for 3 hours until the meat is very tender.
- Meanwhile soak the couscous in the boiling stock and cover with clingfilm for 5 minutes. Remove and separate the grains with a fork.
- When the lamb is tender, adjust the seasoning and stir in the coriander.

Lamb Tagine with Citrus Couscous 589

- Add 3 preserved lemons to the couscous while soaking.

PREPARATION TIME 4 HOURS

COOKING TIME 3 HOURS

INGREDIENTS

Olive oil
2 onions, peeled and sliced
4 cloves garlic, finely sliced
1 courgette (zucchini), sliced
1 aubergine (eggplant), diced
2 carrots, peeled and sliced
3 preserved lemons
1 x 400g can chickpeas (garbanzo beans), drained
2 x 400g cans chopped tomatoes
500ml / 1 pint / 2 cups chicken stock
100g / 3 ½ oz / ½ cup dried apricots
50g / 1 ¾ oz / ¼ cup dates
2 tbsp sultanas
2 tbsp honey
1 bunch coriander (cilantro), chopped
225g / 8 oz / 1 cup cous cous
225ml / 8 fl. oz / 1 cup chicken stock
1kg / 2 ¼ lb Lamb shoulder, cubed
ras el hanout

POULTRY

Lemon Chicken with Sesame & Ginger

590

SERVES 4

- Slice the chicken into strips.
- Combine the egg white, cornflour, a pinch of salt and sesame oil in a bowl then thoroughly coat the chicken strips in the mixture.
- Heat the vegetable oil in a wok until smoking, then add the coated chicken and stir fry over a high heat until the chicken turns white.
- Remove the chicken from the pan and set aside. Discard the oil.
- Add the ginger, lemon juice and zest, stock, sugar and soy and sherry/wine and bring to a rapid boil.
- Whisk in the cornflour until thickened then return the chicken to the pan for a few minutes to cook through. Scatter over the sesame seeds
- Taste the sauce – you may want more lemon, sugar or salt. Serve alongside long grain rice.

PREPARATION TIME 10 MINUTES

COOKING TIME 15 MINUTES

INGREDIENTS

2 tbsp vegetable oil
1 tbsp fresh ginger, grated
3-4 lemons, grated zest and juice
100ml chicken stock
1-2 tsp sugar
Splash soy sauce
Splash dry sherry
1 tsp cornflour
1 tbsp sesame seeds

FOR THE LEMON CHICKEN

4 chicken breasts, skinned
1 egg white
2 tsp cornflour
1 tsp sesame oil

Roast Chicken with Sage Butter

591

SERVES 4-6

PREPARATION TIME 15 MINUTES

COOKING TIME 1 HOUR 30 MINUTES

INGREDIENTS

1 chicken
Olive oil

FOR THE BUTTER

6 sage leaves, finely chopped
150g / 5 oz / ⅔ cup butter, softened
Salt and pepper
½ lemon, grated zest

- Preheat the oven to 200°C (180° fan) / 400F / gas 6.
- Place the chicken in a roasting tin. Using the handle of a teaspoon, gently loosen the skin from the meat, using the spoon to create pockets.
- Mix the butter with the sage, seasoning and lemon zest.
- Push the butter into the pockets under the skin, using your fingers to massage it out and cover the breast.
- Drizzle the skin with oil and season, then roast in the oven for 20 minutes + 20 minutes per 500g/1 lb. The chicken is cooked when the juices run clear at the thickest part.
- Leave to rest for 10 minutes before carving.

Stuffed Roast Pheasant

592

SERVES 2-4

PREPARATION TIME 15 MINUTES

COOKING TIME 30-40 MINUTES

INGREDIENTS

1 pheasant, cleaned and boned out
(ask your butcher)

FOR THE STUFFING

250g / 9 oz / 1 cup mild goats' cheese
2 tbsp parsley, finely chopped
1 tbsp thyme leaves
1 clove garlic, crushed
Salt and pepper

- Preheat oven to 200°C (180° fan) / 400F / gas 6.
- Lay the pheasant out on a surface and open it out.
- Mix together the stuffing ingredients, then spread the stuffing out into the cavity of the bird.
- Season, then roll the bird up into a rough sausage shape and secure with string.
- Place in a roasting tin and season, drizzle with oil and roast for 30-40 minutes until cooked through and the juices run clear.
- Leave to rest for 10 minutes before carving.

593

SERVES 4

Chicken Fajitas

PREPARATION TIME 35 MINUTES

COOKING TIME 10-15 MINUTES

INGREDIENTS

2 chicken breasts, skinned and thinly sliced
2 tsp paprika
2 tsp ground cumin
2 tsp ground coriander
Pinch dried chilli flakes
Salt and pepper
4 tbsp olive oil
1 onion, peeled and finely sliced
1 red pepper, deseeded and finely sliced
1 green pepper, deseeded and finely sliced
4 tbsp canned sweetcorn
1 lime, juiced
8 tortilla wraps
Sour cream
Tomato salsa
Guacamole

- Coat the chicken in half the spices and leave to marinate for 30 minutes.
- Heat half the oil in a pan until nearly smoking, then cook the onion and peppers until golden and tender. Remove from the pan, keep warm and set aside.
- Add the remaining oil and reheat, then add the meat and sprinkle over the remaining spices.
- Stir briskly for 2-3 minutes until either the chicken is cooked through. Mix in the sweetcorn and squeeze over the lime juice. Remove and keep warm.
- Wipe out the pan and use to warm the tortillas through.
- Serve the vegetables with the meat, tortilla wraps and sauces.

Steak Fajitas **594**

- Thinly sliced rump steak makes a luxury substitute.

595

SERVES 4

Chicken with Herbs and Lemon

PREPARATION TIME 5 MINUTES

COOKING TIME 25-30 MINUTES

INGREDIENTS

4 chicken breasts
Handful mixed thyme, rosemary, parsley
Salt and pepper
4 tbsp olive oil
2 preserved lemons
200ml / 7 fl. oz / ¾ cup water, white wine or chicken stock

- Preheat the oven to 200°C (180° fan) / 400F / gas 6.
- Place the chicken snugly in a roasting tin and tuck the herbs in and around the meat.
- Season and drizzle over the oil, then slice the lemons and tuck around the meat.
- Pour over the stock and bake for 25 – 30 minutes or until the chicken is cooked through and the juices run clear.
- Remove the chicken to a warm place to rest. Squish the lemons against the side of the tin and stir into the cooking juices.
- Serve the chicken with the cooking juices poured over.

Citrus Chicken **596**

- If you can't get hold of preserved lemons, simply use 1 quartered lemon and ½ orange if desired

597

SERVES 4-6

Chicken Liver and Port Paté

- Heat a tbsp of butter in a frying pan and cook the chicken livers over a medium heat for 5 minutes, turning them frequently, until golden brown without and just pink within.
- Transfer with a slotted spoon to a food processor, reserving the frying pan and juices.
- Pour the port into the pan, scraping with a wooden spoon and add to the processor.
- Melt 150g butter and pour into the processor. Add the mace, thyme, garlic and salt and pepper. Blend to a smooth puree.
- Spoon into a pot or individual ramekins. Melt the remaining butter and pour over, leave to cool then chill for 24 hours before serving with hot toast.

PREPARATION TIME 20 MINUTES

COOKING TIME 5 MINUTES

INGREDIENTS

225g / 8 oz / 1 cup chicken livers, trimmed
225g / 8 oz / 1 cup butter, softened
2 tbsp port
¼ tsp ground mace
1 tsp thyme leaves
1 clove garlic, crushed
Salt and pepper

Chicken Liver Cognac Pate

 598

- The same quantity of cognac gives a less sweet taste.

599

SERVES 4

Chicken Kiev

- Using a sharp knife, cut a pocket in the side of each chicken breast.
- Mix together the stuffing ingredients until well combined.
- Use a teaspoon to stuff the pocket with the herb butter, then press the edges firmly together.
- Place the flour, eggs and breadcrumbs on separate plates. Season the flour.
- Dip each chicken breast into the flour, eggs then polenta, coating thoroughly each time.
- Heat the oil then add the chicken breasts and cook, turning regularly for about 20 minutes until cooked through.

PREPARATION TIME 10 MINUTES

COOKING TIME 20 MINUTES

INGREDIENTS

4 chicken breasts, skinned
75g / 2 ¾ oz / ⅓ cup plain
(all purpose) flour
3 eggs, beaten
250g / 9 oz / 1 cup breadcrumbs
4 tbsp vegetable oil
Salt and pepper

FOR THE STUFFING

225g / 8 oz / 1 cup butter, softened
2-3 cloves garlic, crushed
½ bunch parsley, finely chopped
½ bunch tarragon, finely chopped
Squeeze of lemon juice

Pork Fillet Kiev

 600

- Batted out pork fillets will give a similar result.

601

SERVES 6-8 # Roast Turkey

Herb Butter-Basted Turkey   602

- Use a teaspoon handle to separate the skin from the flesh and stuff the pockets with softened butter mixed with finely chopped parsley.

Citrus Turkey   603

- Season the butter with lemon zest and plenty of black pepper before rubbing on the bird.

Paprika Turkey   604

- Sprinkle smoked paprika over the turkey for a fuller flavour and a really golden colour.

PREPARATION TIME 10 MINUTES

COOKING TIME 2-3 HOURS

INGREDIENTS

1 turkey, weighing 5.4-6.3kg / 12-14 lb at room temperature
200g / 7 oz / ¾ cup butter, softened or goose fat
Salt and pepper
8-10 rashers smoked streaky bacon

- Preheat the oven to 200°C (180° fan) / 400F / gas 6.
- Rub the turkey all over with the butter or goose fat, season and cover with the smoked bacon.
- Place in the oven and roast for 30 minutes, then reduce the heat to 180°C (160° fan) / 350F / gas 4 and cook for a further 2 hours or so, until the juices run clear at the thickest part.
- Leave to rest for 30 minutes before carving.

SERVES 4

Tandoori Chicken

605

- Prepare the tandoori marinade by mixing together all the ingredients for the marinade in a mixing bowl. Add the chicken, mix well, then cover and chill for at least 1 hour.
- Bring the water to the boil in a large saucepan and add the rice. Bring back to the boil, then cover and simmer for 10-12 minutes.
- Remove from the heat and keep the lid in place and set to one side.
- Pre-heat the grill to hot. Remove the chicken from the marinade, shaking off any excess, and thread onto the wooden skewers.
- Grill for 8-10 minutes, turning occasionally until lightly charred and cooked through.
- Place the tandoori chicken skewers on top and garnish with the finely diced tomato, sprigs of coriander and a sprinkle of ground cinnamon before serving.

Tandoori Chicken in Pitta Breads   606

- Heat and split pitta breads and fill with the tandoori chicken.

PREPARATION TIME 90 MINUTES

COOKING TIME 30 MINUTES

INGREDIENTS

4 skinless chicken breasts, diced
200ml / 7 fl. oz / ¾ cup basmati rice (use a measuring jug), rinsed
400ml / 14 fl. oz / 1 ½ cups boiling water
½ salad tomato, finely diced
Salt and pepper
Pinch of ground cinnamon
Sprigs of coriander (cilantro)
Wooden skewers, soaked in water

FOR THE MARINADE

300ml/10 fl. oz/1 ¼ cups natural yoghurt
1 tsp ground cumin
1 tsp ground coriander
1 tsp garam masala
1 tsp ground cinnamon
1 ½ tsp tandoori chilli powder
1 tsp caster (superfine) sugar
1 clove garlic, minced

607

SERVES 2

Pheasant with Pears and Sage Butter

- Place the pheasant in a roasting tin. Using the handle of a teaspoon, gently loosen the skin from the meat, using the spoon to create pockets.
- Mix the butter with the sage, seasoning and lemon zest.
- Push the butter into the pockets under the skin, using your fingers to massage it out and cover the breast.
- Place in the oven and roast for 20 minutes, then reduce the heat to 180°C / 350F and cook for another 20-25 minutes, until the juices run clear. Cover with foil if it looks like it might burn.
- 15 minutes before the end of cooking, add the pears to the tin, drizzle with honey, then return to the oven to finish cooking.
- Leave to rest, breast-side down for 10 minutes before serving.

Pheasant with Smoky Bacon Lardons   608

- Scatter smokey bacon lardons over the pears before returning to the oven.

PREPARATION TIME 15 MINUTES

COOKING TIME 40 MINUTES

INGREDIENTS

1 pheasant, cleaned
Olive oil
2 pears, halved and cored
1 tbsp honey

FOR THE BUTTER

6 sage leaves, finely chopped
150g / 5 oz / ⅔ cup butter, softened
Salt and pepper
½ lemon, grated zest

609

SERVES 4

Chicken Coconut Milk Curry

PREPARATION TIME 15 MINUTES

COOKING TIME 25-30 MINUTES

....

INGREDIENTS

3 tbsp vegetable oil
1 onion, peeled and finely sliced
2 cloves garlic, finely chopped
2 tbsp red Thai curry paste
3-4 chicken breasts, skinned and cubed
2 tsp tamarind paste
2 tbsp fish sauce
400ml / 14 fl. oz / 1 ½ cups coconut milk
200ml / 7 fl. oz / ¾ cup chicken stock
Salt and pepper
1-2 limes, juiced
Boiled rice to serve

- Heat the oil in a wok or large pan and fry the onion until deep gold and sweet.
- Add the garlic and curry paste and cook out for 2 minutes.
- Add the cubed chicken and allow to colour on all sides.
- Stir in the tamarind and fish sauce, then pour over the coconut milk and chicken stock.
- Lower the heat and leave to simmer for 15-20 minutes until the chicken is cooked through.
- Adjust the seasoning and stir in the lime juice just before serving with the rice.

Thai Green Chicken Curry   610

- Try this with green Thai curry paste for fresher flavours.

611

SERVES 4

Roast Partridge with Plum Sauce

PREPARATION TIME 10 MINUTES

COOKING TIME 30 MINUTES

....

INGREDIENTS

4 partridges, cleaned
4 sprigs thyme
Salt and pepper
4 tbsp butter, softened
4 rashers smoked streaky bacon

FOR THE PLUM SAUCE

1 tbsp butter
250g / 9 oz / 1 cup ripe plums, stoned and quartered
3-4 tbsp light brown sugar
100ml / 3 ½ fl. oz / ½ cup port
Pinch Chinese 5 spice

- Preheat the oven to 200°C (180° fan) / 400F / gas 6.
- Push the thyme sprigs into the cavity of the partridges, then rub the breasts all over with softened butter and season. Cover with the streaky bacon, place in a roasting tin and roast for 25-30 minutes until just cooked.
- Meanwhile heat the butter in a pan, add the plums and cook until starting to soften.
- Add the sugar and caramelise for 4 minutes.
- Pour in the port and 5 spice and simmer until thickened.
- Leave the partridge to rest for 10 minutes before serving with the sauce.
- Serve with steamed or roasted seasonal vegetables.

Partridge with Blackberry Sauce   612

- Use blackberries in place of the plums.

Partridge in Cabbage and Bacon Fondue

613

SERVES 6

Partridge with Cavolo Nero or Kale

614

- Use different greens such as Italian black cabbage or shredded kale for a stronger flavour.

Partridge with White Wine

615

- Use white wine in place of the beer.

Partridge with Juniper

616

- A few lightly crushed juniper berries added to the fondue will add a hit of gin flavour.

PREPARATION TIME 30 MINUTES

COOKING TIME 55 MINUTES

....

INGREDIENTS

6 young partridges
6 thin slices of streaky bacon
50 g of diced smoked bacon
1 green cabbage
3 cloves garlic
1 onion
30 cl pale ale beer
50 g butter
2 tablespoons oil
Salt and pepper

- Wrap a slice of bacon around each partridge and bind them with string to hold them together.
- Chop off the base of the cabbage and separate the leaves. Place them in a pan of boiling water and blanch for 10 minutes. Strain well and chop the leaves.
- Peel the garlic cloves and onion. Finely chop the onion.
- Heat the butter and oil in a large casserole. Brown the partridges all over. When they are nicely browned remove from the casserole.
- Add the diced bacon and onion to the casserole. Fry for 5 minutes over a medium heat, stirring. Add the cabbage and cloves garlic, season and stir.
- Return the partridges to the casserole. Add the beer. Cover and cook on a very low heat for 45 minutes, stirring from time to time.
- Serve immediately.

Breaded Chicken Escalopes

617

SERVES 4

PREPARATION TIME 20 MINUTES

COOKING TIME 8-10 MINUTES

INGREDIENTS

4 chicken breasts, skinned
1 ball mozzarella, sliced
Salt and pepper
3 tbsp flour
2 eggs, beaten
200g / 6 ½ oz / ¾ cup breadcrumbs
Olive oil
Cherry tomatoes, halved

- Place the chicken between 2 pieces of clingfilm and bat out until a bit thinner with a rolling pin.
- Using a sharp knife, cut a pocket into the side of each chicken.
- Stuff the pocket with mozzarella and close the edges of the chicken back over to enclose the cheese.
- Season, then dunk each pieces into flour, then egg then the breadcrumbs.
- Heat the oil in a large pan and fry until golden and crisp and the chicken cooked through – 8-10 minutes.
- Add the halved tomatoes to the pan and cook until just collapsing. Serve with the chicken.

Breaded Chicken with Taleggio Cheese

618

- Taleggio used in place of the mozzarella will give a stronger flavour.

Coq au Vin

619

SERVES 4

PREPARATION TIME 20 MINUTES

COOKING TIME 1 HOUR

INGREDIENTS

50g / 1 ¾ oz / ¼ cup butter
6 rashers smoked streaky bacon or pancetta, diced
2 onions, peeled and finely sliced
3 cloves garlic, finely sliced
2 sprigs thyme
1 chicken, jointed
2 tbsp seasoned flour
300g / 10 oz / 1 ¼ cups chestnut mushrooms, quartered
600ml / 1 pint / 2 cups medium white wine, such as Riesling
300ml / 10 fl. oz / 1 ½ cups double cream
Salt and pepper
2 tbsp parsley, chopped
Squeeze of lemon juice

- Heat the butter in a casserole and fry the bacon until starting to colour.
- Add the onion and garlic and cook until lightly gold. Add the thyme.
- Using a slotted spoon, remove the bacon and onions from the pan to a bowl.
- Add a little oil. Lightly dust the chicken joints with flour, shake off any excess and brown on all sides in the pan.
- Add the mushrooms and cook until golden, then return the bacon and onions to the pan.
- Pour over the wine, bubble up and cook gently for about 30 minutes until the chicken is cooked through.
- Pour in the cream and parsley, season and add a little lemon juice. Heat until the cream starts to thicken, then serve.

Coq Au Vin Rouge

620

- Use red wine in place of the white wine and omit the cream for a punchier dish.

621

SERVES 8

Foie Gras Terrine

- Rinse the foie gras and pat dry. Open the lobes up gently with your fingers and find the large vein that splits up and reaches like tributaries into the lobe.
- Carefully pull out all these veins, using a small sharp knife if necessary and trying to keep the lobes as intact as possible.
- Push the two lobes back together then place in a bowl with the wine, sugar and salt. Leave for 3 hours.
- Line a terrine mould with cling film, then push the marinated foie gras into the mould and place weights on top.
- Press overnight in the refrigerator.
- The next day unmould and slice and serve with brioche and chutney.
- If desired you could very briefly, over a very high heat, flash fry it on each side to heat through.

PREPARATION TIME 3 ½ HOURS + PRESSING TIME

INGREDIENTS

1 lobe of foie gras at room temperature
400ml / 14 fl. oz / 1 ½ cups dessert wine such as Sauternes
60g / 2 oz / ¼ cup salt
30g / 1 oz sugar

TO SERVE
Toasted brioche
Fruit chutney

Foie Gras Terrine with Steak   622

- Serve a very fine slice to melt on top of ribeye steak.

623

SERVES 4

Peking Duck

- Place the duck on a wire rack skin side up and dry thoroughly with kitchen paper. Score the skins with a sharp knife.
- Mix together the ingredients and brush the skin and leave to marinate for about 30 minutes.
- Preheat the oven to 190°C (170° fan) / 375F / gas 5.
- Brush the duck all over with the sauce and transfer the wire rack to a roasting tin. Pour a cup of water into the bottom of the tin and roast/steam for 30 minutes until the duck is cooked through and the skin is crisp.
- You can quickly grill the skin if it hasn't crisped up.
- Serve with rice or pancakes.

PREPARATION TIME 35 MINUTES

COOKING TIME 30 MINUTES

INGREDIENTS

4 duck breasts
2 tbsp runny honey
2 tbsp rice vinegar
1 ½ tbsp soy sauce
1 tbsp Chinese 5 spice
1 tbsp soft dark brown sugar

Chilli Peking Duck   624

- Crushed Szechuan peppercorns will add their distinctive lip-numbing tingling heat to the marinade.

625

SERVES 3-4

Duck a l'Orange

PREPARATION TIME 5 MINUTES

COOKING TIME 1 HOUR 45 MINUTES

....

INGREDIENTS

1 duck, weighing about 2 ¾ kg / 6 lb
Salt and pepper

FOR THE SAUCE

100g / 3 ½ oz / ½ cup caster (superfine) sugar
2 tbsp water
2 oranges, grated zest
250ml / 9 fl. oz / 1 cup orange juice
1 tbsp marmalade
75g / 2 ½ oz / ⅓ cup butter, chilled and cubed

- Preheat the oven to 220°C (200° fan) / 450F / gas 7.
- Prick the duck all over with a knife and place in a roasting tin. Season and roast for 20 minutes.
- Reduce the heat to 180°C / 350F / gas 4 and cook for 1 hour. Remove from the pan, drain to remove excess fat and save the fat for roast potatoes. Rest the duck on a plate.
- Make the sauce: set the sugar and water in a pan over a low heat and swirl until the sugar has melted. Do not stir. Allow to bubble up until golden.
- Once dark golden, remove from the heat and carefully, standing back, add any duck resting juices, orange zest and juice.
- Return to the heat and simmer gently for 10-15 minutes until thickened, stir in the marmalade then whisk in the butter a cube at a time until shiny. Season and serve with the duck.

Duck with Blood Oranges ## 626

- Use blood or even Seville oranges in season for a more grown-up citrus hit.

627

SERVES 4

Sticky Chicken with Cashews

PREPARATION TIME 1 HOUR

COOKING TIME 10 MINUTES

....

INGREDIENTS

8 chicken thighs, boned and skinned
2 tsp Chinese 5 spice
2 tbsp runny honey
1 tbsp soy sauce
1 tbsp groundnut oil
4 spring onions (scallions), finely sliced
2 sticks celery, finely chopped
1 clove garlic, crushed
2 tbsp cashew nuts
1 tbsp sesame seeds

- Cut the chicken into bite size pieces.
- Marinate the chicken for at least 1 hour in the 5 spice, honey and soy.
- Heat the oil in a wok until nearly smoking, then add the spring onions, celery and garlic and stir fry for a few seconds.
- Add the chicken, shaking off any marinade, and stir fry over a high heat until just cooked through then add the cashew nuts and toss to coat.
- Add the reserved marinade and bubble up until thickened and coats the chicken.
- Serve scattered with sesame seeds.

Sticky Quail with Cashews ## 628

- Quail can be treated in the same way – one per person and cooked in a hot oven for 25 minutes.

629

SERVES 4

Satay Chicken

- Mix together the marinade ingredients and pour half over the chicken pieces.
- Leave to marinate for at least 4 hours or overnight.
- Skewer with soaked wooden kebab sticks.
- Griddle over a high heat until blackened in patches and cooked through – 6-8 minutes.
- Meanwhile heat the remaining sauce in a small pan, then squeeze in a little lime juice.
- Serve the satay sauce alongside the chicken.

PREPARATION TIME 4 HOURS

COOKING TIME 10 MINUTES

INGREDIENTS

8 chicken thighs, boned and skinned and cut in half
2 shallots, peeled and finely chopped
½ red chilli, finely chopped
2 cloves garlic, finely chopped
1cm piece fresh ginger, grated
5 tbsp peanut butter
1 tbsp tamarind paste
2 tbsp soy sauce
100ml / 3 ½ fl. oz / ½ cup coconut milk
1 tsp palm or dark brown sugar
1 tbsp fish sauce
1 lime, juiced

Chicken Cordon Bleu

630

SERVES 4

PREPARATION TIME 10 MINUTES

COOKING TIME 20 MINUTES

INGREDIENTS

4 chicken breasts, skinned
4 slices ham
1 ball mozzarella or 150g / 5 oz / ⅔ cup Gruyere, sliced

75g / 2 ¾ oz / ⅓ cup plain (all purpose) flour
2 eggs, beaten
250g / 9 oz / 1 cup breadcrumbs
Vegetable oil
Salt and pepper

- Using a sharp knife, slice each chicken breast open so it opens out like a book.
- Place a piece of ham on top, then cheese and fold over and press the edges together to seal.
- Place the flour, eggs and breadcrumbs on separate plates. Season the flour.
- Dip each chicken breast into the flour, eggs then breadcrumbs, coating thoroughly each time.
- Heat the oil in a thin layer in the base of a pan then add 2 chicken breasts and cook, turning regularly for about 20 minutes until cooked through.
- Keep warm in a low oven while you cook the other 2. Serve hot with a salad.

Turkey Blanquette

631

SERVES 4

PREPARATION TIME 15 MINUTES

COOKING TIME 1 HOUR 15 MINUTES

INGREDIENTS

2 tbsp oil
1 turkey breast, cut into cubes
6 rashers streaky bacon, diced
1 clove garlic, finely chopped

3 shallots, peeled
4 sprigs tarragon, finely chopped
1 bouquet garni
300ml / 10 fl. oz / 1 ¼ cups dry white wine
1 tbsp butter
Handful chestnut mushrooms, sliced
1 tbsp flour
2 egg yolks
3-4 tbsp double cream
½ lemon, juiced

- Heat the oil in a pan and cook the turkey and bacon until slightly golden. Add the garlic and shallots and sauté for a couple of minutes.
- Add the herbs and white wine and enough water just to cover, then reduce the heat and simmer for about 30-40 minutes.
- Strain off 400ml / 14 fl. oz / 1 ½ cups of the turkey cooking liquid.
- Heat the butter in a pan and cook the mushrooms until tender. Add the flour and stir to make a paste.
- Whisk in the measured turkey cooking liquid a bit at a time until the sauce is smooth and thick and leave to simmer gently for 15 minutes.
- Whisk together the egg yolks, cream and a little lemon juice. Whisk in a few tbsp of the mushroom velouté then whisk the liaison back into the pan.
- Pour the sauce back over the turkey and reheat gently before serving.

632

SERVES 4

Chicken Nuggets

PREPARATION TIME 2 HOURS

COOKING TIME 10 MINUTES

....

INGREDIENTS

4 chicken breasts, skinned
300ml / 10 fl. oz / 1 ¼ cups
buttermilk
100g / 3 ½ oz / ½ cup plain
(all purpose) flour
2 eggs, beaten
200g / 7 oz / ¾ cup breadcrumbs
1 tsp mustard powder
Pinch Cayenne
1 tsp dried oregano
Salt and pepper
Vegetable oil

- Bash the chicken breasts between 2 pieces clingfilm with a rolling pin until about 2cm thick.
- Cut each piece into thick strips and place in a bowl with the buttermilk. Refrigerate for at least 2 hours or even overnight.
- The next day, dip them one at a time into the flour, egg then breadcrumbs mixed with the flavourings and lay on a rack to dry slightly.
- Heat 1cm depth oil in a pan and fry the chicken in batches until golden on both sides and cooked through.
- Serve with a squeeze of lemon and ketchup.

Chicken Nuggets with Matzo Cracker Crumb

633

- Use matzo crackers crushed to crumbs for a crisper result.

634

SERVES 4

Guinea Fowl with Orange Lentils

PREPARATION TIME 10 MINUTES

COOKING TIME 40 MINUTES

....

INGREDIENTS

1 Guinea fowl, jointed
Olive oil
Salt and pepper
200g / 7 oz / ¾ cup mixed Puy and
orange lentils
1 onion, peeled and chopped
1 carrot, peeled and chopped
1 stick celery, chopped
1 clove garlic, finely chopped
1 large glass dry white wine
200-300ml / 7-10 ½ fl. oz / ¾ - 1 ¼
cups chicken stock
2 bay leaves
2 tbsp red wine vinegar

- Preheat the oven to 200°C (180° fan) / 400F / gas 6.
- Lay the guinea fowl joints in a roasting tin, drizzle with oil, season and roast for about 30-40 minutes until cooked through.
- Meanwhile, place the lentils in a pan with the vegetables, wine and enough stock to cover with the bouquet garni. Bring to a simmer and cook for about 25 minutes until the lentils are tender,
- If there is any liquid remaining, drain it off, then spoon into a serving dish and season the lentils with salt, pepper and vinegar.
- Lay the guinea fowl on top and serve.

Guinea Fowl with Fresh Orange

635

- Push a quartered orange in and around the joints for a fresh citrus flavour.

SERVES 4

Chicken with Blue Cheese and Bacon

- Preheat the oven to 200°C (180° fan) / 400F / gas 6.
- Lay the chicken on a surface and cut down the side of the chicken open them out like a book.
- Lay the tomato slices into the middle of the chicken, top with blue cheese and fold the chicken back over to encase the filling.
- Wrap the chicken breasts in 2 rashers of bacon to hold the filling in and place in a roasting tin.
- Drizzle with oil, season and bake for 20-25 minutes until cooked through.

PREPARATION TIME 15 MINUTES

COOKING TIME 20-25 MINUTES

INGREDIENTS

4 chicken breasts, skinned
100g / 3 ½ oz / ½ cup blue cheese, crumbled
2 tomatoes, sliced
8 rashers smoked streaky bacon
Olive oil
Salt and pepper

Chicken Stuffed with Mozzarella — 637

- If you don't like blue cheese, use mild mozzarella.

SERVES 4

Turkey with Pesto wrapped in Bacon

- Preheat the oven to 200°C (180° fan) / 400F / gas 6.
- Place the turkey steak on the surface and cut in half down one side, opening it out like a book.
- Mix together the pesto and crème fraîche with a little seasoning and spread into the cavity.
- Roll the turkey back up into a sausage shape and wrap around with the bacon and secure with a cocktail stick.
- Place in a roasting tin, drizzle with oil, season and roast for 45 minutes, until cooked through and the juices run clear.
- Leave to rest for 10 minutes before carving into slices.

PREPARATION TIME 10 MINUTES

COOKING TIME 45 MINUTES

INGREDIENTS

4 turkey breast steaks
6 tbsp pesto
4 tbsp crème fraîche
8 slices streaky bacon
Olive oil
Salt and pepper

Turkey Stuffed with Red Pesto — 639

- The red tomato pesto you can find in supermarkets makes for a different twist.

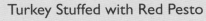

FISH AND SHELLFISH

640

SERVES 2

Littleneck Clams with Garlic & Parsley

- Place the clams in a large bowl of cold water to get rid of any sand.
- Heat the oil and sweat the shallot and garlic until translucent.
- Add the chilli and cook for 1 minute, then toss in the clams, discarding any that remain open when tapped.
- Pour over the white wine, stir in the parsley and cover with a lid and steam for 5-8 minutes until all have opened.
- Discard any that remain closed, season and ladle into bowls, leaving the very bottom of the cooking liquor which will be sandy.

PREPARATION TIME 5 MINUTES

COOKING TIME 10 MINUTES

INGREDIENTS

500g/ 1 lb / 2 cups littleneck clams
2 tbsp olive oil
1 shallot, finely chopped
2 cloves garlic, finely chopped
1 red chilli, deseeded and finely chopped (optional)
200ml / 7 fl. oz / ¾ cup dry white wine
Salt and pepper
½ lemon, juiced
1 bunch flat leaf parsley, finely chopped

Pan-fried Scallops with Leeks

641

SERVES 4

PREPARATION TIME 10 MINUTES

COOKING TIME 10-15 MINUTES

INGREDIENTS

50g / 1 ¾ oz / ¼ cup butter
2 leeks, white part only, finely sliced
30g / 1 oz butter
12 scallops, cleaned and trimmed
Salt and pepper
½ lemon, juiced

- Heat the butter in a pan and when foaming add the leeks. Cook very gently for at least 10 minutes until soft and sweet.
- Heat the 30g butter in another pan and when foaming add the scallops. Cook for 90 seconds on one side and when golden, turn over and cook the other side. Remove from the heat and rest briefly.
- Season the leeks and spoon onto plates. Top with the scallops, squeeze over a little lemon juice and seasoning and serve.

Oysters with Herb Sauce

642

SERVES 4

PREPARATION TIME 5 MINUTES

INGREDIENTS

16 oysters, opened
1 bunch parsley, chopped
1 clove garlic, chopped
75ml / 2 ½ fl. oz / ⅓ cup olive oil
1 lemon, grated zest
Salt and pepper

- Place the opened oysters on a platter of crushed ice.
- Whiz the parsley, garlic, oil and zest in a food processor until the consistency of pesto. Loosen with more oil if necessary.
- Taste – it may need lemon juice as well as seasoning.
- Spoon a little of the sauce on top of each oyster.

643

SERVES 2

Mussels Marinière

PREPARATION TIME 10 MINUTES

COOKING TIME 10 MINUTES

....

INGREDIENTS

1kg / 2 lb / 4 ¼ cups mussels, scrubbed and de-bearded
1 tbsp olive oil
1 onion, peeled and very finely chopped
4 cloves garlic, finely chopped
1 stick celery, finely chopped
300ml / 10 fl. oz / 1 ½ cups dry white wine
Salt and pepper

- Wash the mussels in a bowl of deep cold water. Discard any that remain open when tapped.
- Heat the oil in a large pot and gently fry the onion, garlic and celery until softened.
- Drain the shellfish and add to the pot then toss in the white wine and bubble up.
- Cover with a lid, shake the pot a little and leave the shellfish to open – about 8-10 minutes.
- When they are all just open, taste the sauce and adjust the seasoning if necessary.
- Serve in deep bowls.

Mussels with Cider   **644**

- Use cider in place of the wine.

645

SERVES 4

Red Snapper with Deep Fried Leeks

PREPARATION TIME 10 MINUTES

COOKING TIME 10 MINUTES

....

INGREDIENTS

2 tbsp olive oil
4 red snapper fillets, boned
Salt and pepper
½ lemon, juiced
2 leeks, white part only, very finely sliced lengthways
Vegetable oil for deep frying
Rocket (arugula) to serve

- Heat the oil in a pan and when very hot add the fish fillets skin side down.
- Cook for 2-3 minutes, depending on thickness, then carefully turn over and cook the other side for about 1 minute. Remove from the pan and keep warm.
- Heat the vegetable oil to 180°C / 350F then drop in the leeks a handful at a time until they turn golden and crisp. Remove to drain on kitchen paper.
- Lay the snapper fillets on a thin bed of rocket and squeeze over some lemon juice and a little salt. Top with the deep fried leeks and serve.

Monkfish Tail with Leeks   **646**

- Monkfish tails are meaty and sweet and would go well with the leeks.

647

SERVES 4 # Steamed Halibut with Onions Two Ways

- Heat the butter in a pan and cook the onions over a very low heat for at least 20 minutes until golden and very sweet.
- Place the halibut on a plate in a steamer, season and cook for about 10 minutes or until the fish is just cooked through and a flake comes away easily.
- Serve the halibut on top of the golden onions, topped with spring onions.

PREPARATION TIME 10 MINUTES

COOKING TIME 30 MINUTES

INGREDIENTS

40g / 1 ½ oz butter
1 onion, peeled and finely sliced
4 thick slices halibut
Salt and pepper
½ bunch spring onions (scallions)
finely sliced

Halibut with Red and White Onions

648

- Use 1 red onion as well as the white onion to add to the colour.

649

MAKES 20-24 # Caribbean Haddock Fritters

- Add the yeast to the water with the sugar, stir well and set aside for 10 minutes until it starts to foam.
- Whisk the flour, baking powder, pepper and allspice together, then stir in the yeast mixture and milk and make a smooth batter.
- Flake in the haddock and stir to coat, then stir in the remaining flavourings. Leave to rest for 2 hours.
- Heat the oil to 180°C / 350F and drop in the batter using a tablespoon. Fry on all sides until golden brown, then drain on kitchen paper.
- Serve hot.

PREPARATION TIME 2 HOURS
20 MINUTES

COOKING TIME 10 MINUTES

INGREDIENTS

1 tsp yeast
50ml / 1 ¾ fl. oz / ¼ cup water
½ tsp sugar
250g / 9 oz / 1 cup plain (all purpose)
flour
1 tsp baking powder
1 tsp black pepper
½ tsp allspice
100ml / 3 ½ fl. oz / ½ cup milk
250g / 9 oz / 1 cup haddock, cooked
1 onion, peeled and finely chopped
2 red chillies, finely chopped
½ Habanero pepper, finely chopped
½ bunch spring onions (scallions),
finely chopped
2 tsp dried thyme
1 egg, beaten
Vegetable oil for deep frying

Caribbean Prawn Fritters

650

- Use large langoustines in the batter.

185

651

SERVES 4

Battered Fish

PREPARATION TIME 10 MINUTES

COOKING TIME 20 MINUTES

INGREDIENTS

4 thick fillets white fish such as hake, haddock or cod
A little seasoned flour
225g / 8 oz / 1 cup self-raising (self-rising) flour
300ml / 10 fl. oz / 1 ½ cups cold lager
Pinch Cayenne pepper
Vegetable oil for deep frying

- Dust the fish fillets in a little seasoned flour to help the batter stick.
- Whisk the flour and lager together to make a batter the consistency of double cream.
- Heat the oil to 180°C / 350F.
- Dip the fish fillets in the batter, thoroughly coating both sides then cook 2 at a time for about 10 minutes until deep golden brown and crisp.
- Keep warm in a low oven while you cook the remaining fish.
- Serve with lemon wedges, chips and mushy peas.

Battered Seafood
652
- Why not use a mixture of fish and seafood in the batter to make a platter?

653

SERVES 4

Prawn Cocktail

PREPARATION TIME 10 MINUTES

INGREDIENTS

1 little gem lettuce, leaves separated
½ cucumber, finely diced
250g / 9 oz / 1 cup North Atlantic prawns (shrimp), cooked

FOR THE MARIE ROSE SAUCE
4 tbsp mayonnaise
2 tbsp tomato ketchup
Tabasco
Squeeze of lemon juice
Salt and pepper
Dash of Cognac or dry sherry (optional)
½ tsp paprika, to serve

- Layer the lettuce, cucumber and prawns in individual serving glasses.
- Mix together the ingredients for the sauce, tasting as you go. It should not be too sickly.
- Spoon the sauce over the prawn salad, then sprinkle over a little paprika before serving.

Crayfish Cocktail
654
- Use crayfish tails in place of the prawns.

655

SERVES 4

Tuna Steak with Peppers

Tuna Steak with Harissa Peppers

656

- Stir 1-2 tbsp of harissa into the cooked peppers

Herb and Olive Crusted Tuna

657

- Whiz together thyme leaves, lemon zest and black olives and press onto both sides of the tuna before cooking.

Tuna Steak with Peppers and Tomatoes

658

- Halved cherry tomatoes added to the peppers will add freshness.

PREPARATION TIME 5 MINUTES

COOKING TIME 25 MINUTES

INGREDIENTS

4 tbsp olive oil
2 red peppers, deseeded and finely sliced
2 yellow peppers, deseeded and finely sliced
2 sprigs thyme
Salt and pepper
4 tuna steaks, 2 cm thick
½ lemon, juiced

- Heat the oil in a frying pan and cook the peppers with the thyme until very soft and sweet – about 20 minutes.
- Remove, season and keep warm.
- Reheat the pan, season the tuna on both sides and cook over a high heat for 30-60 seconds per side, depending on how rare you like your tuna.
- Serve over the peppers, squeezing over a little lemon juice.

659

SERVES 4

Fish and Sweet Potato Parmentier

PREPARATION TIME 10 MINUTES

COOKING TIME 40-45 MINUTES

···

INGREDIENTS

600g / 1 lb / 2 ½ cups cod fillet,
boned
200g / 7 oz / ¾ cup smoked haddock
600ml / 1 pint / 2 ½ cups full-fat milk
1 onion, studded with 2 cloves
2 bay leaves
50g / 1 ¾ oz / ¼ cup butter
50g / 1 ¾ oz / ¼ cup flour
Salt and pepper
½ bunch parsley, finely chopped.
1 kg / 2 ¼ lb / 4 ¼ cups sweet potato,
peeled and cut into cubes
2 tbsp Cheddar, grated

- Poach the fish in the milk with the onion and bay leaves for about 8 minutes until just starting to flake. Lift the fish and flavourings out, reserving the milk and leave to cool.
- Heat the butter in a pan and stir in the flour to make a paste. Whisk in the cooking milk a little at a time to make a smooth white sauce.
- Simmer for 15 minutes over a low heat, stirring occasionally. Stir in the parsley and flake in the fish.
- Steam the sweet potato cubes until cooked through – about 10 minutes. Mash thoroughly.
- Preheat the oven to 180°C / 350F / gas 5.
- Spoon the fish in its sauce into individual serving dishes and top with potato. Sprinkle over the cheese and bake for 20-25 minutes until bubbling.

Cod and Potato Parmentier

660

- If you don't like sweet potatoes, this works just as well with floury white potatoes.

661

SERVES 4

Scampi Skewers with Cucumber Salad

PREPARATION TIME 15 MINUTES

COOKING TIME 15 MINUTES

···

INGREDIENTS

100g / 3 ½ oz / 1 ½ cups plain
(all purpose) flour
1 egg, beaten
250g / 9 oz / 1 cup fine breadcrumbs
Pinch Cayenne pepper
800g / 1 ¾ lb / 3 ⅓ cups raw scampi
Vegetable oil for deep frying
1 cucumber, halved lengthways and
finely sliced
1 bunch dill, chopped
3 tbsp white wine vinegar
½ - 1 tbsp caster (superfine) sugar
1 tsp salt

- Lay the flour, egg and breadcrumbs out in separate dishes, seasoning the breadcrumbs and adding the Cayenne.
- Dip the scampi into each bowl in turn, thoroughly coating each time.
- Heat the oil to 180°C / 350F and cook the scampi in batches until golden brown all over. Drain on kitchen paper.
- Meanwhile macerate the cucumber with the dill and other ingredients to make a light quick pickle.
- Serve with the hot scampi.

Monkfish Skewers

662

- Chunks of meaty monkfish won't fall apart and will provide firm sweetness.

663

SERVES 4

Trout Saltimbocca with Piquillo Peppers

- Sandwich a slice of Serrano ham between 2 trout fillets, skin facing out and secure with toothpicks.
- Dust each side with seasoned flour.
- Heat the butter in a pan until foaming, then lay in 2 trout saltimbocca and cook on each side for 3-4 minutes until golden crusted.
- Keep warm in a low oven while you cook the rest.
- To serve, place the saltimbocca on a plate. Decorate around with the peppers and trout roe and top with a few salad leaves. Serve with lemon wedges on the side.

PREPARATION TIME 10 MINUTES

COOKING TIME 25 MINUTES

....

INGREDIENTS

8 trout fillets, pin boned
4 slices Serrano ham
2 tbsp flour, seasoned
50g / 1 ¾ oz / ½ cup butter
1 jar piquillo peppers, drained
4 tsp trout roe
1 lemon, quartered
Salad leaves

664

SERVES 4

Steamed Salmon

PREPARATION TIME 5 MINUTES

COOKING TIME 12-16 MINUTES

....

INGREDIENTS

4 thick salmon steaks
Salt and pepper
4 sprigs thyme or marjoram or chervil

4 tomatoes, thickly sliced
Extra virgin olive oil
½ lemon, juiced

- Set the salmon fillets (probably 2 at a time unless your steamer is industrial) on a plate in a steamer, tucking in the herbs and seasoning.
- Steam over a medium heat for 6-8 minutes, depending on thickness. The inside should be coral pink, not pale pink all the way through otherwise it will be dry.
- Keep the salmon warm while you steam the remaining salmon.
- Meanwhile lay the tomatoes on a plate and drizzle with oil, salt and pepper and lemon juice and leave to macerate.
- Serve the salmon on top of the tomatoes with a squeeze of lemon.

665

SERVES 2

Grilled Sea Bass with Fennel

PREPARATION TIME 10 MINUTES

COOKING TIME 16-18 MINUTES

....

INGREDIENTS

1 sea bass, gutted and cleaned
1 fennel (finocchio) bulb, trimmed and finely sliced
Few sprigs dill

1 lemon, sliced
Salt and pepper
Olive oil

- Heat a barbecue or griddle until very hot.
- Open up the fish and fill the insides with fennel slices, dill, lemon slices and seasoning.
- Rub the outsides with olive oil and grill for about 8 minutes per side, turning carefully until the fish is just cooked through and pulls away easily from the bone.
- Serve at the table for everyone to help themselves.

666

SERVES 4

Lobster Fricassée

Crab Fricassée 667

- Cooked crab claws would be a slightly more economical version.

Lobster Fricassée with Basmati Rice 668

- The perfect accompaniment would be steamed basmati rice to soak up the sauce.

Seafood Fricassée 669

- Mixed seafood such as scallops and prawns would keep the seafood sweetness whilst cutting down on the cost.

PREPARATION TIME 20 MINUTES

COOKING TIME 1 HOUR 15 MINUTES

....

INGREDIENTS

2 lobsters, cooked
1 tbsp oil
30g / 1 oz shallots, finely chopped
30g / 1 oz celery, finely chopped
30g / 1 oz carrots, peeled and diced
60g / 2 oz / ¼ cup button mushrooms, thickly sliced
50g / 1 ¾ oz / ¼ cup butter
1 tomato, chopped
1 tbsp tomato purée
1 sprig thyme
100ml / 3 ½ fl. oz / ½ cup brandy
2 tbsp pastis
200ml / 7 fl. oz / ¾ cup Champagne
500ml / 1 pint / 2 cups fish stock
100ml / 3 ½ oz / ½ cup double cream
Salt and pepper

- Remove the tail and claws from the body. Set aside. Split the bodies in half lengthways.
- Heat the oil in a large pan and fry the lobster bodies for 5 minutes. Add the mirepoix and cook until softened but not browned. Add the mushrooms.
- Add the butter and increase the heat slightly to turn the vegetables golden. Stir in the tomato, tomato puree, thyme and alcohol and cook over a high heat until the liquid has nearly evaporated.
- Add the Champagne and simmer until reduced by half.
- Add the fish stock and simmer for 30 minutes until reduced by half, then add the cream, strain and set aside.
- Carefully remove the flesh from the claws and tail of the lobster. Set the sauce back over a gentle heat and warm the meat through. Season and serve.

670

SERVES 4

Salmon Steaks with Court Bouillon

- Place all the ingredients for the court bouillon in a roasting tin you can set over heat and gently heat until simmering.
- Add the salmon steaks skin side down, cover the tin with foil and poach gently for about 10 minutes until just coral inside – not pale pink as they will be dry.
- Remove from the poaching liquor and serve with salad.

PREPARATION TIME 10 MINUTES

COOKING TIME 10 MINUTES

INGREDIENTS

4 salmon steaks, weighing about 200g / 7 oz each

FOR COURT BOUILLON
250ml / 9 fl. oz / 1 cup dry white wine
1 onion, peeled and sliced
1 carrot, peeled and chopped
1 stick celery, chopped
2 bay leaves
8 black peppercorns
500ml / 1 pint / 2 cups fish stock or water
Salt and pepper

Poached Fish   671

- Any fish can be poached this way, including all white fish.

672

SERVES 6

Pan-fried Prawns

- Peel the prawns, leaving the tail intact.
- Heat the oil in a pan, add the prawns and garlic and sauté over a high heat for two minutes.
- Add the chilli and cook for a further one minute, then season and add lemon juice.
- Serve with good bread.

PREPARATION TIME 10 MINUTES

COOKING TIME 5 MINUTES

INGREDIENTS

36 raw prawns (shrimp)
3 tbsp groundnut oil
2 cloves garlic, finely sliced
1 red chilli, deseeded and finely chopped
Salt
1 lemon, juiced

Pan Fried Scallops   673

- Treat shelled cleaned scallops in the same way.

674

SERVES 4

Crab Meat Coconut Cakes

PREPARATION TIME 15 MINUTES

COOKING TIME 20 MINUTES

....

INGREDIENTS

250g / 9 oz / 1 cup white crabmeat, picked
3 tbsp breadcrumbs
1 tbsp unsweetened desiccated coconut
1 egg, beaten
1 clove garlic, crushed
½ red chilli, deseeded and finely chopped
1 tbsp oyster sauce
1 tbsp coriander (cilantro), finely chopped
Salt and pepper
Vegetable oil for deep frying
1 lime, juiced
Lettuce leaves

- Mix together the crab meat, breadcrumbs, egg, garlic, coconut, chilli, oyster sauce and coriander. Season and combine thoroughly.
- Form into small patties of roughly equal size.
- Heat a 1cm depth of oil in a pan and fry the crab cakes in batches until golden brown on both side.
- Drain on kitchen paper and keep warm in a low oven while you cook the rest.
- Serve wrapped in the lettuce leaves sprinkled with lime juice.

Prawn Coconut Cakes

675

- Mince raw prawns in the food processor and proceed as above.

676

SERVES 4

Cod Stew with Wine and Tomato Sauce

PREPARATION TIME 15 MINUTES

COOKING TIME 30 MINUTES

....

INGREDIENTS

2 tbsp olive oil
1 onion, peeled and finely sliced
1 stick celery, finely chopped
1 carrot, peeled and diced
2 tbsp tomato purée
2 large floury potatoes, peeled and cut into chunks
250ml / 9 fl. oz / 1 cup dry white wine
400ml / 14 fl. oz / 1 ½ cups fish stock
500g / 1 lb / 2 cups cod steak, cut into chunks
1 bouquet garni
2 tbsp parsley, freshly chopped
Salt and pepper

- Heat the oil in a casserole and sweat the onion, celery and carrot until softened.
- Add the tomato puree and cook out for 2 minutes.
- Add the potatoes, then pour over the wine and stock. Add the bouquet garni and fish and bring to a simmer.
- Cook gently for about 20 minutes until the potatoes are tender and the fish is just cooked.
- Season and serve scattered with parsley.

Cod Stew with Red Wine Tomato Sauce

677

- Fish does go well with lighter red wines, so try using one in place of the white wine.

Marinated Sardines with 3 Pepper Salad

678

SERVES 4

- Place the sardines in a dish with a little oil, rosemary and chilli flakes.
- Mix the peppers in a bowl with the oil, lemon juice and seasoning and leave to macerate.
- Heat a griddle pan until smoking, then cook the sardines for 4-5 minutes each side until cooked through.
- Serve with the crunchy pepper salad and good bread.

PREPARATION TIME 10 MINUTES

COOKING TIME 10 MINUTES

INGREDIENTS

12 sardines
Olive oil
Rosemary
Dried chilli flakes
1 red pepper, deseeded and finely chopped
1 yellow pepper, deseeded and finely chopped
1 green pepper, deseeded and finely chopped
2 tbsp extra virgin olive oil
½ lemon, juiced
Salt and pepper

Sardines with Pepper Tomato Salsa

679

- Adding finely chopped tomatoes and a squeeze of lime will make a refreshing accompaniment to the fish.

Herby Fish Cakes

680

SERVES 3-4

- Combine the fish, potatoes, herbs, capers and a little lemon juice in a bowl and season well.
- Chill for 30 minutes.
- Form into equal-sized patties, then dip into the egg, then the breadcrumbs.
- Heat 1cm depth of oil in a pan and gently fry the fishcakes on both sides until golden and crisp.
- Drain on kitchen paper and serve with peas and ketchup

PREPARATION TIME 40 MINUTES

COOKING TIME 10 MINUTES

INGREDIENTS

225g / 8 oz / 1 cup white fish, salmon or tuna, cut into small cubes
225g / 8 oz / 1 cup mashed potato
2 tbsp parsley, chopped
1 tbsp chervil, chopped
3 tsp capers, chopped (optional)
Squeeze of lemon juice
Salt and pepper
1 egg, beaten
3 tbsp breadcrumbs
Vegetable oil

Herby Fish Cakes with a Spicy Crust

681

- A pinch of cayenne with the breadcrumbs will add a kick.

682

SERVES 3

Fish Fingers

PREPARATION TIME 10 MINUTES

COOKING TIME 20 MINUTES

....

INGREDIENTS

400g / 14 oz / 1 ½ cups skinless firm
white fish
100g / 3 ½ oz / ½ cup breadcrumbs
1 tsp dried oregano
Pinch Cayenne
½ lemon, grated zest
Salt and pepper
1 egg, beaten
Olive oil

- Preheat the oven to 200°C (180° fan) / 400F / gas 7.
- Cut the fish into 12 equal sized pieces.
- Mix together the breadcrumbs with oregano, cayenne, lemon zest and seasoning.
- Dip the fish pieces first into the egg, then thoroughly coat in the breadcrumb mix.
- Brush a baking sheet generously with oil and lay the fish fingers on it.
- Bake in the oven for about 20 minutes, turning once, until golden brown.

Fish Fingers with Tartare Sauce **683**

- Serve alongside tartare sauce and wedges of lemon. See page 25 for recipe.

684

SERVES 4-6

Smoked Salmon Mousse

PREPARATION TIME 15 MINUTES
....

INGREDIENTS

250g / 9 oz / 1 cup smoked salmon
trimmings
100g / 3 ½ oz / ½ cup cream cheese
2 tbsp crème fraîche
½ lemon, juiced
2 tbsp chives, chopped
Salt and pepper
8-12 slices smoked salmon
Lemon wedges to serve

- Place the ingredients in a food processor and pulse until roughly chopped.
- Season carefully.
- Lay 2 slices of smoked salmon out on a surface, overlapping, and place a large spoonful in the centre. Wrap the salmon around the mousse to make an enclosed parcel.
- Place on a platter, seam side down, and repeat for the remaining salmon slices.
- Chill until needed then serve with lemon.

Smoked Mackerel Mousse **685**

- Use the same amount of smoked mackerel fillets in place of the smoked salmon.

SERVES 2 # Lobster with Red Pepper Chilli Sauce

Crab with Red Pepper Sauce   687

- Crab claws are a tasty substitute.

Lobster with Brandy Red Pepper Sauce   688

- A splash of flamed brandy would add depth and richness to the sauce.

Creamy Red Pepper Sauce   689

- A splash of cream would soften the heat and intensity.

PREPARATION TIME 20 MINUTES

COOKING TIME 30 MINUTES

....

INGREDIENTS

1 lobster, cooked, tail and claws removed and set aside, body halved lengthways

FOR THE SAUCE
3 tbsp olive oil
Lobster body
1 onion, peeled and chopped
3 cloves garlic, chopped
2 anchovies
2 tbsp tomato purée
300ml / 10 fl. oz / 1 ¼ cups dry white wine
2 jars roasted piquillo peppers, drained
1 tsp smoked paprika
1 Ibarra chillies, drained and chopped or any preserved chilli pepper
4 ripe tomatoes, chopped
Salt and pepper

- Heat the oil in a pan and cook the lobster halves for a few minutes.
- Add the onion, garlic and anchovy and cook until the anchovy breaks down and the onion softens.
- Stir in the tomato puree and white wine and bubble up, then tip in the peppers, paprika, chillies and tomatoes. Season, bring to a simmer and cook until thickened and reduced.
- Whiz the sauce in a blender and adjust the seasoning.
- Serve the hot sauce with the cold lobster tail and claws.

690

SERVES 4

Red Mullet with Pesto

Red Mullet with Red Pesto

691

- Use red pesto in place of the green.

Red Mullet with Black Olives and Pesto

692

- Sliced black olives on the pesto go well with red mullet.

Red Mullet Pesto Baguette

693

- This would make a hearty filling for a fresh crisp baguette.

PREPARATION TIME 5 MINUTES

COOKING TIME 6-8 MINUTES

··

INGREDIENTS

4 red mullet fillets, pin boned
Olive oil
Salt and pepper
4-6 tbsp pesto
Rocket (arugula) salad, to serve

- Lay the fillets in a roasting tin skin side up, drizzle with oil, season.
- Grill under a hot grill until the skin becomes crisp – about 3-4 minutes.
- Working quickly, flip the fillets over and spread with pesto. Return to the grill and cook briefly until the pesto starts to bubble.
- Remove from the grill and serve with salad.

694
SERVES 4
Octopus and Red Onion Stew

- Heat the oil in a pan and cook the onions gently for at least 15 minutes until sweet and golden.
- Add the garlic, paprika and a glass of water and bubble up.
- Add the octopus, cover with a lid and leave to simmer gently for at least 1 hour.
- Season, squeeze in the lemon juice and parsley and serve with bread.

PREPARATION TIME 15 MINUTES

COOKING TIME 1 HOUR 15 MINUTES

INGREDIENTS

1 octopus, cleaned and cut into small pieces
4 tbsp olive oil
3 red onions, peeled and thickly sliced
3 cloves garlic, finely sliced
1 tbsp paprika
Salt and pepper
1 lemon, juiced
Parsley, chopped

Squid Red Onion Stew 695

- Squid can be cooked the same way and is easier to find.

696
SERVES 4-6
Deep-fried Squid with Bearnaise Sauce

- Put the tarragon, shallot, peppercorns, vinegar and wine in a small pan and reduce by a third until there are about 3 tbsp liquid left. Strain.
- Whisk the egg yolks and mustard together in a bowl over a pan of barely simmering water. Whisk in the vinegar reduction, add a tbsp water and whisk.
- Beat in the 25g butter a little at a time, then slowly trickle in the melted butter a drop at a time.
- Season and keep warm until needed.
- Make the batter for the squid: stir the egg into the cold water, then whisk in the flour to form a lumpy tempura-style batter. Dip the squid rings in and coat thoroughly.
- Heat the oil to 180°C / 350F and cook the squid in batches, removing to drain on kitchen paper when golden brown.
- Serve with the warm béarnaise sauce.

PREPARATION TIME 30 MINUTES

COOKING TIME 10 MINUTES

INGREDIENTS

1 tbsp tarragon, chopped
1 shallot, finely chopped
6 black peppercorns, crushed
2 tbsp white wine vinegar
150ml / 5 fl. oz / ⅔ cup white wine
3 egg yolks
1 tsp mustard powder
25g / 1 oz butter at room temperature
180g / 6 oz / ¾ cup butter, melted
Salt
1 kg / 2 ¼ lb squid, cleaned and cut into rings
1 tbsp salt
1 egg
200ml / 7 fl. oz / ¾ cup ice cold water
225g / 8 oz / 1 cup plain (all purpose) flour

Squid with Sweet Chilli Mayonnaise 697

- Stir sweet chilli sauce into mayonnaise for a fiery dipping sauce.

PUDDINGS

698

SERVES 4

Raspberry Fool

- Tip the raspberries into a bowl and lightly crush with a fork so that it is a mixture of liquid and fruit. This will give the fool a more interesting texture.
- Lightly whip the cream to soft peaks, then fold in the yoghurt.
- Fold the raspberries through to make a ripple effect. Taste – you may or may not want the extra sugar.
- Serve in small bowls.

PREPARATION TIME 10 MINUTES

INGREDIENTS

300g / 10 oz / 1 ¼ cups raspberries
150ml / 5 fl. oz / ⅔ cup double cream
125ml / 4 fl. oz / ½ cup Greek natural yoghurt
1 tbsp icing (confectioners') sugar

Chocolate and Mint Mousse

699

SERVES 4

PREPARATION TIME 20 MINUTES

INGREDIENTS

200g / 7oz / ¾ cup dark chocolate
1-2 drops peppermint essence
2 tbsp water
4 eggs, separated
Mint sprigs

- Melt the chocolate and tbsp water in a small bowl over a pan of simmering water.
- Remove the melted chocolate from the heat, leave for 2 minutes, add the peppermint essence, then beat in the egg yolks. Leave to cool for 10 minutes or so.
- Meanwhile whisk the egg whites to soft peaks.
- Fold the egg whites into the chocolate mixture using a metal spoon.
- Spoon into individual glasses or a bowl, cover with clingfilm and chill for at least 6 hours.
- Decorate with mint sprigs.

White Chocolate Mousse

700

SERVES 4

PREPARATION TIME 50 MINUTES

INGREDIENTS

100g / 3 ½ oz / ½ cup good quality white chocolate, broken into pieces
250ml / 9 oz / 1 cup double cream
2 egg whites
1 tbsp caster (superfine) sugar
2 tbsp white chocolate shavings

- Break the chocolate into small pieces and place in a bowl with the cream. Place over a pan of simmering water and whisk until the chocolate has melted. Remove from the heat, leave to cool and then chill for at least 30 minutes.
- Whisk the egg whites, adding the sugar as you whisk, until thick and glossy. Whisk the chocolate mixture until the mixture forms soft peaks, then fold the egg whites in a third at a time, being careful not to lose the air.
- Spoon into individual ramekins and chill until needed.
- Garnish with shavings of white chocolate.

701

SERVES 6

Lemon Charlotte

PREPARATION TIME I HOUR 30 MINUTES

....

INGREDIENTS

1 sachet powdered gelatine
50ml / 1 ¾ oz / ¼ cup warm water
250ml / 9 oz / 1 cup milk
250ml / 9 fl. oz / 1 cup caster (superfine) sugar
2 egg yolks, beaten
1 lemon, grated zest
2 egg whites
450ml / 1 pint / 2 cups double cream
16-20 sponge fingers

- Soak the gelatine in the warm water.
- Pour the milk into a pan and heat gently. Whisk together the egg yolks and sugar, pour over the milk, combine thoroughly, whisking until the sauce thickens.
- Add the gelatine mixture and whisk until combined. Add the zest and stir through. Remove from the heat.
- When the mixture is cold, whisk the egg whites and cream to soft peaks. Fold each one into the lemon mixture and chill for 30 minutes.
- Line the base of a Charlotte Russe mould with baking parchment. Line the base and the sides with the sponge fingers, then spoon in the mixture.
- Chill for 2 hours, then turn out onto a plate when ready to serve.

Orange Lime Charlotte

702

- Substitute the zest of 1 orange and 1 lime for the lemon.

703

SERVES 4

Lemon and Ginger Soufflé

PREPARATION TIME 30 MINUTES

COOKING TIME 15 MINUTES

....

INGREDIENTS

Butter, melted
2 egg yolks + 4 egg whites
6 heaped tbsp caster (superfine) sugar + 2 tbsp for dusting
3 tsp cornflour
1 tbsp plain (all purpose) flour
100ml / 3 ½ fl. oz / ½ cup double cream
100ml / 3 ½ fl. oz / ½ cup milk
Juice and zest of 2 lemons
1 tsp ground cinnamon
4 tsp stem ginger, finely chopped
Icing (confectioners') sugar, to dust

- Preheat oven to 180°C (160° fan) / 350F / gas 5.
- Brush the insides of 4 ramekins with the melted butter then add a little sugar to each and turn them to coat the sides and bottom. Refrigerate.
- Place the cream, flour and cornflour in a bowl and whisk until smooth. Heat the milk in a pan, then whisk into the cream mixture. Pour back into the pan and place over a gentle heat. Whisk until thickened, then whisk in the lemon zest and juice and cinnamon.
- Whisk in the egg yolks and sugar. When it starts to look like custard, set aside to cool.
- Whisk the egg whites to soft peaks. Once the lemon mixture is cool, fold in the remaining egg whites.
- Place a tsp of stem ginger in the bottom of each ramekin. Spoon the soufflé mix into the ramekins.
- Place on a preheated baking tray for 14-15 minutes until risen. Dust with icing sugar and serve immediately.

Lemon Ginger Thyme Soufflé

704

- Add a tsp finely chopped thyme leaves to the mix.

Vanilla Custard

705

SERVES 4

- Heat the cream in a pan until nearly boiling.
- Whisk the egg yolks, cornflour, sugar and vanilla extract.
- Pour the hot cream into the bowl, whisking all the time, then return to the pan. Whisk over a low heat until the sauce has thickened.
- If the sauce does start to curdle, simply remove from the heat and whisk vigorously as it cools. It will become smooth again.

PREPARATION TIME 5 MINUTES

COOKING TIME 10 MINUTES

INGREDIENTS

300ml / 10 fl. oz / 1 ¼ cups single cream
3 egg yolks
1 tsp cornflour
1 tbsp caster (superfine) sugar
½ tsp vanilla extract

Orange Custard

706

- The zest of an orange will add citrus punch.

Bread and Butter Pudding

707

SERVES 4-6

- Preheat the oven to 180°C (160° fan) / 350F / gas 5.
- Cut each slice of bread into two triangles and arrange a layer in the base of the baking dish.
- Sprinkle with the soaked sultanas.
- Add another layer of bread triangles over the top.
- Whisk together the milk, cream, sugar and eggs until well combined, then pour over the bread layers. Push the bread down into the custard to soak it thoroughly. The custard should just reach the top of the bread – if it doesn't add a little more milk and/or cream. Grate over the nutmeg.
- Bake in the oven for 30-40 minutes until set and golden.

PREPARATION TIME 15 MINUTES

COOKING TIME 30-40 MINUTES

INGREDIENTS

8 thick slices white bread, thickly buttered
50g / 1 ¾ oz / ¼ cup sultanas, soaked in a little brandy
300ml / 10 fl. oz / 1 ¼ cups milk
60ml / 3 fl. oz / ¼ cup double cream
50g / 1 ¾ oz / ¼ cup caster (superfine) sugar
3 eggs
Freshly grated nutmeg
1 baking dish liberally buttered

Chocolate Bread and Butter Pudding

708

- Add a couple of handfuls of dark chocolate chips add a luxurious twist.

709

SERVES 4

Crème Caramel

PREPARATION TIME 25 MINUTES

COOKING TIME I HOUR

INGREDIENTS

125g / 4 oz / ½ cup caster (superfine) sugar
2 tbsp hot water
150ml / 5 fl. oz / ⅔ cup milk
300ml / 10 fl. oz / 1 cup single cream
4 eggs
40g / 1 ½ oz soft dark brown sugar
2 drops vanilla extract

- Preheat the oven to 150°C / 300F / gas 2.
- Place the sugar in a stainless steel pan and heat. When the sugar begins to melt, leave to darken to a rich dark gold. Do not stir. Remove from the heat, carefully add the water, and pour into a soufflé dish.
- Pour the milk and cream into a pan and heat gently.
- Whisk the eggs, sugar and vanilla in a bowl. When the milk is very hot but not boiling, pour onto the egg mixture, whisking constantly until blended.
- Pour into the soufflé dish and place in a roasting tin. Pour in enough hot water to come two thirds of the way up the sides of the dish.
- Bake in the oven for 1 hour, until set.
- Remove from the refrigerator 1 hour before serving, then release carefully form the mould onto a plate.

Orange Créme Caramel

710

- Add grated zest of 1 orange to the mix and a little grand marnier to the caramel in the dish.

711

SERVES 4

Raspberry Semolina Pudding

PREPARATION TIME 2 HOURS

COOKING TIME 25 MINUTES

INGREDIENTS

600ml / 1 pint / 2 cups milk
50g / 1 ¾ oz / ¼ cup semolina
1 tbsp caster (superfine) sugar
1 tbsp butter
200g / 7 oz / ¾ cup raspberries
Butter, for greasing

- Lightly butter 4 moulds. Preheat the oven to 160°C (140° fan) / 300F / gas 2.
- Heat the milk in a pan until just warm, then sprinkle in the semolina. Stirring constantly, bring the mixture to the boil and stir until thickened. Add the sugar and butter and stir until combined.
- Divide the raspberries between the moulds and pour the mixture in. Bake for 25 minutes.
- Once cooked, leave to cool, then refrigerate for at least 2 hours until completely cold.
- Turn out of the moulds to serve.

Blackberry Semolina Pudding

712

- For an autumnal variation, use blackberries in season.

713

SERVES 4

Crème Brulée

- Preheat the oven to 180°C (160° fan) / 350F / gas 5.
- Tip the cream into a pan with the milk. Add the seeds from the vanilla pod and the pod itself. Heat almost to boiling point.
- Whisk the egg yolks and sugar in a bowl until pale in colour. Pour the hot cream into the egg yolks, whisking constantly. Strain through a sieve and stir well.
- Sit 4 ramekins in a roasting tin and divide the mixture evenly between them. Pour in enough hot water to come half way up the sides of the ramekins.
- Bake for about 30 minutes, until set.
- Leave to cool on a wire rack, then refrigerate until ready to serve.
- Sprinkle over a thick layer of sugar and either grill or blowtorch until deep golden and melted. Leave to cool and firm then serve.

PREPARATION TIME 2 HOURS

COOKING TIME 30 MINUTES

....

INGREDIENTS

450ml / 1 pint / 2 cups double cream
100ml / 3 ½ fl. oz / ½ cup milk
1 vanilla pod, halved
5 egg yolks
2 tbsp caster (superfine) sugar plus enough for the topping

Strawberry and Rhubarb Bavarois

714

SERVES 4

PREPARATION TIME 2 HOURS
40 MINUTES

COOKING TIME 20 MINUTES

....

INGREDIENTS

FOR THE RHUBARB PURÉE
500g / 1 lb / 2 cups rhubarb
150g / 5 oz / ⅔ cup caster (superfine) sugar

FOR THE BAVAROIS
2 eggs, separated
2 tbsp caster (superfine) sugar
180ml / 6 fl. oz / ¾ cup milk
1 tsp vanilla extract
4 leaves gelatine, soaked in cold water
250ml / 9 fl. oz / 1 cup double cream
16 strawberries, halved

- Make the purée: cook the rhubarb over a gentle heat in a pan with the sugar. Whiz in a food processor, strain and set aside.
- Whisk together the yolks and sugar until pale and creamy.
- Heat the milk in a pan with the vanilla and bring almost to the boil. Pour onto the egg mixture, whisking constantly until combined, then return to the pan over a low heat. Stir until thickened, coating the back of the spoon and remove from the heat.
- Add the gelatine, squeezing out any excess water. Stir until dissolved. Strain into a clean bowl and leave to cool, then refrigerate.
- Whisk the cream to soft peaks. When the vanilla mixture is almost set, fold in the cream.
- Line the sides of individual moulds with the strawberries, cut side facing out. Spoon the rhubarb puree into the base. Spoon the bavarois mix into the moulds and refrigerate.

Panna Cotta with Raspberries

715

SERVES 6

PREPARATION TIME 2 HOURS
15 MINUTES

COOKING TIME 5 MINUTES

....

INGREDIENTS

300ml / 10 fl. oz / 1 ¼ cups double cream
1 tbsp caster (superfine) sugar
1 tsp vanilla extract

1 leaf gelatine, soaked in cold water
200g / 7 oz / ¾ cup raspberries
1 tbsp icing (confectioners') sugar

- Pour the cream, sugar and vanilla into a pan and simmer. Remove from the heat and leave to infuse.
- Stir the softened gelatine into the hot cream and whisk until dissolved. Reheat if the cream has cooled too much.
- Whiz half the raspberries to a puree with the icing sugar.
- Spoon the cream into individual serving glasses, then top with the raspberry puree.
- Refrigerate for 2 hours, then serve with fresh raspberries.

716

SERVES 6

Mascarpone Zabaglione with Strawberries

PREPARATION TIME 3 HOURS

COOKING TIME 35 MINUTES

INGREDIENTS

6 eggs
100g / 3 ½ oz / ½ cup granulated sugar
½ orange, grated zest
100ml / 3 ½ fl. oz / ½ cup dessert or sweet wine
500g / 1 lb / 2 cups mascarpone
24 strawberries
4 tbsp pistachios, shelled and crushed

- Whisk the eggs, sugar and zest with an electric whisk until pale and tripled in volume.
- Tip into a bowl over a pan of simmering water. Very slowly, whisking constantly, pour in the wine, whisking until the eggs have doubled again in volume and the mixture is hot. Take your time as this is when the mixture could curdle.
- Once combined, frothy and voluminous, remove from the heat and whisk for a few more moments to cool.
- Spoon the mascarpone into a bowl and slowly whisk in half the zabaglione. Once combines, fold the remaining half in and spoon into serving glasses.
- Refrigerate for 3 hours before serving. Decorate with strawberries and pistachios.

Mascarpone Zabaglione with Figs   717

- Use quartered figs in place of the strawberries.

718

SERVES 6

Sticky Toffee Pudding

PREPARATION TIME 20 MINUTES

COOKING TIME 40 MINUTES

INGREDIENTS

FOR THE SPONGE
75g / 2 ½ oz / ⅓ cup dates, stoned and finely chopped
1 tsp bicarbonate of soda
50g / 1 ¾ oz / ¼ cup butter
Pinch salt
150g / 5 oz / ⅔ cup Demerara sugar
2 eggs
175g / 6 oz / ¾ cup self raising flour
1 tsp vanilla extract
Butter, softened

FOR THE SAUCE
250ml / 9 fl. oz / 1 cup double cream
80g / 2 ½ oz / ⅓ cup butter
80g / 2 ½ oz / ⅓ cup dark brown sugar

- Preheat the oven to 180°C (160° fan) / 350F / gas 4.
- Pour 275ml / 10 fl. oz / 1 cup boiling water into a bowl and add the dates to soak.
- When the water is lukewarm, add the remaining sponge ingredients, mixing well to combine.
- Pour into a buttered baking dish and bake in the oven for about 40 minutes, or until just firm.
- Heat the sauce ingredients in a pan, whisking regularly.
- When the sponge is cooked, pour over the sauce and flash briefly under a hot grill until bubbling. Serve with ice cream or cream.

Sticky Toffee Pudding with Sherry Cream   719

- To add to the luxury, serve with softly whipped cream folded through with a little sherry.

720

SERVES 4

Summer Fruit Jelly

Autumn Fruit Jelly   721

- Blackberries and late raspberries in a jelly made with a light red beajolais as opposed to rose would make a stunning centrepiece.

Summer Fruit Prosecco Jelly   722

- Use sparkling prosecco instead of the rose wine.

Peach Jelly   723

- Quartered peaches would work well here too.

PREPARATION TIME 3 HOURS

INGREDIENTS

450ml / 1 pint / 2 cups rosé wine
2 tbsp caster (superfine) sugar
3-4 leaves gelatine, soaked in cold water
350g / 12 oz / 1 ½ cups strawberries, hulled and halved
225g / 8 oz / 1 cup raspberries
350g / 12 oz / 1 ½ cups mixed currants, such as blackcurrants, redcurrants, blueberries, blackberries...

- Heat half the wine in a pan, then whisk in the sugar and soaked, squeezed gelatine. Stir to dissolve, then add the remaining wine and pour into a pouring jug to cool.
- Scatter the fruit into the bottom of a large bowl or tureen mould, then pour over the jelly, pushing any fruit down that floats to the surface. Cover with clingfilm and refrigerate for until set.
- To serve, stand the mould in hot water for a few seconds, run a knife around the inside and invert onto a plate.

SERVES 6

724

Cheesecake with Summer Berries

Cheesecake with Figs and Muscat Grapes

725

- Ripe quartered figs and muscat grapes would sit well in the autumn.

Citrus Cheesecake

726

- Add the zest of 1 lime, 1 orange and ½ lemon for a citrusy twist.

Maple Cheesecake

727

- Add 2 tbsp maple syrup to the mix for a smoky sweetness.

PREPARATION TIME 20 MINUTES

COOKING TIME 40 MINUTES

....

INGREDIENTS

100g / 3 ½ oz / ½ cup digestive biscuits, crushed to crumbs
50g / 1 ¾ oz / ¼ cup butter, melted
600g / 1lb / 2 cups cream cheese
2 tbsp plain (all purpose) flour
125g / 4 oz / ½ cup caster (superfine) sugar
1 ½ tsp vanilla extract
2 eggs + 1 egg yolk
150ml / 5 oz / ⅔ cup sour cream
500g / 1 lb / 2 cups mixed summer berries

- Preheat the oven to 180°C (160° fan) / 350F / gas 5.
- Stir the biscuits into the melted butter. Press into the bottom of a large springform cake tin.
- Place on a baking sheet and bake for five minutes.
- Whisk together the cheese, flour and sugar, then beat in the vanilla, eggs and sour cream until pale and smooth.
- Spoon on top of the biscuit base. Return to the oven and bake for about 40 minutes.
- Once the centre is set, remove from the oven and leave to cool. Decorate with berries and serve.

728

SERVES 6-8 # Christmas Pudding

- Lightly grease a 1.5L / 2 ½ pint pudding basin. Tip the fruits and citrus juice into a bowl, add most of the brandy. Leave to macerate for at least 2 hours.
- Sieve the flour into a bowl with the spices, add the suet, zest, breadcrumbs and nuts, stirring to combine well. Add the marinated fruit and stir through.
- Beat the eggs into the bowl. Now is the time to add any coins etc. and for everyone stir and make a wish.
- Spoon into the pudding basin. Cover with a pleated layer of baking parchment (to allow it to rise), then a pleated layer of foil, securing it tightly with string. Tear off a piece of foil and fold three times to make a long strip. Sit the pudding on top and use as a cradle to carry to the steamer.
- Place on an upturned saucer in a large pan and pour in enough boiling water to come two thirds of the way up the sides of the bowl. Cover and steam for about 6 hours, checking it doesn't boil dry.
- Remove from the steamer. Check it is cooked by inserting a skewer – it should come out clean.
- Prick the top of the pudding and pour in a few tbsp extra brandy, then recover with fresh paper and store in a cool dry place until Christmas Day.
- To reheat, steam for 1 hour.

PREPARATION TIME MAKE AT LEAST 1 WEEK IN ADVANCE

COOKING TIME 6 HOURS

INGREDIENTS

500g / 1 lb / 2 cups mixed dried fruit
1 tbsp mixed candied peel, finely chopped
1 apple, peeled, cored and finely chopped
Zest and juice of 1 orange
Zest and juice of 1 lemon
100ml / 3 ½ fl. oz / ½ cup brandy
60g / 2 oz / ¼ cup self raising flour
1 ½ tsp mixed spice
2 tsp ground cinnamon
120g / 4 oz / ½ cup shredded suet
120g / 4 oz / ½ cup soft dark brown sugar
120g / 4 oz / ½ cup fine breadcrumbs
1 tbsp almonds, roughly chopped
2 eggs, beaten
Butter, softened

729

SERVES 6-8 # Cherry Clafoutis

- Preheat the oven to 180°C (160° fan) / 350F / gas 5.
- Grease a baking tin with butter or vegetable oil, then place the cherries in the bottom.
- In a bowl, whisk together the flour, salt and sugar and the beaten eggs until smooth, then whisk in the milk and mix to a smooth batter.
- Pour the mixture over the cherries and bake for 35-40 minutes.
- Allow to cool before serving.

PREPARATION TIME 5 MINUTES

COOKING TIME 35-40 MINUTES

INGREDIENTS

500g / 1 lb / 2 cups cherries, stoned
125g / 4 oz / ½ cup plain (all purpose) flour
Pinch salt
50g / 1 ¾ oz / ¼ cup caster (superfine) sugar
3 eggs, beaten
300ml / 10 fl. oz / 1 ¼ cups milk

Berry Clafoutis

730

- Mixed berries such as raspberries, blueberries and loganberries work well here too.

731

SERVES 4

Apple and Raisin Crumble

PREPARATION TIME 25 MINUTES

COOKING TIME 25-35 MINUTES

INGREDIENTS

750g / 1 ⅓ lb / 3 cups apples, peeled, cored and diced
75g / 2 ½ oz / ⅓ cup raisins, soaked in a little Calvados or brandy
2 tbsp ground cinnamon

FOR THE CRUMBLE

120g / 4 oz / ½ cup plain (all purpose) flour
90g 3 oz / ½ cup chilled butter, diced
3 tbsp muscovado sugar
3 tbsp caster (superfine) sugar

- Preheat the oven to 190°C (170° fan) / 370F / gas 5.
- Cook the apples with a little water until soft.
- Put the flour in a bowl with a pinch of salt.
- Add the cold cubes of butter and, using the tips of your fingers, work the butter into the flour until the mixture resembles porridge oats.
- Place the cooked apple and soaked raisins with the cinnamon in the bottom of a baking dish and cover loosely with the crumble mixture.
- Cook in the oven for 25-35 minutes until golden on top.

Pear Raisin Crumble

732

- Use the same quantity of peeled pears.

733

SERVES 6

Lemon Meringue Pie

PREPARATION TIME 1 HOUR

COOKING TIME 70 MINUTES

INGREDIENTS

125g / 4 oz / ½ cup plain (all purpose) flour
60g / 2 oz / ¼ cup butter
Pinch salt
Cold water

FOR THE FILLING

3 level tbsp cornflour
60g / 2 oz / ¼ cup caster (superfine) sugar
300ml / 10 fl. oz / 1 ¼ cups cold water
Grated zest and juice of 2-3 lemons
2 egg yolks
40g / 1 ½ oz butter

FOR THE MERINGUE

2 egg whites
120g / 4 oz / ½ cup caster (superfine) sugar

- Preheat the oven to 190°C (170° fan) / 370F / gas 5.
- Make the pastry: Sieve the flour and salt into a large bowl, then work the fat into the flour with the pads of your fingers until the mixture resembles breadcrumbs.
- Work in 2 tbsp water and bring the mixture together with a knife, cutting it through to mix, using enough water to just make a smooth ball of dough. Wrap the dough in clingfilm and refrigerate.
- Roll the pastry out to just larger than your pie dish. Cut a 8mm strip all round, dampen the rim of the dish and press the pastry strip on to it. Line the tin with the pastry and press the edges onto the pastry rim. Prick the base with a fork and bake for 25 minutes.
- Place the cornflour and sugar in a bowl and add enough of the water to make a smooth paste. Pour the remaining water into a pan with the lemon zest. Bring to the boil, pour onto the cornflour paste and mix.
- Tip back into the pan and bring back to the boil for 1 minute. Remove from the heat and beat in the egg yolks, lemon juice and butter. Pour into the pastry shell and spread evenly.
- Whisk the egg whites until stiff, then beat in sugar at a time until thick and glossy. Spread over the filling, sealing the top completely.
- Reduce the oven heat to 150°C / 300F / gas 2 and bake for 45 minutes until the meringue is pale gold.

734

SERVES 4

Mississippi Mud Pie

- Stir the crushed biscuits into the melted butter until thoroughly combined, then press into the base of a 23cm pie dish. Chill for 30 minutes.
- Preheat the oven to 180°C (160° fan) / 350F / gas 4.
- Place the chocolate and butter in a bowl over a pan of simmering water and stir until melted. Remove from the heat and leave to cool for 5 minutes.
- Whisk the eggs with the sugar until pale and tripled in volume. Whisk in the melted chocolate in a steady trickle, then whisk in the cocoa powder, cream, vanilla and cayenne if using.
- Pour onto the biscuit base and bake for about 40 minutes until just firm. Leave to cool in the tin and it will sink slightly.
- Serve with softly whipped cream.

Mississippi Mud Pie with Fresh Berries

735

- Serve with raspberries to cut through the chocolate.

PREPARATION TIME 2 HOURS

COOKING TIME 40 MINUTES

INGREDIENTS

75g / 2 ½ oz / ⅓ cup butter, melted
300g / 10 oz / 1 ¼ cups chocolate digestive biscuits

FOR THE FILLING

150g / 5 oz / ⅔ cup dark chocolate, broken up
150g / 5 oz / ⅔ cup butter, cubed
3 eggs
1 tbsp soft brown sugar
1 tbsp cocoa powder
1 tsp vanilla extract
150ml / 5 fl. oz / ⅔ cup double cream
Pinch Cayenne pepper (optional – for a tiny kick)

736

SERVES 4

Poached Pears

- Place the pear peelings and the rest of the poaching ingredients in a large pan and bring to the boil.
- Simmer for 10 minutes to infuse.
- Place the pears upright in the pan and poach gently for around 30 minutes or until completely tender.
- Remove the pears from the liquor and set aside to cool.
- Reduce the poaching liquor by half.
- Serve the pears, with the poaching liquor spooned over.

Poached Pears with Chocolate Sauce

737

- Drizzle some melted dark chocolate over the pears, before serving.

Pears in Red Wine

738

- Red wine works just as well as white with the spices and gives a dramatic colour to the pears.

PREPARATION TIME 10 MINUTES

COOKING TIME 45-50 MINUTES

INGREDIENTS

4 pears, peeled, peelings reserved
500ml / 1 pint / 2 cups white wine
2 tbsp runny honey
75g / 2 ½ oz / ⅓ cup soft brown sugar
Zest of ½ orange + the pared rind of the other half
1 cinnamon stick
1 vanilla pod, split
2 star anise

739

SERVES 4

Chocolate Fondant Puddings

PREPARATION TIME 30 MINUTES

COOKING TIME 8 MINUTES

....

INGREDIENTS

90g / 3 oz / ⅓ cup caster (superfine) sugar
150g / 5 oz / ⅔ cup butter
150g / 5 oz / ⅔ cup dark chocolate, chopped
3 egg yolks
3 eggs
1 tbsp plain (all purpose) flour
1 tsp vanilla extract

- Preheat the oven to 180°C (160° fan) / 350F / gas 4. Grease 4 individual dariole moulds.
- Place the sugar, butter and chocolate in a bowl set over a pan of simmering water and stir occasionally until melted. Remove from the heat and whisk to combine. Leave to cool for 5 minutes.
- Add the egg yolks and eggs and beat well to combine, then fold in the flour.
- Pour into the moulds and chill for 20 minutes.
- Place on a baking tray and cook for 8 minutes.
- Turn out onto plates and serve immediately.

Chocolate Orange Fondant Puddings

740

- The grated zest of an orange is a classic combo with chocolate.

741

SERVES 4

Eton Mess

PREPARATION TIME 15 MINUTES
+ COOLING TIME

COOKING TIME 1 HOUR

....

INGREDIENTS

175g / 6 oz / ¾ cup caster (superfine) sugar
3 egg whites
500g / 1 lb / 2 cups raspberries,
1 tbsp icing (confectioners') sugar
500ml / 1 pint / 2 cups double cream
1 tsp vanilla extract

- Preheat the oven to 150°C (130° fan) / 300F / gas 2.
- Whisk the egg whites to soft peaks, then whisk in the sugar a little at a time, beating each addition in thoroughly, until thick and glossy.
- Spoon onto lined baking trays and bake for 1 hour. Turn the oven off and leave until completely cold.
- Purée half the raspberries with the icing sugar until smooth.
- Whisk the cream to soft peaks, whisking in the vanilla as you go.
- Break up the meringues and layer into individual serving dishes, spooning over a little puree, then adding raspberries and cream, swirling the puree in as you go.
- Serve immediately.

Eton Mess with Strawberries

742

- Lightly crush ripe strawberries with a fork for an even more classically British pudding.

743

SERVES 4

Baked Alaska

- Preheat the oven to its hottest temperature and place a shelf very low down.
- Whisk the egg whites until foamy, then whisk in the salt and cream of tartar until it forms soft peaks. Gradually whisk in the sugar a little at a time until thick and glossy, then fold in the vanilla extract.
- Place the sponge base on a lined baking sheet.
- Using an ice cream scoop, place balls of ice cream on the base, leaving a good edge around the outside.
- Pile the meringue on top, spreading with a palette knife and ensuring the ice cream is completely covered.
- Place under a grill for 2 minutes until golden. Serve immediately.

PREPARATION TIME 20 MINUTES

COOKING TIME 5 MINUTES

INGREDIENTS

6 egg whites
Pinch salt
1 tsp cream of tartar
200g / 7 oz / ¾ cup caster (superfine) sugar
1 tsp vanilla extract
1kg / 2 lb / 4 cups ice cream, slightly softened
1 ready made sponge case

Chocolate Fondant Tart

744

SERVES 4

PREPARATION TIME 2 HOURS

COOKING TIME 30 MINUTES

INGREDIENTS

3 eggs
300g / 10 oz / 1 ¼ cups muscovado sugar
1 tsp vanilla extract
175g / 6 oz / ¾ cup butter, melted
2 tbsp plain (all purpose) flour
2 tbsp cocoa powder
50g / 1 ¾ oz / ¼ cup dark chocolate, chopped
1 pastry case

FOR THE CUSTARD

300ml / 10 fl. oz / 1 ¼ cups single cream
3 egg yolks
1 tsp cornflour
1 tbsp caster (superfine) sugar
½ tsp vanilla extract

- Preheat the oven to 180°C (160° fan) / 350F / gas 4.
- Beat the eggs and sugar until pale and tripled in volume. Stir in the butter and vanilla, then fold in the flour and cocoa. Scatter the chopped chocolate into the pastry base and pour over the filling.
- Bake for 30 minutes or until just firm. Leave to cool while you make the custard.
- Heat the cream in a pan until nearly boiling. Whisk the egg yolks, cornflour, sugar and vanilla extract.
- Pour the hot cream into the bowl, whisking all the time, then return to the pan. Whisk over a low heat until the sauce has thickened.
- Serve with the chocolate fondant tart.

Baked Apples with Toffee Sauce

745

SERVES 4

PREPARATION TIME 10 MINUTES

COOKING TIME 20 MINUTES

INGREDIENTS

4 eating apples, cored
2 tbsp butter, softened
1 tsp ground cinnamon
1 orange, grated zest and juice

FOR THE SAUCE

1 vanilla pod, split
250ml / 9 fl. oz / 1 cup double (heavy) cream
80g / 2 ½ oz / ⅓ cup butter
80g / 2 ½ oz / ⅓ cup dark brown sugar

- Preheat the oven to 200°C (180° fan) / 400F / gas 7.
- Score a line around the centre of each apple to help prevent bursting.
- Mix together the butter, cinnamon and orange zest and squeeze in the juice of ½ the orange. Push some of the butter into the centre of each apple.
- Place in a roasting tin, pour a little water into the bottom and dot with any remaining butter mixture. Cover with aluminium foil and bake for 20 minutes or until tender.
- Meanwhile heat the sauce in a pan, stirring until smooth and thickened.
- Pour over the baked apples and serve.

746

MAKES 1L

Lemon Sorbet

**PREPARATION TIME 10 MINUTES
+ CHURNING TIME**

INGREDIENTS

500g / 1 lb / 2 cups caster (superfine)
sugar
250ml / 9 fl. oz / 1 cup lemon juice
1 lemon, grated zest

- Heat the sugar in a pan with 750ml / 1 ⅓ pints / 3 cups water and stir until dissolved.
- If the lemon is waxed, dip into boiling water briefly to remove it. Stir in the lemon juice and zest, then leave to cool.
- Churn in an ice cream machine to a smooth sorbet. Freeze until required.
- Transfer to the refrigerator 1 hour before eating.

Lemon and Lime Sorbet
747

- Using the same quantity of mixed lime and lemon juice will make this even more refreshing.

748

SERVES 4

Tiramisu

PREPARATION TIME 25 MINUTES

INGREDIENTS

600ml / 1 pint / 2 cups double cream
250g / 9 oz / 1 cup mascarpone
3 tbsp Marsala dolce
5 tbsp caster (superfine) sugar
300ml / 10 fl. oz / 1 ¼ cups strong
coffee
2 tbsp coffee liqueur (optional)
175g / 6 oz sponge fingers
(ladyfingers)
25g / 1 oz dark chocolate, grated
3 tsp cocoa powder

- Place the cream, mascarpone, Marsala and sugar in a bowl and whisk until combined and thick.
- Pour the coffee (and liqueur) into a shallow dish and soak the sponge fingers in it, but be careful they don't disintegrate. Layer half the biscuits into a serving dish, then spoon over half the mascarpone mixture. Grate over half of the chocolate. Repeat until all the ingredients are used up.
- Chill in the refrigerator for 3 hours. Dust with cocoa powder and more chocolate to serve.

Chocolate Tiramisu
749

- Instead of dipping the biscuits in coffee, use hot chocolate and omit the alcohol, for a child-friednly version.

Tiramisu with Preserved Cherries
750

- Try layering the sponge and cream with bottled preserved cherries.

Vanilla Ice Cream

751

MAKES 1L

- Heat the creams in a pan with the vanilla pod and seeds and leave to infuse.
- Whisk together the egg yolks and sugar, then remove the vanilla pod and pour the hot cream onto the eggs, whisking constantly.
- Return to the pan and whisk over a low heat until thickened and smooth.
- Leave to cool slightly then churn in an ice cream machine until done.
- Freeze until required. Transfer to the refrigerator 1 hour before serving.

PREPARATION TIME 2 HOURS

INGREDIENTS

300ml / 10 fl. oz / 1 ¼ cups double cream
300ml / 10 fl. oz / 1 ¼ cups single cream
1 vanilla pod, split
4 egg yolks
40g / 1 ½ oz caster (superfine) sugar

Vanilla Ice Cream with Fruit Swirl

752

- Add a few spoonfuls of raspberry or other fruit puree before churning.

Banoffee Pie

753

SERVES 6-8

- Combine the biscuits and butter in a bowl then press into the bottom of a springform tin. Refrigerate.
- Cover the condensed milk tins completely in boiling water and boil for 2 hours. Make sure they are completely covered at all times, topping up if necessary otherwise they will explode.
- Remove from the water and leave to cool. Open the tins and scoop out the toffee.
- Whiz the bananas with a spoonful of toffee in a food processor until smooth. Whisk the cream to soft peak then fold the banana mixture in until combined.
- Spread half the banana cream over the biscuit base, then smooth over a layer of toffee, using a palette knife to even it out. Repeat, leaving a small amount of banana cream for piping
- Pipe rosettes of banana cream onto the top of the toffee, then decorate with grated chocolate. Refrigerate.

PREPARATION TIME 2-3 HOURS

INGREDIENTS

400g / 14 oz / 1 ½ cups digestive biscuits, crushed
200g / 7 oz / ⅔ cup butter, melted
2 tins of condensed milk
500ml / 1 pint / 2 cups double cream
2-3 ripe bananas
1 tbsp dark chocolate, grated

Bannoffee Pie with a Shortbread Biscuit Base

754

- Try using shortbread instead of digestives for the base.

CAKES

755 · SERVES 4 · Chocolate Coffee Fudge Tart

- Preheat the oven to 180°C / 350F / gas 4.
- Beat the eggs and sugar until pale and tripled in volume. Stir in the butter, coffee and vanilla, then fold in the flour and cocoa. Scatter the chopped chocolate into the pastry base and pour over the filling.
- Bake for 30 minutes or until just firm. Leave to cool.
- Decorate with coffee beans.

PREPARATION TIME 30-40 MINUTES + CHILLING TIME

COOKING TIME 30 MINUTES

INGREDIENTS

3 eggs
300g / 10 oz / 1 ¼ cups muscovado sugar
1 tsp vanilla extract
30ml / 1 fl. oz espresso coffee
175g / 6 oz / ¾ cup butter, melted
2 tbsp plain (all purpose) flour
2 tbsp cocoa powder
50g / 1 ¾ oz / ¼ cup dark (bittersweet) chocolate, chopped
1 pastry case
Coffee beans

756 · SERVES 6-8 · Victoria Sponge

PREPARATION TIME 40 MINUTES

COOKING TIME 25 MINUTES

INGREDIENTS

120g / 4 oz / ½ cup butter, at room temperature
120g / 4 oz / ½ cup caster (superfine) sugar
2 eggs
1 tsp vanilla extract
120g / 4 oz / ½ cup self raising flour
Raspberry or strawberry jam (jelly)
Icing (confectioners') sugar

- Preheat the oven to 170°C / 325F / gas 3. Grease and line 2 x 18cm / 7in sponge tins.
- Cream the butter and sugar together until pale and creamy.
- Whisk the eggs thoroughly, then beat into the butter mixture a little at a time until fully incorporated.
- Stir in the vanilla extract, then sieve the flour a little at a time into the bowl and fold in with a metal spoon. If the batter is a little thick, add a little hot water to loosen.
- Spoon into the tins, then bake for 25 minutes or until springy and golden.
- Leave to cool for 10 minutes. Remove from the tins and cool on a wire rack. Sandwich with the jam and dust with icing sugar to serve.

757 · SERVES 6 · Lemon Drizzle Cake

PREPARATION TIME 25 MINUTES

COOKING TIME 40-45 MINUTES

INGREDIENTS

120g / 4 oz / ½ cup butter, softened
175g / 6 oz / ¾ cup caster (superfine) sugar
2 eggs
1 lemon, grated zest
175g / 6 oz / ¾ cup self raising flour
100ml / 3 ½ fl. oz / ½ cup milk

FOR THE SYRUP
2 lemons, juiced
100g / 3 ½ oz / ½ cup icing (confectioners') sugar

FOR THE GLAZE
½ lemon, juiced
150g / 5 oz / ⅔ cup icing (confectioners') sugar

- Preheat the oven to 180°C / 350F / gas 4. Grease and line a loaf tin.
- Cream the butter and sugar until pale and creamy, then whisk in the eggs a little at a time.
- Whisk in the zest, then, using a metal spoon, fold in the flour, salt and then stir in the milk. Spoon into the loaf tin and bake for 40-45 minutes until a skewer comes out clean when poked into the centre. Set aside.
- Heat the lemon juice and sugar in a pan until the sugar dissolves. Puncture the surface of the cake with a skewer and pour over the hot syrup. Leave to cool completely then remove from the tin.
- Whisk together the lemon juice and sugar to make the glaze, then drizzle over the top of the cake.

758

SERVES 4

Madeira Cake

Madeira with Warm Poached Fruit

759

- Gently cook berries in a little water and sugar to serve with the cake.

Madeira with Whipped Cream

760

- Softly whip some cream with a little grand marnier to serve with the warmed cake.

Madeira with Chocolate Sauce

761

- Melt dark chocolate with enough cream to make a rich thick sauce to dip fingers of the cake in.

PREPARATION TIME 20 MINUTES

COOKING TIME 40 MINUTES

INGREDIENTS

175g / 6 oz / ¾ cup butter, at room temperature
175g / 6 oz / ¾ cup caster (superfine) sugar
3 eggs, beaten
250g / 9 oz / 1 cup self raising flour
3 tbsp milk
½ lemon, grated zest
½ orange, grated zest

- Preheat oven to 180°C (160° fan) / 350F / gas 4. Grease and line a loaf tin.
- Cream the butter and sugar until pale and creamy, then beat in the eggs, a little at a time, beating each addition in thoroughly.
- Sieve the flour into the bowl and fold in with a metal spoon along with the milk to make a loose batter. Fold in the citrus zest.
- Spoon into the loaf tin and bake for 40 minutes or until golden brown and an inserted skewer comes out clean.
- Leave to cool for 5 minutes, then transfer to a wire rack and leave to cool completely.

762 · SERVES 8 · Marble Cake

- Preheat the oven to 180°C (160° fan) / 350F / gas 4. Grease and line a 20cm cake tin.
- Cream the butter and sugar together until pale and creamy. Add the eggs a little at a time, whisking to combine each addition thoroughly.
- Using a metal spoon fold in the flour gently, then add the milk and vanilla extract and combine well.
- Divide the mixture equally between 2 bowls and sieve the cocoa powder into one. Using 2 large spoons, place dollops of the mixtures alternately into the cake tin, then swirl around with a skewer to marble the mixture.
- Bake in the oven for 50-60 minutes until a skewer comes out clean.
- Turn onto a cooling rack and leave to cool.

PREPARATION TIME 30 MINUTES

COOKING TIME 50-60 MINUTES

INGREDIENTS

225g / 9 oz / 1 cup butter, softened
225g / 9 oz / 1 cup caster (superfine) sugar
4 eggs, beaten
225g / 9 oz / 1 cup self raising flour
3 tbsp milk
1 tsp vanilla extract
2 tbsp cocoa powder

763 · Marble Cake with Poached Strawberries

- Cook strawberries in a little orange juice and black pepper to serve alongside.

764 · SERVES 6-8 · Christmas Cake

- Soak all the fruit in the brandy in a bowl overnight.
- The next day preheat the oven to 150°C / 300F / gas 2. Grease and line a 23 cm springform cake tin.
- Cream the butter and sugar, then beat in the zest. Add the eggs a little at a time then add the almond essence.
- Fold in the flour, spices and the soaked fruit.
- Pour into the cake tin and bake for about 3 hours, until an inserted skewer comes out clean.
- Remove from the tin, wrap in foil and store in an airtight container for at least 3 weeks. You could feed the cake with a tbsp brandy every other day.
- Warm the jam in a small pan and paint over the cake. Roll out the marzipan and press onto the cake, cutting away the excess and smoothing away any air bubbles.
- Roll out the icing and cover the cake with it, cutting away any excess. Decorate as desired.

PREPARATION TIME 25 MINUTES

COOKING TIME 3 HOURS

INGREDIENTS

700g / 1 ⅓ lb / 3 cups sultanas
225g / 8 oz / 1 cup raisins
110g / 4 oz / ½ cup currants
110g / 4 oz / ½ cup glacé cherries
110g / 4 oz / ½ cup mixed peel
120ml / 4 fl. oz / ½ cup brandy
225g / 8 oz / 1 cup butter, softened
200g / 7 oz / ¾ cup brown sugar
1 lemon, grated zest
1 orange, grated zest
4 eggs, beaten
1 tsp almond essence
350g / 12 oz / 1 ½ cups plain (all purpose) flour
1 tsp mixed spice
½ tsp ground cinnamon
Pinch salt
200g / 7 oz / ¾ cup apricot jam (jelly)
500g / 1 lb marzipan
1kg / 2 lb ready to roll icing (frosting)

765 · Christmas Cake with Cheese

- Serve alongside a wedge of Wensleydale cheese as per the Yorkshire tradition.

SERVES 8-10

Chocolate Fudge Cake

766

PREPARATION TIME 30 MINUTES

COOKING TIME 30 MINUTES

....

INGREDIENTS

120g / 4 oz / ½ cup self raising flour
1 tsp baking powder
120g / 4 oz / ½ cup butter, softened
120g / 4 oz / ½ cup caster (superfine) sugar
2 eggs
1 ½ tbsp cocoa powder

FOR THE FILLING AND ICING

75g / 2 ½ oz / ⅓ cup granulated sugar
75ml / 2 ½ oz / ⅓ cup evaporated milk
120g / 4 oz / ½ cup dark chocolate, chopped
40g / 1 oz butter, softened
25g / 1 oz chocolate, shaved

- Preheat the oven to 170°C (150° fan) / 325F / gas 3. Grease and line 2 x 18cm / 7 in cake tins.
- Sieve the flour and baking powder into a large bowl, then add the other ingredients.
- Divide the mixture equally between the two cake tins and cook for 30 minutes.
- Remove from the tins and cool on a wire rack.
- Make the icing: Combine the sugar and evaporated milk in a pan and stir to dissolve the sugar.
- Bring to the boil and simmer for 5 minutes, then stir in the chocolate and butter. Chill for at least 1 hour until it has thickened and is spreadable.
- Use the icing to sandwich the cakes together, then smooth the remainder over the top and sides with a palette knife. Decorate with chocolate shavings.

Chocolate Fudge Cake with Raspberry Filling

767

- Spread a thick layer of good quality raspberry or even cherry preserve on the sponge.

SERVES 4

Carrot Cake

768

PREPARATION TIME 20 MINUTES

COOKING TIME I HOUR 30 MINUTES

....

INGREDIENTS

300g / 10 oz / 1 ¼ cups plain (all purpose) flour
1 tsp ground cinnamon
1 tsp baking powder
½ tsp bicarbonate of soda
200g / 7 oz / ¾ cup soft dark brown sugar
4 eggs
250ml / 9 fl. oz / 1 cup vegetable oil
Zest of 2 oranges
200g / 7 oz / ¾ cup carrots, peeled and grated
125g / 4 oz / ½ cup butter, softened
2 tbsp icing (confectioners') sugar
250g / 9 oz / 1 cup cream cheese
Zest of ½ lemon

- Preheat the oven to 150°C (130° fan) / 300F / gas 2. Grease and line a 20cm cake tin.
- Sieve the flour into a bowl with cinnamon, baking powder and bicarbonate of soda, then stir in the sugar.
- Beat the eggs with the oil and fold into the flour with the carrots and orange zest.
- Spoon into the cake tin and bake for about 1 ½ hours until an inserted skewer comes out clean. Leave to cool.
- Beat the butter and sugar together until pale, then beat in the cream cheese and lemon zest. Chill until spreadable and cover the cake using a palette knife to smooth.

Spiced Carrot Cake

769

- A pinch of mixed spice with the cinnamon will add flavour.

770

SERVES 8-10

Coffee Cinnamon Cake

Coffee Cake with Crushed Walnuts

771

- Lightly pulse walnuts in a blender and sprinkle over the top.

Coffee Cake with Caramelised Pecans

772

- Chop pecan nuts and coat in a light caramel before arranging on the cake.

Coffee Cake with Cinnamon Sugar

773

- Mix together brown sugar and cinnamon and sprinkle over the cake.

PREPARATION TIME 30 MINUTES

COOKING TIME 30 MINUTES

....

INGREDIENTS

120g / 4 oz / ½ cup self raising flour
1 tsp baking powder
120g / 4 oz / ½ cup butter, softened
120g / 4 oz / ½ cup caster (superfine) sugar
90 g / 3 oz / ½ cup mixed nuts, chopped
2 eggs
1 tbsp coffee mixed with 1 tbsp hot water
1 tsp ground cinnamon

FOR THE FILLING AND ICING
225g / 8 oz / 1 cup icing (confectioners') sugar
100g / 3 ½ oz / ½ cup butter, softened
2 tbsp instant coffee dissolved in
1 tbsp hot water
¼ tsp ground cinnamon

- Preheat the oven to 170°C (150° fan) / 325F / gas 3. Grease and line 2 x 18cm / 7 in cake tins.
- Sieve the flour and baking powder into a large bowl, then add the other ingredients and whisk until completely combined.
- Divide the mixture equally between the two cake tins and top with the nuts, cook for 30 minutes.
- Remove from the tins and cool on a wire rack.
- Make the icing: Cream the butter and sugar together, then stir in the coffee. Refrigerate until needed.
- Use the icing to sandwich the cakes together, then smooth the remainder over the top and sides with a palette knife. Dust with a little cinnamon

774

SERVES 4-6 # Date and Walnut Cake

PREPARATION TIME 20 MINUTES

COOKING TIME I HOUR

....

INGREDIENTS

250g / 9 oz / 1 cup self raising flour
½ tsp mixed spice
175g / 6 oz / ¾ cup butter, softened
100g / 3 ½ oz / ½ cup muscovado
sugar
2 eggs, beaten
100g / 3 ½ oz / ½ cup dates, stoned
and chopped
60g / 2 oz / ¼ cup walnuts, chopped

- Preheat the oven to 160°C (140° fan) / 325F / gas 3. Grease and line a 2lb loaf tin.
- Sieve the flour into a bowl with the spice, butter, sugar and eggs. Add the dates and walnuts and blend with a wooden spoon or electric whisk.
- Spoon into the loaf tin then bake for 1 hour.
- Leave to cool for 15 minutes, then remove from the tin and cool on a wire rack.

Date and Pecan Cake

775

- Use chopped pecans in place of the walnuts.

776

SERVES 4-6 # Almond Cake

PREPARATION TIME 30 MINUTES

COOKING TIME 45 MINUTES

....

INGREDIENTS

5 eggs, separated
200g / 7 oz / ¾ cup caster (superfine)
sugar
1 tsp almond extract
1 orange, grated zest
200g / 7 oz / ¾ cup ground almonds
1 tbsp plain (all purpose) flour
2 tbsp flaked (slivered) almonds
2 tbsp icing (confectioners') sugar

- Preheat the oven to 180°C (160° fan) / 350F / gas 4. Grease and line a 23cm springform tin.
- Whisk the yolks with half the sugar until pale and creamy. Add the almond extract and zest and combine well.
- Beat the egg whites to stiff peaks, add the remaining sugar a little at a time and beat until thick and glossy.
- Fold a third of the egg whites into the yolks to loosen, then fold in the rest with the ground almonds and flour. Spoon into the loaf tin and bake for about 45 minutes until springy.
- Leave for 10 minutes to cool, then turn onto a wire rack. Decorate with flaked almonds and icing sugar.

Orange Almond Cake

777

- Add grated zest of 1 orange to the mix.

778
SERVES 8

Chocolate Swiss Roll

- Preheat the oven to 180°C (160° fan) / 350F / gas 5. Grease and line a 33x23cm swiss roll tin or baking tray.
- Whisk the eggs and sugar together until tripled in volume.
- Sieve the flour and cocoa powder into a bowl, then fold into the egg mixture a little at a time. Pour into the swiss roll tin and bake for 10 minutes. Whisk the cream to soft peaks and stir in the vanilla.
- Place a large piece of baking parchment on a work surface and sprinkle with sugar. Turn the cake out onto the parchment at one end, removing the paper from the tin.
- Trim the edges of the sponge to neaten, then spread with a layer of cream. Roll up from the short end to make a fat sausage shape while still warm. Leave to cool completely.
- Meanwhile melt the chocolate with the cream in a bowl over a pan of simmering water and stir until smooth. Refrigerate until cold and thickened.
- Spread evenly over the swiss roll, using a palette knife to keep it even.
-

Swiss Roll with Cherry Filling 779

- Use a good quality cherry preserve in place of the cream.

PREPARATION TIME 30 MINUTES

COOKING TIME 10 MINUTES

....

INGREDIENTS

3 eggs
75g / 2 ½ oz / ⅓ cup caster (superfine) sugar
60g / 2 oz / ¼ cup plain (all purpose) flour
1 ½ tbsp cocoa powder
300ml / 10 fl. oz / 1 ¼ cup double cream
1 tsp vanilla extract

For the icing:
300g / 10 oz / 1 ¼ cups dark (70%) (bittersweet) chocolate
300ml / 10 fl oz / 1 ¼ cups double (heavy) cream

780
SERVES 8

Strawberry Jam Swiss Roll

- Preheat the oven to 180°C (160° fan) / 350F / gas 5. Grease and line a 33x23cm swiss roll tin or shallow baking tray.
- Whisk the eggs and sugar together until pale and tripled in volume.
- Sieve the flour into a bowl, then fold into the egg mixture a little at a time until thoroughly combined.
- Pour into the swiss roll tin and bake for 10 minutes until springy.
- Place a large piece of baking parchment on a work surface and sprinkle with a little sugar. Turn the cake out onto the baking parchment at one end, removing the lining paper from the tin.
- Trim the edges of the sponge to neaten, then spread with a layer of jam. Roll up from the short end to make a fat sausage shape while still warm.
- Leave to cool, then slice as required.

Raspberry Jam Swiss Roll 781

- Use raspberry jam in place of the strawberry jam.

PREPARATION TIME 30 MINUTES

COOKING TIME 10 MINUTES

....

INGREDIENTS

3 eggs
75g / 2 ½ oz / ⅓ cup caster (superfine) sugar
60g / 2 oz / ¼ cup plain (all purpose) flour
200g / 7 oz / ¾ cup soft set strawberry jam (jelly)

782

SERVES 8-10 # Chocolate Cake with Buttercream Filling

Chocolate Cake with Citrus Buttercream

783

- Add the grated zest of 1 orange to the buttercream and a squeeze of the juice.

Chocolate Cake with Jam and Buttercream

784

- Double the pleasure by adding a thick layer of strawberry jam.

Chocolate Cake with Chocolate Buttercream

785

- .Sift in 1 tbsp cocoa powder to the filling and fold in.

PREPARATION TIME 30 MINUTES

COOKING TIME 30 MINUTES

INGREDIENTS

120g / 4 oz / ½ cup self raising flour
1 tsp baking powder
120g / 4 oz / ½ cup butter, softened
120g / 4 oz / ½ cup caster (superfine) sugar
2 eggs
1 ½ tbsp cocoa powder

FOR THE FILLING
100g / 3 ½ oz / ½ cup butter, softened
150g / 5 oz / ⅔ cup icing (confectioners') sugar
1 tsp vanilla extract

- Preheat the oven to 170°C (150° fan) / 325F / gas 3. Grease and line 2 x 18cm / 7 in cake tins.
- Sieve the flour and baking powder into a large bowl, then add the other ingredients and whisk until completely combined.
- Divide the mixture equally between the two cake tins and cook for 30 minutes.
- Remove from the tins and cool on a wire rack.
- Make the icing: Cream the butter and sugar until pale and smooth, then stir in the vanilla.
- Use the icing to sandwich the cakes together.
- Decorate with a little caster sugar.

786

SERVES 4

Black Forest Gateau

- Preheat the oven to 190°C (170° fan) / 375F / gas 5. Grease and line 2 x 20cm / 8in sandwich tins.
- Mix the butter, sugar, flour, cocoa powder, baking powder and eggs in a food processor until smooth.
- Divide equally between the bake tins and bake for 25 minutes until risen. Turn onto a wire rack. Leave to cool completely. Slice the cakes in half horizontally.
- Heat the jam with the cherries and Kirsch for 5 minutes. Leave to cool. Spread over three of the sponges. Whisk 300ml / 10 fl. oz of the cream to soft peaks.
- Transfer a cherry-topped sponge to a plate, then smooth on ⅓ of the cream. Sprinkle with chocolate.
- Top with a cherry-topped sponge and repeat, then with the third sponge. Place the final clean sponge on top.
- Whisk the cream to soft peaks. Smooth over the cake top and sides with a palette knife. Finish with grated chocolate.

Black Forest Gateau with Chocolate Curls

787

- Shave chocolate with a peeler to make chocolate curls and a more elaboate decoration.

PREPARATION TIME I HOUR

COOKING TIME 25 MINUTES

....

INGREDIENTS

250g / 9 oz / 1 cup butter, softened
250g / 9 oz / 1 cup caster (superfine) sugar
150g / 5 oz / ⅔ cup self raising flour
3 tbsp cocoa powder
1 tsp baking powder
4 eggs
350g / 12 oz / 1 ½ cups morello cherry jam (jelly)
1 jar or can bottled cherries and their juice
3 tbsp Kirsch
500ml / 1 pint / 2 cups double cream
50g / 1 ¾ oz / ¼ cup dark chocolate, grated

788

SERVES 8

Battenberg Cake

- Preheat the oven to 190°C (170° fan) / 375F / gas 5. Grease and line a 20cm / 8in square cake tin.
- Cut a piece of baking parchment 30x20cm and make an 8cm fold in the centre. Place in the tin with the fold in the centre.
- Mix the butter, sugar, eggs, flour and vanilla in a food processor. Weigh out half the batter and place the two amounts in separate bowls. Add red food dye to one.
- Spoon the batters into each half of the sponge tin. Bake for 30 minutes. Cool for 5 minutes, then place on a wire rack.
- Place one sponge on top of the other and trim off any overhanging edges so they are exactly the same size. Cut in half lengthways to make 4 long rectangles.
- Brush the long side of one of the plain sponges with jam and press against a pink sponge. Repeat with the other two sponges.
- Sandwich the two pairs of sponges to make a checker board pattern, then brush all over with apricot jam.
- Dust the surface with icing sugar and roll out the marzipan to 5mm thick and large enough to completely encase the sponges. Wrap the marzipan around the cake, pressing the edges together to make a firm join.
- Turn seam side down, trim a thin slice off each end and serve.

PREPARATION TIME 45 MINUTES

COOKING TIME 30 MINUTES

....

INGREDIENTS

175g / 6 oz / ¾ cup butter, softened
175g / 6 oz / ¾ cup caster (superfine) sugar
3 eggs
175g / 6 oz / ¾ cup self raising flour
1 tsp vanilla extract
Red food dye
6-8 tbsp apricot jam (jelly), warmed
500g / 1lb ready rolled marzipan
Icing (confectioners') sugar

789

SERVES 4

Banana Loaf Cake

PREPARATION TIME 20 MINUTES

COOKING TIME 1-1 HOUR 30 MINUTES

INGREDIENTS

350g / 12 oz over ripe bananas
180g / 6 oz / ¾ cup plain (all purpose) flour
2 tsp baking powder
1 tsp ground cinnamon
¼ tsp mixed spice
Pinch salt
150g / 5 oz / ⅔ cup soft dark brown sugar
2 eggs, beaten
100g / 3 ½ oz / ¼ cup butter, melted

- Preheat the oven to 170°C (150° fan) / 325F / gas 3. Grease a medium loaf tin.
- Mash the bananas in a bowl until pulpy.
- Sieve the flour into a bowl with the baking powder, spices and salt.
- Whisk the sugar and eggs until pale and creamy and doubled in volume, then whisk in the butter. Fold in the bananas and flour until thoroughly combined.
- Pour into the loaf tin and bake for 1 -1 ½ hours or until an inserted skewer comes out clean.
- Turn onto a wire rack to cool.

Banana Apple Loaf Cake   **790**

- Add ½ grated apple and 1 tbsp rum to the mix.

791

SERVES 6

Raisin Cake

PREPARATION TIME 20 MINUTES

COOKING TIME 1-1 ½ HOURS

INGREDIENTS

175g / 6 oz / ¾ cup soft light brown sugar
175g / 6 oz / ¾ cup butter, softened
3 eggs, beaten
275g / 10 oz / 1 heaped cup self raising flour
2 tsp mixed spice
175g / 6 oz / ¾ cup raisins, soaked in a little brandy
3 tbsp milk

- Preheat the oven to 180°C (160° fan) / 350F / gas 5.
- Cream the butter and sugar until pale and creamy. Add the eggs a little at a time, beating thoroughly after each addition, until well combined. Fold in the flour, spice and raisins. Add a little milk to loosen the batter.
- Spoon into a loaf tin and bake for 1-1 ½ hours until risen and springy or until an inserted skewer comes out clean.
- Turn onto a wire rack and leave to cool.

Chocolate and Raisin Cake   **792**

- Add 175 g / 6 oz of chocolate chips to the batter before baking.

Golden Raisin Cake   **793**

- Golden raisins mixed with ordinary ones make a glorious colour.

SERVES 8

Coconut Cake

Coconut Rum Cake   795

- Whisk 2 tbsp white rum into the icing for a boozy hit.

Coconut Cake with Orange Icing   796

- Stir in grated zest of 1 orange into the icing.

Coconut Cake with Dark Chocolate   797

- Grate over dark chocolate for the 'Bounty' effect.

PREPARATION TIME 30 MINUTES

COOKING TIME 40 MINUTES

INGREDIENTS

200g / 7 oz / ¾ cup plain (all purpose) flour
Pinch salt
2 tsp baking powder
75g / 2 ½ oz / ⅓ cup butter, chilled and cubed
75g / 2 ½ oz / ⅓ cup caster (superfine) sugar
50g / 1 ¾ oz / ¼ cup desiccated coconut
1 lime, grated zest
1 egg
120ml / 4 fl. oz / ½ cup milk
1 tsp vanilla extract

FOR THE ICING

100g / 3 ½ oz / ½ cup butter, softened
150g / 5 oz / ⅔ cup icing (confectioners') sugar
1 tsp vanilla extract
Desiccated coconut to decorate

- Preheat the oven to 180°C (160° fan) / 350F / gas 5. Grease and line a cake tin.
- Sieve the flour, salt, baking powder into a bowl. Using the pads of your fingertips, rub the butter in until it resembles breadcrumbs. Stir in the sugar, coconut and lime zest.
- Whisk the egg and milk together with the vanilla. Make a well in the flour mixture, then add the liquid a little at a time to for a smooth batter.
- Spoon into the cake tin and bake for about 40 minutes, or until an inserted skewer comes out clean. Cool on a wire rack.
- Cream the butter and sugar together until pale and creamy, then whisk in the vanilla. Spread over the cake with a palette knife and decorate with desiccated coconut and grated lime zest.

Chocolate & Orange Cake

798

SERVES 6-8

PREPARATION TIME 30 MINUTES

COOKING TIME 1 HOUR

INGREDIENTS

Zest and juice of 1 orange
225g / 8 oz / 1 cup plain (all purpose) flour
2 tbsp cocoa powder
1 ½ tsp baking powder
300g / 10 oz / 1 ¼ cup caster (superfine) sugar
3 eggs
250ml / 9 fl. oz / 1 cup vegetable oil
1 tsp vanilla extract

FOR THE ICING

200g / 7 oz / ¾ cup icing (confectioners') sugar
3 tbsp cocoa powder
150g / 5 oz / ⅔ cup cream cheese
½ orange, juiced
Candied orange peel, to decorate

- Preheat the oven to 190°C (170° fan) / 375F / gas 5. Grease and line an 18cm springform cake tin.
- Sieve the flour, cocoa powder, baking powder and salt into a large bowl. Stir in the sugar and set aside.
- Whisk the eggs, oil and vanilla extract and beat into the flour mixture until just combined. Stir in the orange zest and juice.
- Pour into the cake tin and bake for about an hour or until an inserted skewer comes out clean. Set aside to cool, then remove from the tin.
- Make the frosting by beating the icing sugar and cocoa powder into the cream cheese with an electric whisk. Whisk in the juice until it smooth and shiny.
- Smooth over the cooled cake and decorate with candied peel.

Chocolate and Orange Cake with Caramelised Walnuts

799

- Chop walnuts and coat in caramelised sugar then sprinkle over the cake.

Orange Loaf Cake

800

SERVES 8

PREPARATION TIME 20 MINUTES

COOKING TIME 50-60 MINUTES

INGREDIENTS

120g/ 4 oz / ½ cup butter, softened
250g / 9 oz / 1 cup caster (superfine) sugar
3 eggs, beaten
Zest and juice of 1 orange
250g / 9 oz / 1 cup plain (all purpose) flour
1 tsp baking powder
Juice of 1 orange
3-4 tbsp honey
2 drops orange blossom water (optional)

1 orange, sliced into rounds and baked on a rack at 120°C/250F for 2 hours

- Preheat the oven to 180°C (160° fan) / 350F / gas 5. Grease and line a 1L loaf tin.
- Cream the butter and sugar together until pale and creamy, then add the beaten eggs a little at a time, beating thoroughly after each addition.
- Fold in the zest and juice, flour and baking powder. Pour into the loaf tin.
- Bake for 50-60 minutes or until an inserted skewer comes out clean.
- Turn out of the tin onto a wire rack.
- Meanwhile heat the juice and honey, then add the orange blossom water if using. Pierce the cake with a skewer a few times and drizzle the syrup over and leave to soak in.
- Decorate with the dried orange slices.

Orange Loaf Cake with Orange Cream

801

- Stir orange jucie and zest into mascarpone and serve alongside.

802 · SERVES 8 · Bakewell Tart Pie

- Butter and flour the pan. To prepare the dough sift together the flour and icing sugar.
- Add the cold butter into cubes, work with fingertips. Add the salt and beaten egg, working by hand until forming a ball, film and refrigerate for 30 minutes.
- Chop the unblanched whole almonds finely. Meanwhile, whisk the butter and sugar until the mixture becomes creamy. Add the eggs and the almonds, and whisk.
- Spread the dough on a floured surface and line the mold with it. Refrigerate for 1 hour.
- Blind bake the pastry covered in foil and weighted down with rice or beans for 10 minutes in a preheated oven at 180°C / 350°F / th.6.
- Let cool a few minutes then pour over the raspberry jam and smooth. Spread the almond mix, and sprinkle with almonds. Bake at 180°C / 350°F / th.6 for 35 minutes.

PREPARATION TIME 20 MINUTES

COOKING TIME 45 MINUTES

INGREDIENTS

FOR THE DOUGH
200g / 7 oz of flour
100g / 4 oz / 1 stick of butter, diced
40g / 1 ½ oz / of icing (confectioners') sugar
1 small egg, beaten
A pinch of salt

FOR THE FILLING
300g / 11 oz of raspberry jam (jelly)
200g / 7 oz / 1 cup of whole almonds
130g / 4 ½ oz of soft butter, unsalted
120g / 4 ½ oz of sugar
40-50g / 2 oz of flaked (slivered) almonds
3 eggs

803 · Gingerbread Cake · SERVES 6

PREPARATION TIME 20 MINUTES

COOKING TIME 45 MINUTES

INGREDIENTS

250g / 9 oz / 1 cup self-raising flour
1 tsp baking powder
½ tsp bicarbonate of soda
½ tsp ground ginger
½ tsp mixed spice
75g / 2 ½ oz / ⅓ cup caster (superfine) sugar
75g / 2 ½ oz / ⅓ cup unsalted butter, melted
200ml / 7 fl. oz / ¾ cup milk
1 egg
2-3 tbsp stem ginger, finely chopped

- Preheat the oven to 200°C (180° fan) / 400F / gas 6. Grease and line a loaf tin.
- In one bowl combine the dry ingredients.
- Pour the milk in to a measuring jug and crack in the egg and whisk with a fork to amalgamate.
- Pour the liquid ingredients into the dry ingredients, stirring with a wooden spoon. The batter should remain somewhat lumpy – do not whisk until smooth. Add the stem ginger to the batter and stir in.
- Pour into the loaf tin and bake in the oven for about 45 minutes or until an inserted skewer comes out clean.
- Remove to a wire rack and allow to cool.

804 · Dundee Cake · SERVES 8

PREPARATION TIME 20-30 MINUTES

COOKING TIME 1-2 HOURS

INGREDIENTS

175g / 6 oz / ¾ cup butter, softened
175g / 6 oz / ¾ cup light brown sugar
3 tbsp marmalade
3 eggs, beaten
225g / 8 oz / 1 cup self raising flour
1 tbsp ground almonds
1 tsp mixed spice
½ tsp ground cinnamon
400g / 14 oz / 1 ½ cups mixed dried fruit
3 tbsp glacé cherries
2 tbsp whisky
2 tbsp blanched almonds

- Preheat the oven to 150°C (130° fan) / 300F / gas 2. Grease and line a 20cm/8in springform cake tin.
- Cream the butter and sugar in a food processor until pale and creamy. Add the marmalade and pulse, then add the eggs a little at a time, beating thoroughly after each addition.
- Add the flour, almonds, spices and mix well until combined. Stir in the dried fruit and cherries with a metal spoon, then stir in the whisky.
- Spoon into the cake tin, level out the surface and arrange the almonds in concentric circles on top.
- Bake for 1 ½ - 2 hours or until firm and golden brown.
- Leave to cool for 10 minutes, then remove from the tin and cool on a wire rack.

805

SERVES 8

Mirabelle Plum Cake

PREPARATION TIME 25 MINUTES

COOKING TIME 1 HOUR

....

INGREDIENTS

200g / 7 oz / ¾ cup Mirabelle plums,
halved and stoned
3-4 tbsp sugar
120g / 4 oz / ½ cup self raising flour
120g / 4 oz / ½ cup caster (superfine)
sugar
¼ tsp baking powder
1 tbsp milk
1 tsp vanilla extract
2 eggs
100g / 3 ½ oz / ½ cup butter, softened

- Preheat the oven to 180°C (160° fan) / 350F / gas 4.
  Grease and line a 20cm / 8 in cake tin.
- Toss the stoned plums in the sugar to macerate.
- Sieve the flour into a bowl and add the rest of the dry
  ingredients. Whisk the eggs, milk and vanilla.
- Beat the butter and some of the egg mixture into the
  dry ingredients until combined, then whisk in the rest
  until completely incorporated.
- Spoon into the tin and decorate the top with the plums.
- Bake for about 1 hour or until an inserted skewer comes
  out clean. Leave to cool completely before removing
  from the tin.

Greengage Cake 806

- Any kind of stone fruit works here, but
  sweet greengages are particularly good.

807

SERVES 6-8

Pear Cake

PREPARATION TIME 20 MINUTES

COOKING TIME 1 HOUR

....

INGREDIENTS

200g / 7 oz / ¾ cup butter, softened
100g / 3 ½ oz / ½ cup caster
(superfine) sugar
100g / 3 ½ oz / ½ cup soft dark
brown sugar
2 eggs, beaten
1 tsp vanilla extract
½ tsp ground cinnamon
200g / 7 oz / ¾ cup self raising (self
rising) flour
½ tsp baking powder
Pinch salt
2-3 ripe pears, peeled cored and
chopped

- Preheat the oven to 160°C (140° fan) / 310F / gas 3.
  Grease and line a 2lb loaf tin.
- Beat the butter and sugar together, then whisk in the
  eggs a little at a time, beating thoroughly after each
  addition. Stir in the vanilla extract and cinnamon.
- Using a metal spoon, fold in the flour, baking powder
  and salt. Stir in the pears.
- Pour into a loaf tin, trying to ensure the pears are evenly
  distributed and bake for 1 hr or until an inserted skewer
  comes out clean.
- Leave to cool in the tin before turning out onto a wire
  rack to cool completely.

Apple Cake 808

- The same quantity of chopped
  apple will give a similar result.

Pineapple Upside-Down Cake

809

SERVES 8

- Preheat the oven to 220°C (200° fan) / 425F / gas 7.
- Arrange the pineapple rings in the base of an oven proof frying pan and sprinkle over the sugar. Heat gently until the sugar has melted and the pineapple caramelises.
- Whisk the flour, eggs and milk in a bowl, add the sugar and whisk thickened, adding more milk if necessary. It should be the consistency of whipped cream.
- Pour the batter over the pineapple and bake in the oven for about 20 minutes until golden and risen.
- Meanwhile make the sauce: Place the mangoes, sugar and water in a pan and cook until the mangoes have softened. Whiz with a hand held blender until smooth, then stir in the rum and raisins.
- Remove the cake from the oven and invert onto to a plate. Serve with the hot sauce.

Apple Upside-Down Cake
810

- Slices of apple work well here in place of the pineapple.

PREPARATION TIME 25 MINUTES

COOKING TIME 20 MINUTES

INGREDIENTS

½ ripe pineapple, peeled and sliced into thin rings
2 tbsp caster (superfine) sugar
180g / 6 oz / ¾ cup self raising flour
2 eggs
150ml / 5 fl. oz / ⅔ cup milk
1 tsp vanilla extract
2 tbsp caster (superfine) sugar

FOR THE SAUCE

500g / 1 lb ripe mangoes, peeled, stoned and chopped
150g / 5 oz / ⅔ cup sugar
200ml / 7 fl. oz / ⅔ cup water
4 tbsp rum
4 tbsp raisins

Polenta Cake

811

SERVES 6-8

- Preheat the oven to 160°C (140° fan) / 310F / gas 3. Grease and line a 23cm cake tin.
- Cream the butter and sugar together until pale and creamy. Add the eggs a little at a time, beating thoroughly after each addition.
- Whisk in the polenta, flour, baking powder and citrus zest until thoroughly incorporated then add the orange juice to make a smooth loose batter.
- Pour into the cake tin, spread evenly and bake for 45-50 minutes or until an inserted skewer comes out clean.
- Remove from the oven and transfer to a wire rack to cool. Dust with icing sugar before serving.

Spiced Polenta Cake
812

- Turn up the volume with 1 tsp ground cinnamon and a pinch of mixed spice.

PREPARATION TIME 25 MINUTES

COOKING TIME 45-50 MINUTES

INGREDIENTS

250g / 9 oz / 1 cup butter, softened
250g / 9 oz / 1 cup caster (superfine) sugar
4 eggs, beaten
150g / 5 oz / ⅔ cup fine polenta
200g / 7 oz / ⅔ cup plain (all purpose) flour
2 tsp baking powder
2 oranges, grated zest and juice
½ lemon, grated zest
Icing (confectioners') sugar, to dust

SWEET TREATS

813

MAKES 12

Blueberry Muffins

- Preheat the oven to 200°C (180° fan) / 400F / gas 6. Line a 12 hole muffin tin.
- In a bowl, whisk together the sugar, oil, egg and buttermilk.
- Stir through the blueberries, then sieve in the flour with the baking powder and bicarbonate. Fold until lightly blended, but still a little lumpy. This will help keep the muffins light.
- Spoon evenly into the muffin cases then bake for about 25 minutes or until golden and risen.

PREPARATION TIME 15 MINUTES

COOKING TIME 25 MINUTES

INGREDIENTS

250g / 9 oz / 1 cup caster (superfine) sugar
80ml / 2 ½ fl. oz / ⅓ cup vegetable oil
1 egg
250ml / 9 fl. oz / 1 cup buttermilk
200g / 7 oz / ⅔ cup blueberries
300g / 10 oz / 1 ¼ cups plain (all purpose) flour
2 tsp baking powder
1 tsp bicarbonate of soda

Chocolate Chip Muffins

814

MAKES 12

PREPARATION TIME 15 MINUTES

COOKING TIME 25 MINUTES

INGREDIENTS

250g / 9 oz / 1 cup caster (superfine) sugar
80ml / 2 ½ fl. oz / ⅓ cup vegetable oil
1 egg

250ml / 9 fl. oz / 1 cup buttermilk
200g / 7 oz / ⅔ cup dark chocolate chips
300g / 10 oz / 1 ¼ cups plain (all purpose) flour
2 tsp baking powder
1 tsp bicarbonate of soda

- Preheat the oven to 200°C (180° fan) / 400F / gas 6. Line a 12 hole muffin tin.
- In a bowl, whisk together the sugar, oil, egg and buttermilk.
- Stir through the chocolate chips, then sieve in the flour with the baking powder and bicarbonate. Fold until lightly blended, but still a little lumpy. This will help keep the muffins light.
- Spoon evenly into the muffin cases then bake for about 25 minutes or until golden and risen.

Walnut Brownies

815

MAKES 16

PREPARATION TIME 15 MINUTES

COOKING TIME 30 MINUTES

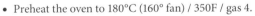

INGREDIENTS

120g / 4 oz / ½ cup butter
50g / 2 oz / ¼ cup dark chocolate
2 eggs, beaten
225g / 8 oz / 1 cup granulated sugar

50g / 2 oz / ½ cup plain (all purpose) flour
1 tsp baking powder
Pinch salt
150g / 5 oz / ⅔ cup walnuts, chopped

- Preheat the oven to 180°C (160° fan) / 350F / gas 4.
- Melt the butter and chocolate in a bowl over a pan of simmering water.
- Once melted, stir in the other ingredients until smooth and combined.
- Pour into a tin and bake for 30 minutes until the centre feels springy to the touch.
- Leave to cool in the tin before dividing into 16 squares and cooling on a wire rack.

Lemon Cupcakes

PREPARATION TIME 20 MINUTES

COOKING TIME 20 MINUTES

INGREDIENTS

120g / 4 oz / ½ cup self raising flour
120g / 4 oz / ½ cup caster (superfine) sugar
120g / 4 oz / ½ cup butter, softened
2 eggs, beaten
1 lemon, grated zest
2 tbsp milk

FOR THE TOPPING
120g / 4 oz / ½ cup butter, softened
250g / 9 oz / 1 cup icing (confectioners') sugar
1 lemon, juice

- Preheat the oven to 200°C (180° fan) / 400F / gas 6. Line a 12 hole muffin tin with cases.
- Place all the cupcake ingredients except the milk in a food processor and blitz until smooth and combined.
- Add the milk a little at a time to make a dropping consistency.
- Divide the mixture evenly between the cases and bake for 20 minutes or until risen and golden.
- Meanwhile cream the butter with the icing sugar until pale and creamy, then stir in the lemon juice.
- Remove the cakes from the tin to a wire rack to cool then decorate with the lemon icing.

Lime Cupcakes

817

- Use lime in place of the lemon – you may need an extra one.

Chocolate Cupcakes

PREPARATION TIME 25 MINUTES

COOKING TIME 20 MINUTES

INGREDIENTS

120g / 4 oz / ½ cup self raising flour
120g / 4 oz / ½ cup caster (superfine) sugar
120g / 4 oz / ½ cup butter, softened
2 eggs, beaten
1 tbsp cocoa powder
2 tbsp milk

FOR THE TOPPING
90g / 3 ½ oz / white chocolate, chopped
350g / 12 oz / / 1 ½ cups butter, softened
300g / 10 ½ oz / 1 ¼ cups icing (confectioners') sugar
120ml / 4 fl. oz / ½ cup double cream
Chocolate buttons, for decorating

- Preheat the oven to 200°C (180° fan) / 400F / gas 6. Line a 12 hole muffin tin with cases.
- Place all the cupcake ingredients except the milk in a food processor and blitz until smooth and combined. Add the milk a little at a time to make a dropping consistency.
- Divide the mixture evenly between the cases and bake for 20 minutes or until risen and golden.
- Meanwhile place the chocolate in a bowl set over a pan of simmering water and stir until melted. Set aside to cool slightly.
- Whisk the butter, icing sugar until pale, then whisk in the melted chocolate. Whisk in the cream until smooth and lightened.
- Remove the cakes from the tin to a wire rack to cool then decorate with the icing and chocolate buttons.

Chocolate Cupcakes with Chocolate Buttons

819

- Decorate with good quality chocolate buttons and spray silver if desired.

820

MAKES 16

Almond Chocolate Chip Brownies

Almond Brownies with Cherries

821

- Stir in 2 tbsp chopped glace cherries for extra chew.

Pecan Chocolate Brownies

822

- Use pecan nuts in place of the almonds.

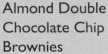

Almond Double Chocolate Chip Brownies

823

- Try adding a handful of white chocolate chips to the mix to melt as it cooks.

PREPARATION TIME 15 MINUTES

COOKING TIME 30 MINUTES

....

INGREDIENTS

120g / 4 oz / ½ cup butter
50g / 2 oz / ¼ cup dark chocolate
2 eggs, beaten
225g / 8 oz / 1 cup granulated sugar
50g / 2 oz / ½ cup plain (all purpose) flour
1 tsp baking powder
Pinch salt
120g / 4 oz / ½ cup almonds, chopped
120g / 4 oz / ½ cup dark or white chocolate chips

- Preheat the oven to 180°C (160° fan) / 350F / gas 4.
- Melt the butter and chocolate in a bowl over a pan of simmering water.
- Once melted, stir in the other ingredients apart from the chocolate chips until smooth and combined.
- Tip in the chocolate chips and stir to distribute then pour into a tin and bake for 30 minutes until the centre feels springy to the touch.
- Leave to cool in the tin before dividing into 16 squares and cooling on a wire rack.

824

MAKES 12-16 # Chocolate Chip Cookies

Double Chocolate Cookies

825

- Add a handful of white chocolate chips as well as the dark.

Cranberry Chocolate Cookies

826

- Use chopped dried cranberries in place of the chocolate chips.

Nutty Chocolate Cookies

827

- Use chopped hazelnuts in place of the chocolate chips.

PREPARATION TIME 20-30 MINUTES

COOKING TIME 20 MINUTES

INGREDIENTS

120g / 4 oz / ½ cup dark chocolate, chopped
150g / 5 oz / ⅔ cup plain (all purpose) flour
1 tbsp cocoa powder
1 tsp bicarbonate of soda
Pinch salt
120g / 4 oz / ½ cup butter, softened
120g / 4 oz / ½ cup caster (superfine) sugar
1 egg
350g / 12 oz / 1½ cups chocolate chips, white or dark

- Preheat the oven to 170°C (150° fan) / 325F / gas 3.
- Place the chocolate in a bowl over a pan over simmering water and stir until melted. Set aside to cool.
- Tip the flour, cocoa powder and bicarbonate into a bowl and stir in the salt.
- Cream the butter and sugar in a bowl until pale and creamy, then whisk in the melted chocolate.
- Whisk in the egg, then the dry ingredients, then the chocolate chips.
- Splodge fairly even amounts onto a lined baking sheet about 6cm apart. Cook for 20 minutes or until an inserted skewer comes out not wet with batter – it won't be clean.
- Leave to cool then transfer to a wire rack. Best eaten warm and soft.

828

MAKES 12 # Vanilla Cupcakes

- Preheat the oven to 200°C (180° fan) / 400F / gas 6. Line a 12 hole muffin tin with cases.
- Place all the ingredients except the milk in a food processor and blitz until smooth and combined.
- Add the milk a little at a time to make a dropping consistency.
- Divide the mixture evenly between the cases and bake for 20 minutes or until risen and golden.
- Remove the cakes from the tin to a wire rack to cool.

PREPARATION TIME 20 MINUTES

COOKING TIME 20 MINUTES

INGREDIENTS

120g / 4 oz / ½ cup self raising flour
120g / 4 oz / ½ cup caster (superfine) sugar
120g / 4 oz / ½ cup butter, softened
2 eggs, beaten
1 tsp vanilla extract
2 tbsp milk

Buttercream Cupcakes **829**

- Decorate with mixed candied peel and a flavoured buttercream.

830

MAKES 24 # Shortbread Biscuits

- Preheat the oven to 190°C (170° fan) / 375F / gas 5.
- Cream the butter and sugar until pale and creamy.
- Whisk in the flour a little at a time until thoroughly incorporated. Turn the dough out onto a floured surface and roll out to 1cm thickness.
- Cut out equal sized rounds or fingers and place on a baking tray. Refrigerate for 20 minutes.
- Bake in the oven for about 20 minutes or until pale gold. Set aside to cool on a wire rack, then dust with sugar.

PREPARATION TIME 15 MINUTES

COOKING TIME 20 MINUTES

INGREDIENTS

120g / 4 oz / ½ cup butter, softened
60g / 2 oz / ¼ cup caster (superfine) sugar
180g / 6 oz / ¾ cup plain (all purpose) flour
1 tsp vanilla extract (optional)
Sugar, for dusting

Shortbread Biscuits with Poached Fruit **831**

- Gently warm berries in a little water and sugar for an instant dessert.

832

MAKES 10-12 Gingerbread Men

PREPARATION TIME 50 MINUTES

COOKING TIME 12 MINUTES

INGREDIENTS

30g butter / 1 oz, softened
25g / 1 oz caster (superfine) sugar
½ tsp bicarbonate of soda
25g / 1 oz golden syrup
1 egg yolk
125g / 4 oz / ½ cup plain
(all purpose) flour
1 tsp ground ginger
½ tsp mixed spice

Mixed sugar balls for decoration
Golden syrup

- Preheat the oven to 180°C (160° fan) / 350F / gas 4.
- Whisk together the butter and sugar until pale, then stir in the bicarbonate, syrup and egg yolk.
- Sieve in the flour and spices, then mix with a wooden spoon until the mixture comes together in a ball.
- Roll into a cylinder, wrap in clingfilm and chill in the refrigerator for 30 minutes.
- Roll out to 1cm thickness and cut out gingerbread men with appropriate cutters and place on a lined baking sheet.
- Bake in the oven for about 12 minutes, then remove to a wire rack and leave to cool. Use the syrup as glue if necessary to decorate.

Gingerbread Snowmen   833

- Just use different cutters to create gingerbread decorations for the tree.

834

MAKES 24 Millionaire's Shortbread

PREPARATION TIME 30 MINUTES

COOKING TIME 35-40 MINUTES

INGREDIENTS

225g / 8 oz / 1 cup plain (all purpose) flour
100g / 3 ½ oz / ½ cup caster (superfine) sugar
225g / 8 oz / 1 cup butter, softened

FOR THE TOPPING

175g / 6 oz / ¾ cup butter
175g / 6 oz / ¾ cup caster (superfine) sugar
4-5 tbsp golden syrup
400g / 14 oz / 1 ½ cups condensed milk
200g / 7 oz / ¾ cup dark chocolate

- Preheat the oven to 160°C (140° fan) / 310F / gas 2. Lightly grease an oblong Swiss roll tin.
- Whiz the flour, sugar and butter in a food processor until they form a smooth dough.
- Gather into a smooth ball and pat out flat with your hands. Press into the base of the swiss roll tin and prick the base with a fork all over. Bake for 35-40 minutes until golden. Set aside to cool.
- Place the butter, sugar, syrup and condensed milk in a pan and stir over a low heat until the butter has melted. Bring the mixture gently to a bubble, then stir constantly until the mixture thickens and starts to look like fudge. Pour over the shortbread.
- Melt the chocolate in a bowl set over a pan of simmering water.
- Pour the chocolate over the fudge mixture and leave to set. Cut into 24 equal squares and serve.

Millionaire's Shortbread with   835
Milk Chocolate

- Use milk chocolate in place of the dark for the topping.

836

MAKES 30 Almond Tuile

- Preheat the oven to 170°C (150° fan) / 325F / gas 3. Line 2 baking trays.
- Beat the butter and sugar until pale and creamy, then add the egg whites a little at a time, beating thoroughly after each addition. Stir in the flour and chill for at least 20 minutes.
- Drop the mixture onto the baking trays with a teaspoon, leaving a lot of space in between for them to spread.
- Bake for 3 minutes, then scatter on the almonds and bake for a further 5-6 minutes until golden brown but not too dark.
- Transfer to a wire rack to cool. If desired, once out of the oven for a minute, wrap around the handle of a wooden spoon to create the distinctive curved shape then leave on the wire rack to harden.

PREPARATION TIME 40 MINUTES

COOKING TIME 8 MINUTES

INGREDIENTS

100g / 3 ½ oz / ½ cup butter, softened
100g / 3 ½ oz / ½ cup caster (superfine) sugar
3 egg whites
100g / 3 ½ oz / ½ cup plain (all purpose) flour
2 tbsp flaked (slivered) almonds

Almond Tuiles with Chocolate 837
- Drizzle dark melted chocolate over the top then leave to cool and harden.

838

MAKES 16-20 Chocolate Whoopee Pies

- Preheat the oven to 180°C (160° fan) / 350F / gas 4. Line a baking tray.
- Melt the chocolate and butter in a bowl over a pan of simmering water. Set aside to cool a little.
- Whisk the sugar, eggs and vanilla together, then fold in the chocolate and cinnamon.
- Sieve the flour, cocoa and baking powder into a bowl, then fold into the chocolate mixture.
- Spoon tablespoons of the mixture on to the baking tray – around 32-40, and bake for 8 minutes.
- Remove from the oven and place half the biscuits on a wire rack. Turn the remaining biscuits flat side up and top with a marshmallow. Return to the oven for 3 minutes or until the marshmallows are soft.
- Press the cooled biscuits on top of the marshmallow and leave to cool.

PREPARATION TIME 30 MINUTES

COOKING TIME 8-12 MINUTES

INGREDIENTS

1 tbsp butter
150g / 5 oz / ⅔ cup dark chocolate
225g / 8 oz / 1 cup caster (superfine) sugar
3 eggs
1 tsp vanilla extract
½ tsp ground cinnamon (optional)
250g / 9 oz / 1 cup plain (all purpose) flour
1 tbsp cocoa powder
½ tsp baking powder
16-20 marshmallows

Spiced Whoopee Pies 839
- Add a kick with a pinch of cayenne pepper.

840

MAKES 16-20

Whoopee Pies with Summer Fruit Jam

Whoopee Pies with Hedgerow Filling

841

- Use any kind of bramble jelly for the filling.

Whoopee Pies with Hedgerow Cream

842

- Stir the bramble jelly or any kind into softly whipped cream to fill.

Whoopee Pies with Chocolate Filling

843

- Sandwich together with a thick spreading of Nutella.

PREPARATION TIME 30 MINUTES

COOKING TIME 10 MINUTES

INGREDIENTS

100g / 3 ½ oz / ½ cup butter
200g / 7 oz / ¾ cup caster (superfine) sugar
2 eggs, beaten
2 tsp vanilla extract
120ml / 4 fl. oz / ½ cup buttermilk
300g / 10 oz / 1 ¼ cups plain (all purpose) flour
1 ½ tsp baking powder
1 tsp bicarbonate of soda
1 jar mixed summer fruit conserve, such as strawberry, raspberry, redcurrant

- Preheat the oven to 180°C (160° fan) / 350F / gas 4. Line a tray with baking parchment.
- Cream the butter and sugar until pale and creamy, then add the eggs a little at a time, beating thoroughly after each addition.
- Whisk in the vanilla and buttermilk.
- Sieve the flour, baking powder and bicarbonate together then fold into the creamed mixture with a metal spoon a little at atime.
- Drop tablespoons of the mixture onto the baking tray and bake for 8 minutes until golden.
- Remove half to a wire rack to cool. Turn the remaining half flat side up and spread with summer fruit conserve. Return to the oven to warm the conserve through – 2 minutes – then press the cooled halves onto the jam. Leave to cool.

844

MAKES 10-12 Sultana Scones

- Preheat the oven to 220°C (200° fan) / 425F / gas 2. Lightly grease a baking sheet.
- Mix the flour and salt in a bowl then rub in the cubed butter using the pads of your fingertips until the mixture resembles breadcrumbs.
- Stir in the sultanas and sugar, then the milk for a soft dough.
- Turn on to a floured surface and knead briefly, but do not overwork. Pat out to about 2cm thick then use a cutter to cut out rounds. Place on a baking sheet. Keep gathering up the leftover dough to use up and stamp out more rounds.
- Brush with a little extra milk and bake for about 15 minutes or until golden and well risen.
- Cool on a wire rack before splitting in half and serving as desired.

PREPARATION TIME 20 MINUTES

COOKING TIME 15 MINUTES

INGREDIENTS

225g / 8 oz / 1 cup self raising flour
Pinch salt
60g / 2 oz / ¼ cup butter, chilled and cubed
1 tbsp sultanas
1 tbsp caster (superfine) sugar
150ml / 5 fl. oz / ⅔ cup milk

Sultana Apricot Scones **845**

- A handful of chopped dried apricots ups the fruit content.

846

MAKES 10-12 Honey Scones

- Preheat the oven to 220°C (200° fan) / 425F / gas 2. Lightly grease a baking sheet.
- Mix the flour and salt in a bowl then rub in the cubed butter using the pads of your fingertips until the mixture resembles breadcrumbs.
- Stir in the honey and sugar, then the milk for a soft dough.
- Turn on to a floured surface and knead briefly, but do not overwork. Pat out to about 2cm thick then use a cutter to cut out rounds. Place on a baking sheet. Keep gathering up the leftover dough to use up and stamp out more rounds.
- Brush with a little extra milk and the seeds and bake for about 15 minutes or until golden and well risen.
- Cool on a wire rack before splitting in half and serving as desired.

PREPARATION TIME 20 MINUTES

COOKING TIME 15 MINUTES

INGREDIENTS

225g / 8 oz / 1 cup self raising flour
Pinch salt
60g / 2 oz / ¼ cup butter, chilled and cubed
1 tbsp sultanas
1 tbsp clear honey
150ml / 5 fl. oz / ⅔ cup milk
2 tbsp mixed seeds, to decorate

Heather Honey Scones **847**

- For a stronger honey flavour try heather honey.

848

MAKES 12

Hot Cross Buns

PREPARATION TIME 1 HOUR
45 MINUTES

COOKING TIME 15 MINUTES

....

INGREDIENTS

500g / 1 lb / 2 cups strong white
bread flour
75g / 2 ½ oz / ⅓ cup butter
3 tbsp caster (superfine) sugar
1 tsp salt
1 tsp ground cinnamon
½ tsp ground mixed spice
¼ tsp grated nutmeg
1 ½ tsp fast action dried yeast
1 egg, beaten
275ml / 9 ½ fl. oz / 1 scant cup milk
120g / 4 oz / ½ cup golden sultanas

TO DECORATE

120g / 4 oz / ½ cup plain (all
purpose) four
8 tbsp water
4 tbsp milk
2 tbsp sugar

- Place the flour in a large bowl and rub in the butter using the pads of your fingertips until the mixture resembles breadcrumbs.
- Stir in the sugar, salt, spices and yeast, whisk in the egg and then gradually add the milk.
- Knead on a floured surface for 5 minutes until the dough is smooth and elastic. Work in the sultanas, then return to the bowl, cover with clingfilm and leave in a warm place to rise for 1 hour or until doubled in size.
- Tip the dough out onto the surface and knead well for 5 minutes. Cut into 12 equal pieces, then shape each one into a smooth ball, tucking any joins or seams underneath. Place, spaced well apart, on a greased baking sheet. Cover again with oiled clingfilm and leave in a warm place for 30 minutes.
- Preheat the oven to 200°C / 400F / gas 6.
- To make the crosses, sieve the flour into a small bowl and mix in the water to make a smooth paste. Pipe crosses onto the buns.
- Bake in the oven for about 15 minutes.
- Meanwhile place the milk and sugar in a pan and heat until the sugar has dissolved and the liquid is syrupy. Brush over the baked buns, transfer to a wire rack and cool.

849

MAKES 30-40

Butter Cookies

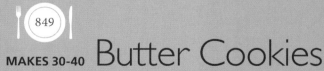

PREPARATION TIME 1 HOUR
20 MINUTES

COOKING TIME 15 MINUTES

....

INGREDIENTS

370g / 13 oz / 1 ½ cups plain (all
purpose) flour
Pinch salt
250g / 9 oz / 1 cup butter, softened
1 egg yolk
120g / 4 oz / ½ cup caster (superfine)
sugar
1 tsp vanilla extract
Or 1 lemon, grated zest

- Sieve the flour and salt into a bowl. Set aside.
- Cream the butter and sugar until pale and creamy. Whisk in the egg yolk and flavouring, then work in the flour a little at a time.
- Bring the dough together into a ball, wrap in clingfilm and refrigerate for 1 hour.
- Preheat the oven to 180°C (160° fan) / 350F / gas 4.
- Roll the dough out on a floured surface to about 3mm thickness. Cut out with your preferred cookie cutter shapes, or simply stamp out circles and place on lined baking sheets.
- Bake for about 15 minutes until pale gold. Transfer to a wire rack to cool.

Citrus Butter Cookies

850

- Add the zest of ½ orange as well as the lemon.

MAKES 8-10

Raspberry Mini Loaf Cakes

Cherry Loaf Cake   852
- Use stoned cherries in place of the raspberries.

Strawberry Loaf Cake   853
- Use hulled halved strawberries.

Blackberry Loaf Cake   854
- Use blackberries in place of the raspberries.

PREPARATION TIME 20 MINUTES

COOKING TIME 20 MINUTES

....

INGREDIENTS

120g / 4 oz / ½ cup self raising flour
120g / 4 oz / ½ cup caster (superfine) sugar
120g / 4 oz / ½ cup butter, softened
2 eggs, beaten
1 tsp vanilla extract
2 tbsp milk
1 punnet raspberries

- Preheat the oven to 200°C (180° fan) / 400F / gas 6. Line individual mini-loaf cake tins or simply line a muffin tin with cases if you don't have any.
- Place all the ingredients except the milk in a food processor and blitz until smooth and combined.
- Add the milk a little at a time to make a dropping consistency.
- Divide the mixture evenly between the cases and push 3-4 raspberries down the middle of each loaf cake. Bake for 20 minutes or until risen and golden.
- Remove the cakes from the tin to a wire rack to cool.

855

MAKES 12

Lemon Meringue Cupcakes

PREPARATION TIME 30 MINUTES

COOKING TIME 20 MINUTES

·······································

INGREDIENTS

120g / 4 oz / ½ cup self raising flour
120g / 4 oz / ½ cup caster (superfine) sugar
120g / 4 oz / ½ cup butter, softened
2 eggs, beaten
1 lemon, grated zest
2 tbsp milk

FOR THE TOPPING
2 egg whites
120g / 4 oz / ½ cup caster (superfine) sugar

- Preheat the oven to 200°C (180° fan) / 400F / gas 6. Line a 12 hole muffin tin with cases.
- Place all the cupcake ingredients except the milk in a food processor and blitz until smooth and combined.
- Add the milk a little at a time to make a dropping consistency.
- Divide the mixture evenly between the cases and bake for 20 minutes or until risen and golden.
- Whisk the egg whites until stiff, then beat in a little sugar at a time until thick and glossy. Spread over the cupcakes, piling it up to make it look decorative.
- Go over the meringues with a blowtorch to colour. Serve.

Lime Meringue Cupcakes

 856

- Use lime zest in place of the lemons.

857

MAKES 12

Blueberry Cupcakes

PREPARATION TIME 30 MINUTES

COOKING TIME 20 MINUTES

·······································

INGREDIENTS

120g / 4 oz / ½ cup self raising flour
120g / 4 oz / ½ cup caster (superfine) sugar
120g / 4 oz / ½ cup butter, softened
2 eggs, beaten
1 tsp vanilla extract
2 tbsp milk

FOR THE TOPPING
200g / 7 oz / ⅔ cup blueberries
120g / 4 oz / ½ cup butter, softened
250g / 9 oz / 1 cup icing (confectioners') sugar
Blue food dye

- Preheat the oven to 200°C (180° fan) / 400F / gas 6. Line a 12 hole muffin tin with cases.
- Place all the cupcake ingredients except the milk and blueberries in a food processor and blitz until smooth and combined.
- Add the milk a little at a time to make a dropping consistency, then stir in the blueberries, reserving a few for decoration.
- Divide the mixture evenly between the cases and bake for 20 minutes or until risen and golden.
- Meanwhile cream the butter with the icing sugar until pale and creamy, then stir in the food dye to the desired tone.
- Remove the cakes from the tin to a wire rack to cool. Spread the icing over the top and decorate with blueberries.

Blackcurrant Cupcakes

857 858

- Blackcurrants make a very adult version of these treats.

859

SERVES 8

Mini Bakewell Tarts

- Tip the flour, butter, almonds and sugar into a food processor with a pinch of salt and whiz to breadcrumbs. Add the egg yolk and 1 tbsp cold water and pulse. Flatten to a disc, cover with clingfilm and chill for 1 hour.
- Roll the pastry out on a floured surface to about 3mm thick. Line a 20cm tart tin with the pastry, prick the base with a fork and chill for 20 minutes. Preheat the oven to 180°C/350F/Gas 4.
- Line individual pastry cases with baking parchment and baking beans or rice. Blind bake for 20 minutes, remove the parchment and beans and bake for 5 minutes. Cool.
- Spread the jam over the bases. Cream the butter and sugar together. Add the beaten eggs and yolk, beating well after each addition. Fold in the almonds and zest.
- Spoon onto the jam, spread evenly and bake for 20 minutes. Mix the icing sugar with enough water to make a spreadable paste. Spoon evenly onto the tarts, then scatter over the flaked almonds and leave to set.

Mini Plum Bakewells   860

- Although traditionally made with raspberry jam, feel free to use. plum jam instead.

PREPARATION TIME 30-40 MINUTES

COOKING TIME 65 MINUTES

....

INGREDIENTS

125g / 4 oz / ½ cup plain (all purpose) flour
75g / 2 ½ oz / ⅔ cup butter
1 tbsp caster (superfine) sugar
1 egg, separated
Pinch salt
2 tbsp ground almonds

For the filling:
2 heaped tbsp raspberry jam
150g / 5 oz / 2/3 cup butter
150g / 5 oz / 2/3 cup caster (superfine) sugar
3 eggs, beaten
1 egg yolk
150g / 5 oz / ⅔ cup ground almonds
Zest of 1 orange
1 tbsp flaked almonds, toasted
175g / 6 oz / ¾ cup icing sugar

861

MAKES 36-40

Cigarettes Russe

- Combine the sugar, flour and salt and make a well in the centre. Stir in the melted butter, lightly beaten egg whites, cream and vanilla and mix until thoroughly combined. Cover and chill for at least 2 hours.
- Preheat the oven to 210°C (190° fan) / 425F / gas 7. Lightly grease two baking sheets.
- Spoon a tablespoon of batter onto the baking sheets, using the back of the spoon to spread the circle very thinly. Repeat to make 3 more. Bake for 5-6 minutes, until just brown around the edges.
- Once the biscuits have baked, working very quickly, use a palette knife to transfer each one to the work surface, then roll them around a wooden spoon handle or similar to make a cigarette shape. Cool.
- If the batter gets too stiff and cold to shape, simply return to the oven for 1 minute to soften up again. Continue until all the biscuits have been rolled.

Spiced Cigarettes   862

- Add ½ tsp ground cinnamon to the mix.

PREPARATION TIME 2 HOURS

COOKING TIME 5-6 MINUTES

....

INGREDIENTS

500g / 1 lb/ 2 cups icing (confectioners') sugar
300g / 10 oz / 1 ¼ cups plain (all purpose) flour
Pinch salt
250g / 9 oz / 1 cup butter, melted
6 egg whites
1 tbsp double cream
1 tsp vanilla extract

863

MAKES 16-20 Coconut Whoopee Pies

Whoopee Pies with Chocolate Filling

864

- Try spreading one side with nutella before adding the marshmallows.

Whoopee Pies with Raspberry Filling

865

- Spread thickly with raspberry jam.

Citrus Coconut Whoopee Pies

866

- Dust with grated lime or orange zest.

PREPARATION TIME 30 MINUTES

COOKING TIME 10 MINUTES

....

INGREDIENTS

100g / 3 ½ oz / ½ cup butter
200g / 7 oz / ¾ cup caster (superfine) sugar
2 eggs, beaten
2 tsp vanilla extract
120ml / 4 fl. oz / ½ cup buttermilk
100g / 3 ½ oz / ½ cup desiccated coconut
300g / 10 oz / 1 ¼ cups plain (all purpose) flour
1 ½ tsp baking powder
1 tsp bicarbonate of soda
16-20 marshmallows
Desiccated coconut, to garnish

- Preheat the oven to 180°C (160° fan) / 350F / gas 4. Line a tray with baking parchment.
- Cream the butter and sugar until pale and creamy, then add the eggs a little at a time, beating thoroughly after each addition.
- Whisk in the vanilla and buttermilk, then the desiccated coconut.
- Sieve the flour, baking powder and bicarbonate together then fold into the creamed mixture with a metal spoon a little at atime.
- Drop tablespoons of the mixture onto the baking tray and bake for 8 minutes until golden.
- Remove half to a wire rack to cool. Turn the remaining half flat side up and top with marshmallows. Return to the oven melt the marshmallows – 2 minutes – then press the cooled halves on top. Leave to cool.
- Sprinkle with desiccated coconut before serving.

867
MAKES 8
Almond Cake Pops

- Melt the chocolate in a bowl set over a pan of simmering water. Crumble the cake into a bowl, making sure it is fairly evenly sized crumbs.
- Stir in the melted chocolate a bit at a time; the mixture should be smooth and like fudge. If you use too much the mixture will be too heavy for the sticks.
- Roll golf-ball size pieces into balls and stick a lollipop stick into the middle of each one.
- Roll in the chopped almonds and refrigerate for 1 hour.

PREPARATION TIME 1 HOUR

INGREDIENTS

100g / 3 ½ oz / ½ cup dark chocolate
250g / 9 oz / 1 cup mixed shop-bought cakes, such as fruit cake, Madeira cake, chocolate cake, ginger cake – whatever you fancy
4 tbsp almonds, finely chopped

Almond and Chocolate Chip Cake Pops
868

- Add 2 tbsp of chocolate chips to the mixture.

Hazelnut Cake Pops
869

- Use crushed hazelnuts instead almonds.

870
MAKES 50
Canistrelli Biscuits

- Preheat the oven to 180°C (160° fan) / 350F / gas 4. Line a baking sheet.
- Combine the flours, salt, baking powder and lemon zest in a bowl. Make a well in the centre and pour in the liquids, stirring with a fork, until the dough comes together.
- Turn onto a lightly oiled surface and knead to a smooth ball.
- Pat the dough into a disc about 1.5cm thick. Slice into 2.5cm / 1in diamonds. Transfer to the baking sheet, leaving about an inch of space in between them.
- Bake for 15 minutes, reduce the heat to 160°C / 325F / gas 2 and bake for 15 minutes until golden.
- Cool on a wire rack.

PREPARATION TIME 30 MINUTES

COOKING TIME 30 MINUTES

INGREDIENTS

150g / 5 oz / ⅔ cup plain (all purpose) flour
100g / 3 ½ oz / ½ cup wholewheat flour
1 tsp salt
1 ½ tsp baking powder
1 lemon, grated zest
80ml / 2 ½ fl. oz / ⅓ cup olive oil
80ml / 2 ½ fl. oz / ⅓ cup white wine

Canistrelli Biscuits with Orange
871

- Use orange zest instead of lemon.

872

SERVES 4

Chocolate Truffles

PREPARATION TIME 20 MINUTES
+ CHILLING TIME

INGREDIENTS

300g / 10 oz / 1 ¼ cups dark
chocolate, chopped
300ml / 10 fl. oz / 1 ¼ cups double
cream
2 tbsp butter
Cocoa powder, for dusting

- Tip the chocolate into a bowl.
- Heat the cream and butter in a pan until simmering then pour over the chocolate and stir until the chocolate has melted and is fully incorporated.
- Now is the time to add 1-2 tbsp of any liqueurs or flavourings if desired.
- Chill for about 4 hours.
- Roll the mixture into walnut-sized balls with oiled hands. Set on a baking sheet and dust with cocoa powder. Refrigerate until needed.

Liqueur Chocolate Truffles

873

- Try adding 2 tbsp of your favourite liqueur, such as coffee or even Baileys.

874

MAKES 36

Vanilla Fudge

PREPARATION TIME 45 MINUTES
+ SETTLING TIME

INGREDIENTS

300ml / 10 fl. oz / 1 ¼ cups milk
350g / 12 oz / 1 ½ cups caster
(superfine) sugar
100g / 3 ½ oz / ½ cup butter
1 tsp vanilla extract

- Lightly grease an 18cm / 7in cake tin or roasting tin
- Place the ingredients, except the vanilla in a saucepan and heat slowly, stirring constantly, until the sugar has dissolved and the butter has melted.
- Bring to the boil and boil for 15-20 minutes, stirring constantly, until the mixture reaches 'soft ball' stage (115°C) or until a small amount of mixture dropped into a glass of cold water will form a soft ball that you can pick up on the end of a teaspoon. Remove from the heat, stir in the vanilla and leave to cool for 5 minutes.
- Using a wooden spoon, beat the mixture until it thickens and the shine disappears and it starts to look more opaque.
- Pour into the tin and set at room temperature. Once set cut into squares and serve.

Maple Fudge

875

- Halve the vanilla and add 2 tsp maple syrup to the mix.

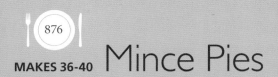

876
MAKES 36-40 Mince Pies

Mincemeat Tart
877

- Spread the mincemeat thickly over puff pastry, crimp the edges and bake until golden.

Mince Pies with Rum Cream
878

- Serve warm with softly whipped cream with rum folded in.

Mince Pies with Brandy Butter
879

- Three minutes before they are cooked, gently lift the star shapes and spoon over a little brandy butter. Replace the stars, continue cooking, then serve warm, soaked with brandy butter.

PREPARATION TIME 45 MINUTES

COOKING TIME 15 MINUTES

INGREDIENTS

250g / 9 oz / 1 cup plain (all purpose) flour
60g / 2 oz vegetable shortening, chilled
60g / 2 oz butter, chilled
Juice of 1 orange
Pinch salt
250g / 9 oz / 1 cup mincemeat

- Whiz the flour, butter and shortening in a food processor until the mixture resembles breadcrumbs. Pour in the orange juice and salt until the mixture starts to come together.
- Remove from the bowl and form into 3 balls. Press into a disc, cover with clingfilm and refrigerate for 20 minutes.
- Preheat the oven to 220°C (200° fan) / 425F / gas 7.
- Roll out the discs as thinly as possible and use to line 4.5cm tart tins – you may well make these in batches unless you have enough tart tins. Place a spoonful of mincemeat in the base.
- Reroll any leftover pastry and use to cut out star shapes. Press lightly on top of the mincemeat.
- Bake for 15 minutes or until pale gold. Remove from the oven and cool on a wire rack while making the next batch.

PASTRY

880

SERVES 4

Apple Strudel

- Preheat the oven to 190°C (170° fan) / 375F / gas 5.
- Place the apples in a bowl and coat well with the orange juice to prevent browning. Add the zest, sugar, spices and sultanas. Mix well.
- Brush each sheet of filo with melted butter, keeping the rest under a damp tea towel while not using.
- Lay out a large piece of baking parchment and layer the sheets of filo on top of one another. Sprinkle the top sheet with breadcrumbs.
- Spoon the apple mixture down the middle of the sheet.
- Roll the pastry around the apple to make a fat sausage, using the parchment to help you roll.
- Lift onto a baking sheet, brush with more melted butter and bake for 35 minutes or until golden and crisp.

PREPARATION TIME 30 MINUTES

COOKING TIME 35 MINUTES

INGREDIENTS

750g / 1 ⅓ lb / 3 cups eating apples, peeled, cored and chopped
Zest and juice of 1 orange
100g / 3 ½ oz / ½ cup caster (superfine) sugar
¼ tsp ground cloves
2 tsp ground cinnamon
Grated nutmeg
60g / 2 oz / ¼ cup sultanas
6-8 sheets ready made filo pastry
60g / 2 oz / ¼ cup butter, melted
3 tbsp breadcrumbs

881

MAKES 28-30 BUNS

Choux Buns with Whipped Cream

PREPARATION TIME 15 MINUTES

COOKING TIME 25 MINUTES

INGREDIENTS

60g / 2 oz / ¼ cup strong plain (bread) flour
1 tsp caster (superfine) sugar
150ml / 5 fl. oz / ⅔ cup cold water
50g / 1 ¾ oz / ¼ cup butter, cubed
2 eggs, beaten
300ml / 10 fl. oz / 1 ¼ cups double cream
30g / 1 oz icing (confectioners') sugar
1 tsp vanilla extract

- Preheat oven to 200°C (180° fan) / 400F / gas 6.
- Crease a piece of baking parchment in half across the diagonal and open out again. Sift the flour onto the paper, add the sugar and fold into the crease to hold it.
- Pour the water into the pan with the butter and heat gently until the butter melts, stirring occasionally. As it comes to the boil, remove from the heat and tip the flour in quickly. Beating vigorously with a wooden spoon or electric whisk until the mixture forms a smooth ball. Beat in the eggs a little at a time.
- Grease a baking sheet place teaspoons of the mixture at 1 inch intervals.
- Bake in the oven for 10 minutes then increase to 220°C /450F/Gas 7 and bake for a further 15 minutes.
- Allow to cool on a wire rack. Whisk the cream with the sugar and vanilla extract.
- When completely cool, cut the top third off the choux buns and pipe the cream inside. Place the tops on and serve.

882

SERVES 4

Steak and Kidney Pie

PREPARATION TIME 2 ½ HOURS

COOKING TIME 45 MINUTES

INGREDIENTS

FOR THE FILLING
2 tbsp vegetable oil or beef dripping
750g / 1 ⅓ lb3 cups stewing beef
200g / 7 oz / ¾ cup ox kidney, chopped
2 onions, peeled and chopped
1 tbsp tomato purée
1 ½ tbsp plain (all purpose) flour
2 bay leaves
2 tbsp Worcestershire sauce
450ml / 15 fl. oz / 1 ¾ cups beef stock
225g / 8 oz / 1 cup mushrooms, sliced
Salt and pepper
1 pastry case

- Make the filling: Heat the fat in a pan and brown the meat on all sides. Remove with a slotted spoon and add the onions. Cook until softened and golden.
- Stir in the tomato purée, cook out for a few seconds, then tip the meat back into the pan with all its juices. Stir in the flour to make a paste, then the bay leaves, Worcestershire sauce and stock. Season and simmer very gently for 1 ½ - 2 hours until the meat is tender.
- Tip the filling into the pie dish to come level with the top of the pastry – reserve any excess liquid for gravy. Use a couple of upturned egg cups in the filling to support the lid of the pastry, then carefully place the larger half of pastry onto the pie. Seal the edges by crimping, brush the pastry with beaten egg and make a little hole in the top for the steam to escape.
- Bake in the oven for about 40-45 minutes until the pastry is golden brown.

883

MAKES 20

Croissants

Croissants with Spiced Apples

884

- Serve with caramelised sautéed apples.

Savoury Croissants

885

- Serve stuffed with ham and cheese, grilled until melted.

Croissant Bread and Butter Pudding

886

- Use in bread and butter pudding in place of bread, see page 201 for the recipe.

PREPARATION TIME 2 HOURS

COOKING TIME 15 MINUTES

······························

INGREDIENTS

625g / 1 lb 5 oz / 2 ¾ cups strong white (bread) flour
12g / ½ oz salt
75g / 3 oz / ⅓ cup sugar
20g / ¾ oz dried yeast
500g / 1 lb / 2 cups butter, cold, cubed
1 egg, beaten

- Place the flour, salt, sugar and yeast in a bowl and stir in enough water to make a pliable dough.
- Tip onto a floured surface, bring together and knead for 5-8 minutes. Refrigerate for 1 hour.
- Remove from the fridge, roll out on a floured surface into a 60x30 cm rectangle.
- Roll out the butter into a 20x 30cm rectangle and place in the middle of the dough rectangle so it covers two thirds of the dough. Fold the remaining dough third over the butter layer so the dough now has 3 layers. Wrap in clingfilm and refrigerate for another hour.
- Flour the work surface and roll the dough out again to 60x30 cm and repeat the folding process, then refrigerate again for another hour.
- Repeat twice more, wrap in film and rest overnight.
- The next day roll out the dough to around 3mm thickness and cut into 20x20cm squares.
- Cut each square in half diagonally to make 2 triangles and place on a lightly floured surface.
- Roll each dough triangle up without pressing down too hard and curl round to make the traditional crescent shape. Place on lined baking trays and leave to rise for 1 hour in warm place. Preheat the oven to 200°C (180° fan) / 400F / gas 6.
- Lightly brush with beaten egg and bake for about 15 minutes or until golden brown and crisp.

887

SERVES 4

Broccoli and Salmon Quiche

- Preheat the oven to 200°C (180° fan) / 400F / gas 6 and put in a baking sheet to warm.
- Rub the butter into the flour with the salt until you have coarse breadcrumbs. Add water a little at a time using a round-bladed knife to mix until the mixture just comes together. Form into a ball, cover with clingfilm and refrigerate for 20-30 minutes.
- Meanwhile bake the salmon in a dish in the oven with a little butter for about 15 minutes or until the fish just starts to flake apart. Leave to cool, then flake and remove any bones and skin. Steam the broccoli for two minutes.
- Roll out the pastry and press it into a greased flan tin. Prick all over with a fork and bake in the oven for 20 minutes until pale gold.
- Spread the broccoli and salmon evenly over the pastry base. Whisk together the eggs, egg yolk, cream, seasoning and Parmesan then pour over the vegetables.
- Bake in the oven for 35 minutes. Leave to cool.

PREPARATION TIME 1 HOUR

COOKING TIME 1 HOUR

....

INGREDIENTS

1 head broccoli, separated into small florets
400g / 14 oz / 1 ½ cups salmon fillet
2 eggs + 1 egg yolk
275ml / 10 fl. oz / 1 ¼ cups double cream
Salt and pepper
1 tbsp Parmesan, grated

FOR THE QUICHE PASTRY
110g / 3 ½ oz / ½ cup plain (all purpose) flour
50g 1 ¾ oz / ¼ cup cold, diced butter
Pinch salt
Cold water, to mix

Salmon and Pea Quiche

888

- Use 150g peas in the quiche.

889

MAKES 12

Pain au Chocolat

- Make the croissant dough according to the recipe on P 250 up to the final rolling out.
- Roll the dough out to about 6mm thick and cut into 12x12cm squares.
- Place a chocolate baton at the base of each dough square and fold the pastry over to make a sausage shape.
- Brush with beaten egg and place on a lined baking sheet to rest for 1 hour in a warm place.
- Preheat the oven to 200°C (180° fan) / 400F / gas 6.
- Bake the pastries for about 15 minutes or until risen and golden.
- Cool on a wire rack for 5 minutes before eating.

PREPARATION TIME MAKE THE DAY BEFORE 2 HOURS

COOKING TIME 15 MINUTES

....

INGREDIENTS

1 x recipe croissant dough (page 250)
250g / 9 oz / 1 cup dark chocolate, 70%, cut into thick batons

Pain Au Chocolat with Peanut Butter

890

- Spread a stripe of peanut butter thickly under the chocolate baton before rollings.

891

MAKES 24

Cinnamon Buns

PREPARATION TIME 2 HOURS

COOKING TIME 30 MINUTES

····································

INGREDIENTS

75ml / 3 fl. oz / ⅓ cup lukewarm water
½ tsp dried yeast
50ml / 1 ¾ fl. oz / ¼ cup maple syrup
50ml / 1 ¾ fl. oz / ¼ cup butter, melted
1 egg, beaten
½ tsp salt
500g / 1lb / 2 cups plain (all purpose) flour

FOR THE FILLING

40g / 1 ½ oz / butter, melted
1 tbsp ground cinnamon
¼ tsp grated nutmeg
2 tbsp soft dark brown sugar
2 tbsp maple syrup
3 tbsp pecans, chopped
2 tbsp sultanas

- Tip the water, yeast and half the maple syrup into a bowl and leave for 15 minutes until it starts to bubble.
- Add the syrup, melted butter, egg and salt and mix. Tip the flour into a bowl and make a well in the centre. Pour in the yeast mixture and bring the flour into the liquid working until everything is combined.
- Tip out of the bowl onto a floured surface and knead for 8-10 minutes. Place back into the bowl, cover and leave to rise for 1 hour.
- Preheat the oven to 170°C (150° fan) / 325F / gas 4.
- Knock the dough back and roll on a floured surface to make 38x25cm rectangle. Brush with melted butter, then sprinkle over the filling ingredients. Roll the dough up like a fat sausage. Gently stretch it out with your hands to about 60cm in length.
- Cut the roll into 5-6cm lengths and place in greased muffin tins. Bake in the oven for 30 minutes. Remove to a wire rack to cool.

Cinnamon Buns with Cranberries   892

- Use cranberries in place of the sultanas.

893

MAKES 28

Salt and Pepper Palmiers

PREPARATION TIME 1 HOUR 20 MINUTES

COOKING TIME 15 MINUTES

····································

INGREDIENTS

500g / 1 lb/ 2 cups puff pastry
Sea salt
Coarsely ground black pepper
Plain (all purpose) flour
1 egg, beaten

- Roll the pastry out on a floured surface to around 30x35cm.
- Scatter over the sea salt and pepper. With the shortest end facing you, take the long edges of the pastry and roll them towards each other to meet in the middle. Press gently together and refrigerate for 1 hour.
- Preheat the oven to 200°C (180° fan) / 400F / gas 6.
- Slice the pastry roll into 1cm thick slices and place on a lined baking sheet. Brush with beaten egg and bake for about 15 minutes until puffed and golden.

Parmesan Palmiers   894

- Add 2 tbsp finely grated Parmesan with the seasoning.

Goats' Cheese & Spinach Pesto Turnovers

895

SERVES 4-6

Mozzarella Pesto Turnovers

896

- Thinly sliced mozzarella is a milder substitute for the goats cheese.

Goats' Cheese Ham and Spinach Turnovers

897

- Add a small square of ham with the filling.

Goats' Cheese, Walnuts and Honey Turnovers

898

- Place a piece of goats cheese, drizzle with 1 tsp honey and scatter over a few chopped walnuts before baking.

PREPARATION TIME 25 MINUTES

COOKING TIME 15-20 MINUTES

INGREDIENTS

FOR THE FILLING
2 tbsp olive oil
1 onion, peeled and finely chopped
500g / 1 lb / 8 cups spinach leaves, washed
Salt and pepper
2 tbsp pine nuts
4 tbsp Parmesan, grated
Olive oil
200g / 7 oz / ¾ cup goats' cheese, crumbled

FOR THE PASTRY
300g / 10 oz / 1 ¼ cups self-raising flour
½ tsp salt
4 tbsp olive oil
2 tbsp white wine
100ml / 3 ½ fl. oz / ½ cup water

- Preheat the oven to 200°C (180° fan) / 400F / gas 6.
- Make the filling: Heat the olive oil in a pan and fry the onion until softened. Wilt the spinach in the same pan and season, then tip the whole lot into a food processor. Add the pine nuts, Parmesan and a little oil and blitz to make a rough paste, adding more oil if necessary.
- Make the pastry: Sieve the flour and salt into a bowl. Heat the olive oil, wine and water in a pan until hand hot. Pour the warm liquid into the flour and knead until soft and elastic. Shape into a ball.
- Turn out onto a floured surface and divide into 20 pieces.
- Roll each piece into a circle about 8cm in diameter.
- Place a teaspoon of spinach pesto onto one half of the pastry, place a piece of goats' cheese on top and fold over the other half to enclose it, pressing down around the edges to seal it in. Repeat to make 20 little turnovers.
- Place on an oiled baking sheet and make small slashes in the top of the pastry. Bake for 15-20 minutes until golden brown.

899
SERVES 4-6

Ham and Mushroom Slice

PREPARATION TIME 10 MINUTES

COOKING TIME 20-25 MINUTES

....

INGREDIENTS

500 ml / 17 ½ fl. oz / 2 cups milk
35 g / 1 ¼ oz butter
2 tbsp plain (all purpose) flour
100 g / 3 ½ oz button mushrooms,
chopped
100 g / 3 ½ oz ham, cubed
450 g / 1 lb all-butter puff pastry
1 egg, beaten

- Preheat the oven to 220°C (200° fan), 430F, gas 7.
- Heat the milk to simmering point and set aside.
- Heat the butter in a small saucepan and stir in the flour. Slowly add the hot milk, stirring constantly, and cook until the sauce is thick and smooth.
- Stir in the mushrooms and ham and season with salt and pepper, then leave to cool completely.
- Roll out the pastry and divide into 2 equal rectangles.
- Transfer one rectangle to a baking tray and spread over the filling, leaving a 2 cm border round the outside.
- Brush the edge of the pastry with beaten egg and lay the other pastry sheet on top. Squeeze the edges to seal and trim the pastry to neaten.
- Score a pattern on top with a sharp knife.
- Bake in the oven for 25 - 35 minutes or until the top is golden brown.

Chicken and Mushroom Slice   900

- Replace the ham with an equal weight of chopped cooked chicken breast.

901
SERVES 4-6

Apple Tart

PREPARATION TIME 50 MINUTES

COOKING TIME 30-40 MINUTES

....

INGREDIENTS

FOR THE PASTRY
75g / 2 ½ oz / ⅔ cup plain
(all purpose) flour
20g / ¾ oz lard
20g / ¾ oz butter
Pinch salt
Cold water

FOR THE FILLING
700g / 1 ⅓ lb / 3 cups Bramley apples,
peeled, cored and quartered
1 tbsp soft brown sugar
¼ tsp ground cloves
1 tsp ground cinnamon
Grated nutmeg
Apricot jam (jelly), warmed

- Preheat the oven to 200°C (180° fan) / 400F / gas 6.
- Sieve the flour and salt into a large bowl, then cut the lard and butter into cubes and work into the flour until the mixture resembles breadcrumbs.
- Work in 2 tbsp water and bring the mixture together with a knife, cutting it through to mix, using enough water to just make a smooth dough. Refrigerate.
- Slice the apples thinly and tip into three quarters into a pan with the sugar and cloves and cinnamon. Add 1 tbsp water and cook very gently with a lid on until the apples collapse completely to make a purée.
- Roll out the pastry on a floured surface to line a 20cm / 8 inch greased pie dish. Spoon in the filling, then arrange the apple slices on top. Sprinkle over a little grated nutmeg and bake for 30-40 minutes, reducing the heat to 180°C / 350F after the first 10.
- Brush with warmed jam when out of the oven to give a shine to the apples.

Apple Sultana Tart   902

- Add 6 tbsp golden sultanas with the apples.

903

SERVES 4-6 Apricot Pie

- Make the filling: cook half the apricots in a pan with the water and sugar over a very low heat until tender, stirring occasionally. Leave to cool.
- Roll out the rested pastry and divide into two thirds and one third. Flatten into circles and leave for 30 minutes.
- Preheat oven to 180°C (160° fan) / 350F / gas 5.
- Roll out the larger pastry circle to line a 20cm / 8 inch greased pie dish and press into the dish. Roll the other dough circle out on baking parchment and chill.
- Spoon the cooked apricots over the pastry base, then top with the uncooked apricot halves.
- Arrange the dough strips on top of the tart to form a lattice pattern and brush with egg.
- Bake on a preheated baking sheet for 1 hour until crisp.
- Leave to cool, brushing with a little warmed apricot jam (jelly) for shine.

Peach Pie 904

- Peaches can be used in much the same way.

PREPARATION TIME I HOUR 30 MINUTES

COOKING TIME I HOUR

INGREDIENTS

FOR THE PASTRY
Double the recipe shortcrust pastry (see Apple Tart)

FOR THE FILLING
500g / 1 lb / 2 cups apricots, halved and stoned
2 tbsp water
4 tbsp sugar
75g / 2 ½ oz / ⅓ cup apricot jam (jelly)
1 egg, beaten

905

MAKES 6 Sausage Rolls

- Preheat the oven to 200°C (180° fan) / 400F / gas 6.
- Roll the pastry out on a floured surface to the thickness of a coin.
- Cut the sausages into short lengths about 3-4cm, then place a sausage piece in the top corner of the pastry rectangle.
- Score a line down the pastry the width of the sausage piece. Roll the pastry around the sausage, cutting it when you have encased the sausage. Place on a lined baking sheet. Repeat until all the sausages are used up.
- Make 2 small slashes in the top of each sausage roll and brush with beaten egg.
- Bake in the oven for 25 minutes or until golden brown. Leave to cool on a wire rack before eating.

Sausage Rolls with Fennel Seeds 906

- Try sprinkling the sausages with lightly crushed fennel seeds before rolling.

PREPARATION TIME 30 MINUTES

COOKING TIME 25 MINUTES

INGREDIENTS

6 Cumberland or traditional sausages
1 x 375g ready-rolled puff pastry
1 egg, beaten

907

SERVES 4

Mushroom Pie

PREPARATION TIME 25 MINUTES

COOKING TIME 30 MINUTES

....

INGREDIENTS

60g / 2 oz / ¼ cup butter
1kg / 2 ¼ lb / 4 ¼ cups field
mushrooms, thickly sliced
1 sprig thyme
2 sprigs tarragon
2 cloves garlic, finely sliced
1 tbsp plain (all purpose) flour
50ml / 1 ¾ oz / ¼ cup red wine
300ml / 10 fl. oz / 1 ¼ cups vegetable
stock
2 tbsp double cream
Salt and pepper
500g / 1 lb ready made puff pastry
1 egg, beaten

- Preheat 200°C (180° fan) / 400F / gas 6.
- Heat the butter in a large frying pan and cook the mushrooms with the herbs and garlic gently until all the excess liquid has evaporated.
- Add the flour and cook out for 2 minutes, then add the wine and the stock gradually, stirring as you go until smooth. Leave to simmer for 10 minutes until smooth and thick.
- Cut the pastry into two pieces slightly larger than a 20cm / 8in pie dish and roll out on a floured surface to about 5mm thickness.
- Line the pie dish with one circle, then spoon the mushroom filling in, reserving any excess sauce. lay the second circle on top and crimp the edges together. Brush with beaten egg and make a small slash in the top for the steam to escape.
- Bake on a preheated baking sheet for 30 minutes.

Mushroom Spinach Pie   908

- Add 200g wilted drained spinach to the base of the pie before the mushrooms.

909

SERVES 4

Quiche Lorraine

PREPARATION TIME 50 MINUTES

COOKING TIME I HOUR

....

INGREDIENTS

FOR THE QUICHE PASTRY
110g / 3 ½ oz / ½ cup plain (all
purpose) flour
50g / 1 ¾ oz / ¼ cup cold, diced
butter
Pinch salt
Cold water, to mix

FOR THE FILLING
8 rashers smoked streaky bacon,
diced
100g / 3 ½ oz / ½ cup Gruyére
cheese, grated
2 eggs + 1 egg yolk
300ml / 10 fl. oz / 1 ¼ cups double
cream
salt and pepper

- Preheat the oven to 200°C (180° fan) / 400F / gas 6 and put in a baking sheet to warm.
- Rub the butter into the flour with the salt until you have coarse breadcrumbs. Add water a little at a time until the mixture just comes together.
- Form into a ball, cover with clingfilm and refrigerate.
- Grill the bacon until crisp and cut into small pieces.
- Roll out the pastry and press it gently into a lightly greased flan tin. Prick all over with a fork and bake in the oven on the baking sheet for 20 minutes.
- Place the cheese and bacon evenly over the pastry base. Whisk together the eggs and cream and season, then pour in, adding a little pepper but careful on the salt.
- Bake in the oven for 25-30 minutes until just set. Leave to cool before serving.

Quiche Lorraine with Broccoli   910

- Steamed broccoli florets folded in make a good colourful addition.

911

MAKES 8

Beef Empanadas

- Preheat the oven to 200°C (180° fan) / 400F / gas 6.
- Heat the oil in a pan and cook the onion and garlic until translucent. Add the beef, increase the heat and cook until browned. Add the beans, spices and seasoning and cook for 5-10 minutes until cooked through.
- Roll the pastry out onto a lightly floured surface to about 1cm thickness and cut out eight circles about 10cm wide.
- Spread a small spoonful of the beef mixture into the centre of each circle, leaving a 1cm border around the edge. Brush the edges with a little beaten egg and fold the pastry over to enclose the filling.
- Using a fork, crimp the edges of the pastry together to seal the filling in and brush the parcels with beaten egg.
- Bake in the oven on a greased baking sheet for about 10 minutes, then lower the oven temperature to 180°C / 350F / gas 4 and cook for another 10 minutes.

PREPARATION TIME 30 MINUTES

COOKING TIME 20 MINUTES

INGREDIENTS

1 x 500g / 1lb ready-made puff pastry
1 egg, beaten

FOR THE FILLING

1 tbsp olive oil
1 onion, peeled and finely chopped
1 clove garlic, finely chopped
500g / 1 lb / 2 cups minced beef
1 x 400g can kidney beans, drained
½ tsp cayenne pepper
1 tsp ground cumin

Lemon Curd Tart

912

SERVES 6

PREPARATION TIME 1 HOUR

COOKING TIME 25 MINUTES

INGREDIENTS

125g / 4 oz / ½ cup plain (all purpose) flour
60g / 2 oz / ¼ cup butter

Pinch salt
Cold water
400g lemon curd

- Preheat the oven to 190°C (170° fan) / 375F / gas 5.
- Make the pastry: Sieve the flour and salt into a large bowl, then cut the lard and butter into cubes and work into the flour with the pads of your fingers until the mixture resembles breadcrumbs.
- Work in 2 tbsp water and bring the mixture together with a knife, cutting it through to mix, using enough water to just make a smooth ball of dough that leaves the bowl clean. Wrap the dough in clingfilm and refrigerate for 20 minutes.
- Roll the pastry out on a floured surface to just larger than your pie dish. Cut a 8mm strip all round, dampen the rim of the dish and press the pastry strip on to it. Line the tin with the pastry and press the edges onto the pastry rim. Prick the base with a fork and bake for 25 minutes until pale gold and cooked through.
- Pour lemon curd into the pastry shell and spread evenly.
- Allow to set at room temperature, then serve.

Mushroom Vol au Vents

913

SERVES 6

PREPARATION TIME 20 MINUTES
+ CHILLING TIME

COOKING TIME 30-35 MINUTES

INGREDIENTS

350g / 12 oz / 1 ½ cups ready made puff pastry
1 egg, beaten

3 tbsp butter
500g / 1 lb / 2 cups mixed wild mushrooms, chopped
2 sprigs thyme leaves
2 tbsp plain (all purpose) flour
300ml / 10 fl. oz / 1 ¼ cups milk
2 tbsp Parmesan, grated
Salt and pepper

- Roll the pastry out on a floured surface to 2.5cm / ¼ in thick. Cut out six 7cm / 3inch circles with a pastry cutter and score a smaller circle just inside the rim.
- Place on a baking sheet and chill for 30 minutes. Preheat the oven to 200°C (180° fan) / 400F / gas 6.
- Brush the pastry cases with a little egg and bake for 20 minutes or until risen and golden. Leave to cool, then carefully remove the lids and scoop out the centres.
- Melt the butter in a pan and cook the mushrooms with thyme and seasoning until any excess liquid has evaporated.
- Stir in the flour and cook out for 2 minutes, then whisk in the milk and simmer for 5-10 minutes until thickened and smooth. Whisk in the Parmesan.
- Spoon into the pastry cases, replace the lids and cook for 10-15 minutes until the filling is bubbling.

914

SERVES 4

Vanilla Mille Feuille

Mille Feullie with Summer Fruit

915

- Layer the vanilla cream with lightly crushed summer berries.

Citrus Vanilla Cream Mille Feuille

916

- Add grated zest of 1 orange to the vanilla cream.

Mille Feullie with Chopped Nuts

917

- For extra crunch scatter over chopped hazelnuts and pecans tossed in caramelised sugar.

PREPARATION TIME 45 MINUTES

COOKING TIME 25-30 MINUTES

INGREDIENTS

1 sheet ready made puff pastry
Icing (confectioners') sugar

FOR THE CRÈME PATISSIÈRE
250ml / 9 fl. oz / 1 cup full fat milk
½ vanilla pod, seeds removed
2 egg yolks
60g / 2 oz / ¼ cup caster (superfine) sugar
2 tsp custard powder
1 dstsp cornflour
25g / 1 oz butter

FOR THE VANILLA CREAM
50ml / 1 ¾ oz / ¼ cup double cream, whipped

- Make the crème patissière: in a heavy bottomed pan, bring the milk, vanilla pod and seeds to the boil.
- In a bowl, whisk the egg yolks, sugar, custard powder and cornflour, then add a third of the milk to the bowl and whisk.
- Remove the vanilla pod, bring the milk back to the boil and pour the egg mixture into the pan, whisking constantly until it re-boils. Remove from the heat and whisk in the butter. Pour into a bowl and cover with clingfim to prevent a skin forming. Set aside. Once cool, whisk until smooth, then fold in the whipped cream.
- Preheat the oven to 190°C (170° fan) / 375F / gas 5. Roll the pastry to 1.5mm thick and prick with a fork all over. Place on a lined baking sheet, then top with another layer of baking parchment and cover with a baking sheet.
- Bake in the oven according to packet instructions. Remove from the oven and increase the heat to 240°C (220° fan) / 475F / gas 9.
- Dust the smoothest side of the cooked pastry liberally with icing sugar and caramelise in the oven for a few seconds. Allow to cool then cut into three equal strips.
- When cold, pipe the vanilla cream onto one pastry strip. Top with a second layer, then pipe over more cream and top with the final pastry strip.

918

MAKES 8 # Sicilian Cannoli

- Mix the ricotta and flavourings, together.
- Fill a piping bag with the mixture, and using a plain nozzle pipe into the brandy snap tubes. Alternatively use the handle of a teaspoon but it will be a messier result...

PREPARATION TIME 15 MINUTES

INGREDIENTS

8 brandy snap tubes
500g / 1 lb / 2 cups ricotta
50g / 1 ¾ oz / ¼ cup icing (confectioners') sugar
1 tbsp candied peel, finely chopped
60g / 2 oz / ¼ cup dark chocolate, cut into chips
¼ tsp ground cinnamon
75g / 2 ½ oz / ⅓ cup shelled pistachios, chopped

Cannoli with Chopped Cranberries   919

- The sharpness of dried cranberries are wonderful against the sweetened ricotta.

920

SERVES 8 # Apple Tarte Tatin

- Preheat the oven to 220°C (200° fan) / 425F / gas 7.
- Tip the granulated sugar into a stainless steel pan with 6 tbsp water. Stir over a low heat until the sugar dissolves, then remove the spoon and increase the heat a little. Boil to a deep gold, then pour into a 23cm / 9in sponge sandwich tin.
- Core the apples and slice thinly. Arrange a layer over the caramel – this will be the top so make it decorative – then toss the remaining apples in the zest, juice and cinnamon and scatter in the tin. Press down gently.
- Cut the pastry sheet out to slightly larger than the tin, then place over the apples and tuck the edges in. Make a small hole to let the steam out. Bake in the oven for 40 minutes until crisp and golden brown.
- Tip any juices from the tin into a saucepan. Add the caster sugar and boil until syrupy. Turn the tatin out onto a plate and spoon the syrup over the apples.

PREPARATION TIME 25 MINUTES

COOKING TIME 40 MINUTES

INGREDIENTS

1 x sheet ready rolled puff pastry
175g / 6 oz / ¾ cup granulated sugar
1 kg / 2 ½ lb / 4 ¼ cups eating apples
Finely grated zest and juice of 1 lemon
1 tsp ground cinnamon
75g / 2 ½ oz / ⅓ cup caster (superfine) sugar

Banana Tart Tatin   921

- Bananas, peeled and thickly sliced, caramelise to sweet stickiness in place of the apples.

922

SERVES 6

Chicken and Olive Filo Pie

PREPARATION TIME 20 MINUTES

COOKING TIME 25 MINUTES

INGREDIENTS

6 sheets filo pastry
Melted butter
2 tbsp olive oil
1 onion, peeled and chopped
2 cloves garlic, finely sliced
1 tsp dried oregano
1 tsp ground coriander
1 egg
Salt and pepper
300g / 10 oz / 1 ¼ cups cooked chicken, such as leftovers
200g / 7 oz / ¾ cup mixed green and black olives, stoned

- Preheat the oven to 200°C (180° fan) / 400F / gas 6. Keep the filo sheets under a damp tea towel.
- Heat the oil in a pan and sweat the onion. Add the garlic, oregano and coriander; cook for 2 minutes. Beat the egg, then add the onion mix and the olives.
- Line a pie dish with baking parchment. Brush a sheet of filo pastry with melted butter and place in the base of the dish. Brush another sheet, turn the dish a quarter turn and place the filo sheet on top of the first. Repeat with the next 2 sheets.
- Spoon the olive mixture into the base of the pie, then tear the chicken into bite size pieces and place evenly on top. Pour the remaining olive mixture over the top.
- Brush the remaining 2 sheets of filo with butter and place on top of the pie, tucking the pastry in around the sides. Brush again with melted butter and bake for 25 minutes.
- Leave to cool slightly before serving.

Chicken and Olive Pepper Pie   923

- Add 3 finely chopped red peppers to the onion.

924

SERVES 6

Chicken and Mushroom Pie

PREPARATION TIME 50 MINUTES

COOKING TIME 30 MINUTES

INGREDIENTS

2 tbsp butter
3-4 chicken thighs, deboned and skinned, cut into chunks
1 shallot, finely chopped
100g / 3 ½ oz / ½ cup button mushrooms, quartered
3 sprigs thyme
2 sprigs tarragon leaves
1 ½ tbsp plain (all purpose) flour
300ml / 10 fl. oz / 1 ¼ cups milk
Salt and pepper
1 egg, beaten

FOR THE PASTRY

120g / 4 oz / ½ cup plain (all purpose) flour
60g / 2 oz / ¼ cup butter
Pinch salt
Cold water

- Sieve the flour and salt into a bowl, then cut the lard and butter into cubes and work into the flour until the mixture resembles breadcrumbs.
- Work in 2 tbsp water and bring the mixture together using enough water to make a smooth ball of dough. Wrap in clingfilm and chill for 30 minutes.
- Preheat the oven to 200°C (180° fan) / 400F / gas 6.
- Heat the butter in a pan and fry the chicken until golden.
- Remove the chicken then sweat the shallot and mushrooms with the herbs. Stir in the flour, then whisk in the milk to make a smooth sauce. Return the chicken to the pan, season and simmer for 10 minutes.
- Tip the chicken into a pie dish. Roll the pastry out on a floured surface to slightly larger than the pie dish and sit on top of the filling.
- Brush with beaten egg, make a hole in the pastry to let the steam escape and bake in the oven for 30 minutes.

Chicken, Ham and Mushroom Pie   925

- Adding some cooked chopped ham ramps up the flavour.

926

SERVES 4 Pecan Tart

Walnut Tart 927
- Use walnuts in place of the pecans.

Pecan Fig Tart 928
- Decorate the top with quartered ripe figs.

Date Pecan Tart 929
- Add 2 tbsp chopped dates to the filling.

PREPARATION TIME 20 MINUTES

COOKING TIME 45 MINUTES

INGREDIENTS

250g / 12 oz ready-made shortcrust pastry, rolled out thinly

FOR THE FILLING
120g / 4 oz / ½ cup butter
120g / 4 oz / ½ cup golden syrup
1 tsp vanilla extract
225g / 8 oz / 1 cup soft brown sugar
3 eggs, beaten
300g / 10 oz / 1 ¼ cups pecans, halved

- Preheat the oven to 180°C (160° fan) / 350F / gas 4.
- Line a 9in pie tin with the pastry.
- Place the butter, syrup, vanilla extract and sugar in a pan over low heat and stir until the butter has melted. Remove from the heat and leave to cool.
- Add the eggs and mix well.
- Setting aside a few for decoration, tip the pecans into the pastry case then pour over the syrup mixture.
- Bake for 45 minutes until the pastry is golden.
- Decorate the top with the remaining pecans and serve when cool.

930

MAKES 10-12 # Onion Tartlets

Red Onion Tartlets   931
- Use red onions in place of the white.

Onion Pepper Tartlets   932
- Use 1 finely chopped red pepper with the onion.

Onion Olive Tartlets   933
- Use a handful chopped green or black olives.

PREPARATION TIME 50 MINUTES

COOKING TIME 35 MINUTES

INGREDIENTS

1 x recipe shortcrust pastry (see Chicken & Mushroom Pie, page 251)

FOR THE FILLING
1 tbsp butter
1 onion, peeled and finely sliced
3 eggs
100ml / 3 ½ fl. oz / ½ cup double cream
Salt and pepper
2 tbsp Parmesan cheese, finely grated
Handful sun-dried tomatoes

- Preheat the oven to 200°C (180° fan) / 400F / gas 6.
- Roll out the rested pastry to about 5mm thick. Using individual tartlet cases as a guide, cut out circles large enough to line the cases, then proceed to do so.
- Prick the bases of the pastry cases and bake for 10-15 minutes until pale gold and cooked.
- Meanwhile cook the onion slowly in butter until golden and sweet. Whisk the eggs in a bowl with cream, seasoning and cheese and add the onion.
- Pour the mixture into the baked, cooled tartlet cases, then push a sun dried tomato into the centre of the mixture.
- Bake for about 20 minutes, until just set. Cool on a wire rack before releasing from the tartlet moulds.

**MAKES
28-30 BUNS**

Savoury Choux Pastry

- Preheat oven to 200°C (180° fan) / 400F / gas 6.
- Crease a piece of baking parchment in half across the diagonal and open out again. Sift the flour onto the paper, add the salt and fold into the crease to hold it.
- Pour the water into the pan with the butter and heat gently until the butter melts, stirring occasionally.
- As it comes to the boil, remove from the heat and tip the flour in quickly. Beating vigorously. Beat in the eggs a little at a time, mixing well, until you have a smooth glossy pastry dough. MIx in the dried herbs.
- Grease a baking sheet and quickly run under the tap to create moisture in the oven to help the buns rise. Place teaspoons of the mixture at 1 inch intervals.
- Bake in the oven for 10 minutes then increase to 220°C (200° fan) / 450F / gas 7 and bake for a further 15 minutes until golden brown.

PREPARATION TIME 10-15 MINUTES

COOKING TIME 25 MINUTES

INGREDIENTS

60g / 2 oz / ¼ cup strong plain (bread) flour
Pinch salt
150ml / 5 fl. oz / ⅔ cup cold water
50g / 1 ¾ oz / ¼ cup butter, cubed
2 eggs, beaten
1 tbsp dried herbs

Pesto Choux Rolls   935

- Stir 1-2 tbsp pesto into the pastry.

MAKES 8

Vegetable Empanada

- Preheat the oven to 200°C (180° fan) / 400F / gas 6.
- Cook the potatoes in boiling salted water for 5 minutes with the carrots, then add the broccoli and cook for a further 2 minutes. Drain thoroughly.
- Tip into a bowl and lightly mash. Cook the onion in oil in a pan until translucent then add to the crushed vegetables with the peas. Season and add the spices.
- Roll the pastry out onto a lightly floured surface to about 1cm thickness and cut out eight circles.
- Spread a small spoonful of the vegetable mixture into the centre of each circle, leaving a 1cm border around the edge. Brush the edges with a little beaten egg and fold the pastry over to enclose the filling.
- Using a fork, crimp the edges of the pastry together to seal the filling in and brush the parcels with beaten egg.
- Bake in the oven on a greased baking sheet for 10 minutes, then lower the oven temperature to 180°C and cook for another 10 minutes.

PREPARATION TIME 30-40 MINUTES

COOKING TIME 20 MINUTES

INGREDIENTS

1 x 500g pack puff pastry
1 egg, beaten

FOR THE FILLING

500g / 1 lb / 2 cups floury potatoes, peeled and cubed
2 carrots, peeled and diced
1 head broccoli, divided into florets
1 tbsp olive oil
1 onion, peeled and finely chopped
2 tbsp frozen peas
Salt and pepper
Pinch Cayenne pepper
1 tsp curry powder

Vegetable Empanada with Cheese   937

- Top the vegetables with a good melting cheese such as gruyere or fontina.

BREADS

938

SERVES 8

Sultana Brioche

- Lightly grease a 23x13x7cm loaf tin. Warm the milk with 3 tbsp water, add the egg and whisk.
- Place the flours, salt, sugar and yeast in a food processor and mix, then add the butter a little at a time and pulse to cut the butter into the flour – Don't let it become breadcrumbs.
- Tip the flour-butter mixture into a bowl, make a well in the centre and add the milk and egg and the sultanas and fold together with a fork. It needn't be completely smooth.
- Pour into the loaf tin, cover with cling film and leave to prove in a wam draught-free place for 1 hour. Preheat the oven to 200°C (180° fan) / 400F / Gas 7.
- Remove the clingfilm and bake for about 30 minutes or until risen and golden. Leave to cool before eating.

PREPARATION TIME 4 HOURS

COOKING TIME 30 MINUTES

INGREDIENTS

125ml / 4 fl oz / ½ cup milk
1 egg at room temperature
160g / 5 oz / ⅔ cup plain
(all purpose) flour
160g / 5 oz / ⅔ cup strong white
bread flour
1 tsp salt
1 ½ tbsp sugar
1 x 7g sachet easy-blend dried yeast
200g / 7 oz / ¾ cup unsalted butter,
chilled and cubed
4-5 tbsp sultanas

939

MAKES 12

Bread Rolls

PREPARATION TIME 2 HOURS

COOKING TIME 10 MINUTES

INGREDIENTS

450g / 1 lb / 2 cups strong white
bread flour
2 tbsp butter
1 tsp sugar
1 tsp salt
1 ¼ tsp fast action dried yeast
275ml / 9 ½ fl. oz / 1 cup warm water
1 egg yolk, beaten

- Place the flour in a bowl and rub in the butter using the pads of your fingertips until the mixture resembles breadcrumbs.
- Stir in the sugar, salt and yeast and enough water to make a soft, smooth dough.
- Turn out onto a floured surface and knead for 5 minutes until smooth and elastic. Return to the bowl, cover with clingfilm and leave in a warm place to rise for 1 hour or until doubled in size.
- Tip the dough back out onto the surface and knead, then cut into 12 equal pieces. Shape into smooth balls with any seams tucked underneath and place on greased baking sheets, cover loosely and leave to rise for 30 minutes.
- Preheat the oven to 200°C (180° fan) / 400F / gas 6.
- Brush with beaten egg, spray the tray lightly with water and bake for 10 minutes until golden and they sound hollow when tapped. Transfer to a wire rack to cool.

940

MAKES 12

Sesame Seed Rolls

PREPARATION TIME 2 HOURS

COOKING TIME 10 MINUTES

INGREDIENTS

450g / 1 lb / 2 cups strong white
bread flour
2 tbsp butter
1 tsp sugar
1 tsp salt
1 ¼ tsp fast action dried yeast
275ml / 9 ½ fl. oz / 1 cup warm water
1 egg yolk, beaten
3 tbsp sesame seeds

- Place the flour in a bowl and rub in the butter using the pads of your fingertips until the mixture resembles breadcrumbs.
- Stir in the sugar, salt and yeast and enough water to make a soft, smooth dough.
- Turn out onto a floured surface and knead for 5 minutes until smooth and elastic. Return to the bowl, cover with clingfilm and leave in a warm place to rise for 1 hour or until doubled in size.
- Tip the dough back out onto the surface and knead, then cut into 12 equal pieces. Shape into smooth balls with any seams tucked underneath and place on greased baking sheets, cover loosely and leave to rise for 30 minutes.
- Preheat the oven to 200°C (180° fan) / 400F / gas 6.
- Brush with beaten egg, sprinkle over the sesame seeds, spray the tray lightly with water and bake for 10 minutes until golden and they sound hollow when tapped. Transfer to a wire rack to cool.

941

MAKES 2

Rosemary Focaccia

PREPARATION TIME 40 MINUTES
+ 2 HOURS PROVING TIME

COOKING TIME 20 MINUTES

....

INGREDIENTS

750g / 1 ¼ lb / 3 cups '00' flour
½ tsp salt
2 tsp fast-action dried yeast
150ml / 5 fl. oz / ⅔ cup extra virgin olive oil
450ml / 1 pint / 2 cups lukewarm water
Coarse sea salt
1 bunch rosemary leaves

- Sift the flour and salt into a bowl and make a well in the centre. Pour 50ml of the oil into the flour, add the yeast and rub together with your fingers until the mixture resembles breadcrumbs. Pour in about 400ml of the water and mix until the dough comes together. You may need a little more water.
- Tip the dough onto a floured surface and knead for about 10 minutes until smooth and elastic, pushing the dough away from you with the heel of your hand. The dough will be very soft.
- Place in a lightly oiled bowl, cover with clingfilm and leave to rise in a warm, draught-free place until doubled in size – about 1 ½ hours.
- Take the dough out of the bowl, punch out the air and divide in to two balls. Roll into 2 x 25 cm circles and place in 2 lightly oiled cake tins or pizza pans. Cover with clingfilm again and leave to rise for 30 minutes. Preheat the oven to 200°C (180° fan) / 400F / gas 6.
- Uncover the dough and push your fingertips in at regular intervals to make deep dimples. Drizzle generously with oil so that the dimples almost fill up. Top with sprigs of rosemary. Sprinkle with a generous amount of salt. Spray with a little water and bake for about 20 minutes or until risen and golden.

942

SERVES 10

Wholemeal Bread

PREPARATION TIME 2 HOURS

COOKING TIME 25 MINUTES

....

INGREDIENTS

325g / 11 oz / 1 ⅓ cup strong wholemeal bread flour
2 tsp caster (superfine) sugar
½ tsp salt
2 tsp fast action dried yeast
1 tbsp vegetable oil
200ml / 7 fl. oz / ¾ cup warm water

- Mix the flour, sugar, salt and yeast in a bowl, add the oil and gradually add enough water to make a soft dough.
- Knead on a floured surface for 10 minutes until smooth and elastic. Place in a greased 500g / 1lb loaf tin, cover loosely and leave in a warm place for 45 minutes or until the top of the dough reaches the top of the tin.
- Preheat the oven to 200°C (180° fan) / 400F / gas 6.
- Remove the covering and bake for 25 minutes or until browned and sounds hollow when tapped.
- Remove from the tin and transfer to a wire rack to cool.

Wholemeal and Cheese Bread Loaf

943

- Sprinkle 2 tbsp of Parmesan cheese over the top to create a golden cheesy crust.

Wholemeal Hazelnut Bread

944

- add 100g chopped hazelnuts to the mix.

945

SERVES 10

White Loaf

White Loaf with Fennel Seeds

946

- Add 2 tbsp fennel seeds to the mix.

Herby White Loaf

947

- Add 1 tbsp mixed dried herbs.

Pesto White Loaf

948

- Add 2 tbsp pesto to the mix.

PREPARATION TIME 2 HOURS

COOKING TIME 25 MINUTES

INGREDIENTS

300g / 10 oz / 1 ¼ cups strong white bread flour
1 tbsp butter
1 tsp sugar
½ tsp salt
1 tsp fast action dried yeast
175ml / 6 fl. oz / ¾ cup warm water

- Tip the flour in a bowl, add the butter and rub in using the pads of your fingertips until it resembles breadcrumbs. Stir in the sugar, salt and yeast. Gradually add enough water to make a soft dough.
- Knead on a floured surface for 5 minutes until smooth and elastic. Place in a greased 500g / 1lb loaf tin, cover loosely and leave in a warm place for 30 minutes or until the top of the dough reaches the top of the tin.
- Preheat the oven to 200°C (180° fan) / 400F / gas 6.
- Remove the covering and bake for 25 minutes or until browned and sounds hollow when tapped.
- Remove from the tin and transfer to a wire rack to cool.

949
SERVES 10

Hazelnut & Walnut Bread

PREPARATION TIME 2 HOURS

COOKING TIME 25 MINUTES

....

INGREDIENTS

475g / 16 oz / 2 cup malthouse flour
1 tbsp soft brown sugar
1 ½ tsp salt
1 ½ tsp fast action dried yeast
2 tbsp vegetable oil
325ml / 11 fl. oz / 1 ⅓ cup warm water
200g / 7 oz / 3.4 cup mixed hazelnuts (cob nuts) and walnuts, chopped

- Mix the flour, sugar, salt and yeast in a bowl, add the oil and stir in enough water to make a smooth dough.
- Knead on a floured surface for 5 minutes until smooth and elastic. Work in the walnuts and hazelnuts, then return to the bowl. Cover loosely and leave in a warm place to rise for 1 hour or until doubled in size.
- Tip onto a floured surface, knead well for 5 minutes then shape into an oval loaf.
- Transfer to a greased baking sheet and make deep slashes in the top. Cover loosely and leave to rise for 30 minutes or until half as big again.
- Preheat the oven to 200°C (180° fan) / 400F / gas 6.
- Sprinkle with a little extra flour, lightly spray with water and bake for 25 minutes or until browned and the bread sounds hollow when tapped. Transfer to a wire rack to cool.

Hazelnut and Walnut Bread with Sultanas   950

- Add 60g sultanas to the mix.

951
SERVES 10

Rye Bread

PREPARATION TIME 2 HOURS

COOKING TIME 25 MINUTES

....

INGREDIENTS

275g / 9 ½ oz / 1 cup rye flour
200g / 7 oz / ¾ cup strong white bread flour
2 tsp caraway seeds, lightly crushed
1 ½ tsp salt
1 ½ tsp fast action dried yeast
2 tbsp soft brown sugar
2 tbsp vegetable oil
350ml / 12 fl. oz / 1 ½ cups warm water

- Place the flours in a bowl and stir in the caraway seeds, salt and yeast with the sugar. Stir in the oil and gradually add enough water to make a dough.
- Knead on a floured surface for 5 minutes until smooth and elastic, then return to the bowl. Cover loosely and leave in a warm place to rise for 1 hour or until doubled in size.
- Tip onto a floured surface, knead well for 5 minutes then shape into an round loaf.
- Transfer to a greased baking sheet and make deep slashes in the top. Cover loosely and leave to rise for 30 minutes or until half as big again.
- Preheat the oven to 200°C (180° fan) / 400F / gas 6.
- Sprinkle with a little extra flour, lightly spray with water and bake for 25 minutes or until browned and the bread sounds hollow when tapped. Transfer to a wire rack to cool.

Pumpkin Rye Bread   952

- Add 1 tbsp of pumpkin seeds to the top of the loaf before baking.

953

MAKES 16 # Pretzels

- Place the flours in a bowl, then stir in the sugar, salt and yeast. Gradually mix in enough water to make a dough.
- Knead on a floured surface for 5 minutes until smooth and elastic, then return to the bowl. Cover loosely and leave in a warm place to rise for 1 hour.
- Tip the dough out on to a floured surface and knead well. Divide into 16 equal pieces. Roll each piece into a thin sausage about 30cm / 12 in long. Shape to form a rainbow, then twist the ends of the rainbow together in the centre and press the ends to seal.
- Transfer to a greased baking sheet and cover loosely. Leave to rise for 30 minutes or until half as big again.
- Preheat the oven to 200°C (180° fan) / 400F / gas 6. Bake the pretzels for 10 minutes or until browned.
- Meanwhile warm the salt and water in a small pan and stir until dissolved. Brush over the baked pretzels and sprinkle over the sea salt.

PREPARATION TIME 2 HOURS

COOKING TIME 10 MINUTES

INGREDIENTS

325g / 11 oz / 1 ½ cups strong white bread flour
75g / 2 ½ oz / ⅓ cup rye flour
2 tsp soft light brown sugar
1 tsp salt
1 tsp fast action dried yeast
275ml / 9 ½ fl. oz / 1 cup warm water
3 tsp fine salt
3 tbsp water
Sea salt

Sweet Pretzels   954

- Sprinkle with granulated sugar rather than salt.

955

SERVES 8 # Poppy Seed Milk Bread

- Mix together the flour, yeast, sugar and salt in a bowl, then stir in the milk gradually with the butter and honey to make a smooth soft dough.
- Turn onto a floured surface and knead for 10 minutes until smooth and elastic.
- Shape the dough into a long oval – you could twist it along its length if desired – and place on a greased baking sheet. Cover loosely and leave to rise for 1 hour or until doubled in size.
- Preheat the oven to 220°C (200° fan) / 450F / gas 8.
- Brush the loaf with a little extra milk and scatter with poppy seeds. Bake for 25-30 minutes or until golden and sounds hollow when tapped.

PREPARATION TIME 2 HOURS

COOKING TIME 25-30 MINUTES

INGREDIENTS

500g / 1 lb / 2 cups strong white bread flour
1 ½ tsp fast action dried yeast
1 tbsp honey
1 tbsp butter
1 tsp salt
350ml / 12 fl. oz / 1 ½ cups warm milk
4 tbsp poppy seeds

Fennel Seed Milk Bread   956

- The same amount of fennel seeds offer an aniseedy taste.

957

SERVES 10

Stollen

Citrus Stollen 958
- Add zest of 1 orange as well as the lemon.

Almond Stollen 959
- Add 2 tbsp flaked almonds to the mix.

Rum Stollen 960
- Add 4 tbsp rum to the mix.

PREPARATION TIME 2 HOURS

COOKING TIME 30 MINUTES

···

INGREDIENTS

120g / 4 oz / ½ cup mixed dried fruit
4 tbsp rum
500g / 1lb / 2 cups strong white bread flour
½ tsp salt
120g / 4 oz / ½ cup caster (superfine) sugar
½ tsp grated nutmeg
½ tsp ground cardamom
½ tsp ground cinnamon
Zest of 1 lemon
2 tbsp sultanas
2 tbsp almonds, finely chopped
1 ½ tsp fast action dried yeast
175g / 6 oz / ¾ cup butter
1 egg, beaten
175ml / 6 fl. oz / ¾ cup warm milk
250g / 9 oz / 1 cup marzipan
1 tbsp butter, melted
1 tbsp icing (confectioners') sugar

- Place the dried fruits and candied peel in a bowl with the rum and leave to soak overnight.
- Place the flour in a bowl with the salt, sugar, spices, lemon zest, sultanas, almonds and yeast. Add 2 tbsp of melted butter and the egg and whisk in enough milk to make a soft dough.
- Knead for 5 minutes until smooth and elastic. Return to the bowl, cover loosely and leave to rise in a warm place for 1 hour or until doubled in size.
- Knead the dough well, then cut the remaining butter into pieces and knead a little at a time into the dough along with the dried fruit and peel.
- Wrap in baking parchment and chill for 20 minutes. Roll out on a floured surface to about 15x40cm oval. Shape the marzipan into a sausage approximately the same length and place in the centre of the oval and wrap the dough around the marzipan. Transfer to a greased baking sheet, leave to rise for 30 minutes.
- Preheat the oven to 180°C (160° fan) / 350F / gas 4.
- Bake the stolen for about 30 minutes, then transfer to a wire rack. Brush with butter and sugar and serve warm.

961

SERVES 10

Walnut Bread

- Mix the flour, sugar, salt and yeast in a bowl, add the oil and stir in enough water to make a smooth dough.
- Knead on a floured surface for 5 minutes until smooth and elastic. Work in the walnuts, then return to the bowl. Cover loosely and leave in a warm place to rise for 1 hour or until doubled in size.
- Tip onto a floured surface, knead well for 5 minutes then shape into an oval loaf.
- Transfer to a greased baking sheet and make deep slashes in the top. Cover loosely and leave to rise for 30 minutes or until half as big again.
- Preheat the oven to 200°C (180° fan) / 400F / gas 6.
- Sprinkle with a little extra flour, lightly spray with water and bake for 25 minutes or until browned and the bread sounds hollow when tapped. Transfer to a wire rack to cool.

PREPARATION TIME 2 HOURS

COOKING TIME 25 MINUTES

INGREDIENTS

400g / 14 oz / 1 ½ cup malthouse flour
75g / 2 ½ oz / ⅓ cup granary flour
1 tbsp soft brown sugar
1 ½ tsp salt
1 ½ tsp fast action dried yeast
2 tbsp vegetable oil
325ml / 11 fl. oz / 1 ⅓ cup warm water
200g / 7 oz / ¾ cup walnuts, chopped

Walnut Bread with Cheese

962

- Walnut bread makes the best accompaniment to a cheeseboard.

963

MAKES 3

Ciabatta

- Mix the first amounts of flour with the water in a large bowl and add the yeast. Mix together well for a few minutes, then cover and leave to rise overnight.
- Next day add the next amount of flour and yeast and mix well. Gradually add the water and oil, mixing it together in a food mixer for a few minutes. Then add the salt and mix until you have a very sticky dough.
- Transfer the dough to a large oiled bowl and leave to rise, covered, for one hour.
- Move from the bowl and leave to rest on a floured work surface for 30 minutes.
- Preheat the oven to 240°C (220° fan) / 465F / gas 8.
- Pull the dough into 3 approximate long flat slipper shapes. Place on a lined baking sheet and leave to rest for 10 minutes.
- Bake in the oven for 25 minutes or until risen and golden brown. Transfer to a wire rack to cool.

PREPARATION TIME 9 HOURS
50 MINUTES

COOKING TIME 25 MINUTES

INGREDIENTS

250g / 9 oz / 1 cup '00' flour
190ml / 6 ½ fl. oz / ¾ cup water
15g / ½ oz fresh yeast
250g / 9 oz / 1 cup '00' flour
10g / ½ oz yeast
190ml / 6 ½ fl. oz / ¾ cup water
1 tbsp olive oil
12g / ½ oz salt

Olive Ciabatta

964

- A couple of handfuls chopped stoned olives and ½ tsp dried chilli flakes add punch.

965

SERVES 3-4

Tomato Mozzarella Pizza

PREPARATION TIME 2 HOURS

COOKING TIME 8-10 MINUTES

INGREDIENTS

FOR THE PIZZA DOUGH
400g / 13 ½ oz / 1 ½ cups strong
white bread flour
100g / 3 ½ oz / ½ cup fine ground
semolina flour
½ tbsp salt
1 x 7g sachet dried yeast
½ tbsp caster (superfine) sugar
350ml / ½ pint / ⅓ cup lukewarm
water

FOR THE TOPPING: PER PIZZA
6 tbsp passata
150g / 5 oz / ⅔ cup cherry tomatoes,
halved
1 clove garlic, finely chopped
½ ball mozzarella, sliced
1 tsp dried oregano
Extra virgin olive oil
Black pepper

- Pour the flour(s) and salt into a bowl and make a well in the centre. Add the yeast and sugar to the water, mix with a fork. When frothing, pour into the well. Using a fork in a circular movement, slowly bring in the flour from around the insides and mix into the water.
- When it starts to come together, use your hands and pat it into a ball.
- Knead the dough by pushing it away from you with the heel of your hand for around 10 minutes until the dough is smooth and elastic. Flour the dough, cover with clingfilm and leave to rest for 30 minutes.
- Roll the pizzas out about 30 minutes before you want to cook them. Preheat the oven to 250°C (230° fan) / 500F / gas 9. Flour the surface, tear off a piece of dough and roll into a rough circle about 0.5cm thick.
- Spread the base of each pizza with the passata, then with tomatoes. Scatter over the garlic and oregano, then lay over the mozzarella.
- Place either directly on the bars of the oven or on a preheated baking sheet for 8-10 minutes until golden and crisp. Drizzle with extra virgin olive oil, grind over some pepper and serve hot.

966

SERVES 4

Garlic Parsley Bread

PREPARATION TIME 10 MINUTES

COOKING TIME 25 MINUTES

INGREDIENTS

1 large baguette
250g / 9 oz / 1 cup butter, softened
3-4 cloves garlic, crushed
1 bunch parsley, chopped
Salt and pepper
Squeeze of lemon juice

- Preheat the oven to 180°C (160° fan) / 350F / gas 4.
- Make deep slashes along the length of the baguette about 2-3cm apart.
- Mix the softened butter with the rest of the ingredients, mashing well to combine.
- Liberally spread the inside of the slashes with the garlic butter. Any leftover can be spread along the top of the loaf.
- Wrap in foil and bake for about 20 minutes. Open the foil and bake for a further 5 minutes to crisp the top of the baguette.

Garlic Bread with Cheese ## 967

- Add thinly sliced mozzarella inbetween all of the slashes in the loaf.

Garlic Bread with Parmesan ## 968

- Add 4 tbsp grated Parmesan to the butter.

969
MAKES 6-8 Naan Bread

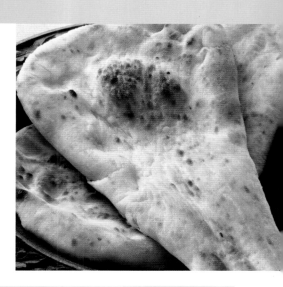

- Sieve the flour, sugar, salt and baking powder into a large bowl. Whisk the milk and oil together, make a well in the centre and pour in almost all the liquid, reserving a tbsp or two.
- Working from the centre outwards, mix the dough together, bringing in the flour round the edges bit by bit to form a smooth dough.
- Place in a greased bowl, cover with a damp tea towel and leave in a warm, draught-free place for 1 hour.
- When risen, punch the air out of the dough and form into 6-8 even-sized balls, depending on how large you want your naan to be.
- Preheat your grill to its highest setting. Place a heavy baking sheet on the shelf.
- Pull the dough into oval or teardrop shapes with your fingers, then grill for 2 minutes. Brush with melted butter before serving warm.

PREPARATION TIME 2 HOURS

COOKING TIME 2 MINUTES

INGREDIENTS

250g / 9 oz / 1 cup plain (all purpose) flour
2 tsp sugar
½ tsp salt
½ tsp baking powder
120ml / 4 fl. oz / ½ cup milk
2 tbsp vegetable oil

TOPPINGS

Nigella or black onion seeds
Poppy seeds
Chopped garlic

Sesame Seed Breadsticks

970
MAKES 20-24

PREPARATION TIME 2 HOURS

COOKING TIME 15-20 MINUTES

INGREDIENTS

450g / 1 lb / 2 cups strong white bread flour
1 x 7g sachet dried yeast
1 ½ tsp salt

250ml / 9 fl. oz / 1 cup lukewarm water
Olive oil
2 tbsp sesame seeds

- Place the flour, yeast and salt in a bowl, then add the water a little at a time to form a dough.
- Bring the dough together with your hands and knead well for 10 minutes until smooth and elastic.
- Divide the mixture into about 20 equal portions then roll into sausage shapes. ou can leave them like this or twist them like barley sugar.
- Place well-spaced on floured baking sheets, cover with a damp tea towel and leave in a warm place for 30 minutes.
- Preheat the oven to 200°C (180° fan) / 400F / gas 7.
- Brush with the olive oil and sprinkle with sesame seeds, then bake for about 15-20 minutes or until cooked.

Brioche

971
MAKES 2

PREPARATION TIME 2 HOURS +
OVERNIGHT CHILLING

COOKING TIME 35 MINUTES

INGREDIENTS

2 tbsp milk
2 ½ tsp fast action dried yeast
400g / 14 oz / 1 ½ cup strong white

bread flour
4 eggs + 3 yolks
2 tbsp caster (superfine) sugar
1 tsp salt
250g / 9 oz / 1 cup butter, softened

- The day before, heat the milk to boiling, then pour into a measuring jug and leave until warm. Top up with warm water to 50ml, then stir in the yeast. Add 2 tbsp of flour, cover and leave for 30 minutes.
- Once bubbling, beat the eggs, yolks, sugar and salt together in a bowl then pour in the yeast. Add the remaining flour and stir to a rough dough. Cover and leave for 30 minutes. Add the butter a little at a time. When all the butter is incorporated, tip onto a floured surface and knead until smooth and elastic. Place back in the bowl, cover and chill overnight.
- Grease two 2lb loaf tins, divide the dough in half and shape each half into a rough loaf shape. Place in the tins, tucking them seam side down and leave for 2 hours.
- Preheat the oven to 200°C (180° fan) / 400F / gas 6. Brush the tops with beaten egg and bake for 15 minutes. Reduce the heat to 180°C (160° fan) / 350F / gas 4 and bake for 20 minutes until golden brown. Remove from the tins and cool on a wire rack.

972

SERVES 6

Honey Gingerbread

PREPARATION TIME 20 MINUTES

COOKING TIME 45 MINUTES

INGREDIENTS

250g / 9 oz / 1 cup self-raising flour
1 tsp baking powder
½ tsp bicarbonate of soda
½ tsp ground ginger
½ tsp mixed spice
75g / 2 ½ oz / ⅓ cup honey
75g / 2 ½ oz / ⅓ cup unsalted butter, melted
200ml / 7 fl. oz / ¾ cup milk
1 egg
2-3 tbsp stem ginger, finely chopped

- Preheat the oven to 200°C (180° fan) / 400F / gas 6. Grease and line a loaf tin.
- In one bowl combine the dry ingredients.
- Pour the milk in to a measuring jug and crack in the egg and whisk with a fork to amalgamate.
- Pour the liquid ingredients into the dry ingredients, stirring with a wooden spoon. The batter should remain somewhat lumpy – do not whisk until smooth. Add the stem ginger to the batter and stir in.
- Pour into the loaf tin and bake in the oven for about 45 minutes or until an inserted skewer comes out clean.
- Remove to a wire rack and allow to cool.

Gingerbread with Mascarpone

 973

- Serve with mascarpone whisked with a little orange zest and juice.

974

MAKES 2

Sesame Brioche Bread

PREPARATION TIME 2 HOURS + OVERNIGHT CHILLING

COOKING TIME 35 MINUTES

INGREDIENTS

2 tbsp milk
2 ½ tsp fast action dried yeast
400g / 14 oz / 1 ½ cup strong white bread flour
4 eggs + 3 yolks
2 tbsp caster (superfine) sugar
1 tsp salt
250g / 9 oz / 1 cup butter, softened
2 tbsp sesame seeds
1 egg, beaten

- The day before, heat the milk to boiling, then pour into a measuring jug and leave until warm. Top up with warm water to 50ml, then stir in the yeast. Add 2 tbsp of flour, cover and leave for 30 minutes.
- Once bubbling, beat the eggs, yolks, sugar and salt together in a bowl then pour in the yeast. Add the flour and stir to a dough. Cover and leave for 30 minutes.
- Add the butter a little at a time. When all the butter is blended, tip onto a floured surface and knead.
- Place back in the bowl, cover and chill overnight.
- Divide the dough in half and shape into figures of eight. Place on a greased baking sheet. Leave for 2 hours.
- Preheat the oven to 200°C (180° fan) / 400F / gas 6. Brush the tops with beaten egg and sesame seeds and bake for 15 minutes. Reduce the heat to 180°C (160° fan) / 350F / gas 4 and bake for 20 minutes until golden brown. Remove from the tins and cool on a wire rack.

Poppyseed Brioche Bread

975

- Use poppyseeds instead of the sesame.

976

SERVES 10 # Granary Bread

- Tip the flour in a bowl, add the butter and rub in using the pads of your fingertips until it resembles breadcrumbs. Stir in the sugar, salt and yeast. Gradually add enough water to make a soft dough.
- Knead on a floured surface for 5 minutes until smooth and elastic. Place in a greased 500g / 1lb loaf tin, cover loosely and leave in a warm place for 30 minutes or until the top of the dough reaches the top of the tin.
- Sprinkle the top with oats and seeds.
- Preheat the oven to 200°C (180° fan) / 400F / gas 6.
- Remove the covering and bake for 25 minutes or until browned and sounds hollow when tapped.
- Remove from the tin and transfer to a wire rack to cool.

PREPARATION TIME 2 HOURS

COOKING TIME 25 MINUTES

INGREDIENTS

300g / 10 oz / 1 ¼ cups granary flour
1 tbsp butter
2 tsp soft brown sugar
½ tsp salt
1 tsp fast action dried yeast
175ml / 6 fl. oz / ¾ cup warm water
Oats and seeds for decoration

Light Granary Loaf   977

- Use half granary, half strong white bread flour for a less dense loaf.

978

MAKES 3 # Ciabatta

- Mix the first amounts of flour with the water in a large bowl and add the yeast. Mix together well for a few minutes, then cover and leave to rise overnight.
- Next day add the next amount of flour and yeast and mix well. Gradually add the water and oil, mixing it together. Then add the salt and mix.
- Transfer the dough to a large oiled bowl and leave to rise, covered, for one hour.
- Move from the bowl and leave to rest on a floured work surface for 30 minutes.
- Preheat the oven to 240°C (220° fan) / 465F / gas 8.
- Pull the dough into 3 approximate long flat slipper shapes. Place on a lined baking sheet and leave to rest for 10 minutes.
- Bake in the oven for 25 minutes or until risen and golden brown. Transfer to a wire rack to cool.

PREPARATION TIME 9 HOURS
50 MINUTES

COOKING TIME 25 MINUTES

INGREDIENTS

250g / 9 oz / 1 cup '00' flour
190ml / 6 ½ fl. oz / ¾ cup water
15g / ½ oz fresh yeast
250g / 9 oz / 1 cup '00' flour
10g / ½ oz yeast
190ml / 6 ½ fl. oz / ¾ cup water
1 tbsp olive oil
12g / ½ oz salt

Rosemary Ciabatta   979

- Add 2 tbsp finely chopped rosemary leaves to the mix.

980

MAKES 3

Olive Ciabatta

PREPARATION TIME 9 HOURS
50 MINUTES

COOKING TIME 25 MINUTES

INGREDIENTS

250g / 9 oz / 1 cup '00' flour
190ml / 6 ½ fl. oz / ¾ cup water
15g / ½ oz fresh yeast
250g / 9 oz / 1 cup '00' flour
10g / ½ oz yeast
190ml / 6 ½ fl. oz / ¾ cup water
1 tbsp olive oil
12g / ½ oz salt
100g / 3 ½ oz / ½ cup mixed green
and black olives, stoned and halved

- Mix the first amounts of flour with the water in a large bowl and add the yeast. Mix together well for a few minutes, then cover and leave to rise overnight.
- Next day add the next amount of flour and yeast and mix well. Gradually add the water and oil, mixing it together. Add the salt and mix. Work in the olives.
- Transfer the dough to a large oiled bowl and leave to rise, covered, for one hour.
- Move from the bowl and leave to rest on a floured work surface for 30 minutes.
- Preheat the oven to 240°C (220° fan) / 465F / gas 8.
- Pull the dough into 3 approximate triangles. Place on a lined baking sheet and leave to rest for 10 minutes.
- Bake in the oven for 25 minutes or until risen and golden brown.

Olive and Anchovy Ciabatta   981

- Add a few very finely chopped anchovies to the mix.

982

MAKES 10

Bagels

PREPARATION TIME 3 HOURS

COOKING TIME 12-15 MINUTES

INGREDIENTS

500g / 1 lb / 2 cups strong white
bread flour
2 tbsp caster (superfine) sugar
1 tsp salt
1 ¼ tsp fast action dried yeast
300ml / 10 fl. oz / 1 ¼ cups warm
water
1 egg yolk, beaten

- Place the flour, half the sugar, salt and yeast in a large bowl. Mix in enough water to make a dough.
- Knead on a floured surface for 5 minutes, then return to the bowl. Cover loosely and leave in a warm place for 1 hour.
- Tip the dough onto a floured surface and knead then cut into 10 equal places. Roll each piece into a ball, then make a hole in the centre with your finger.
- Transfer to lined baking sheets, cover loosely and leave to rise for 30 minutes or until half as big again.
- Preheat the oven to 200°C (180° fan) / 400F / gas 6.
- Bring 2L / 3 ½ pints water to the boil in a pan with the remaining sugar. Lower the bagels into the water one at a time and cook until they float – 2-3 minutes. Remove with a slotted spoon and drain on kitchen paper.
- Transfer back to the baking sheets, brush with egg and bake for 12-15 minutes until golden brown.

Sesame Seed Bagels   983

- Brush with vegetable oil and scatter with sesame seeds.

984

MAKES 16

Individual Brioches

Brioche with Poached Fruit

985

- Serve for breakfast alongside poached fruit.

Brioche with Caramelised Apples

986

- Serve with apples sautéed in butter and sugar.

Cinnamon Brioche

987

- Add 1 tsp ground cinnamon to the mix.

PREPARATION TIME 2 HOURS + OVERNIGHT CHILLINGS

COOKING TIME 15-20 MINUTES

INGREDIENTS

2 tbsp milk

2 ½ tsp fast action dried yeast

400g / 14 oz / 1 ½ cup strong white bread flour

4 eggs + 3 yolks

2 tbsp caster (superfine) sugar

1 tsp salt

250g / 9 oz / 1 cup butter, softened

- The day before, heat the milk to boiling, then pour into a measuring jug and leave until warm. Top up with warm water to 50ml, then stir in the yeast. Add 2 tbsp of flour to the yeast, stir well, cover and leave for 30 minutes.
- Once bubbling, beat the eggs, yolks, sugar and salt together in a bowl then pour in the yeast. Add the remaining flour and stir to a rough dough. Cover at this point and leave for 30 minutes.
- Preferably using a dough hook, tip the dough into a mixing bowl and add the butter a little at a time as it mixes. When all the butter is incorporated, tip onto a floured surface and knead until smooth and elastic.
- Place back in the bowl, cover and chill overnight.
- Cut off 16 tiny pieces of dough to make the tops. Cut the rest into 16 larger pieces. Shape each into a small ball and transfer to greased brioche tins.
- Shape the tiny dough pieces into balls and place on top. Leave for 2 hours until doubled in height.
- Preheat the oven to 200°C (180° fan) / 400F / gas 6. Brush the tops with beaten egg and bake for 10 minutes. Reduce the heat to 180°C (160° fan) / 350F / gas 4 and bake for 5-10 minutes until golden brown. Remove from the tins and cool on a wire rack.

Dried Sausage Ciabatta

Bacon Ciabatta 989

- Add the same quantity of cooked smoked bacon lardons.

Blue Cheese Ciabatta 990

- Add small cubes of blue cheese to the mix.

Fontina Ciabatta 991

- Fontina is a good melting cheese so add in small cubes.

PREPARATION TIME 9 HOURS 50 MINUTES

COOKING TIME 25 MINUTES

....

INGREDIENTS

250g / 9 oz / 1 cup '00' flour
190ml / 6 ½ fl. oz / ¾ cup water
15g / ½ oz fresh yeast
250g / 9 oz / 1 cup '00' flour
10g / ½ oz yeast
190ml / 6 ½ fl. oz / ¾ cup water
1 tbsp olive oil
12g / ½ oz salt
100g / 3 ½ oz / ½ cup chorizo or
salami sausage, finely diced

- Mix the first amounts of flour with the water in a large bowl and add the yeast. Mix together well for a few minutes, then cover and leave to rise overnight.
- Next day add the next amount of flour and yeast and mix well. Gradually add the water and oil, mixing it together in a food mixer for a few minutes. Then add the salt and mix until you have a very sticky dough. Stir in the diced sausage.
- Transfer the dough to a large oiled bowl and leave to rise, covered, for one hour.
- Move from the bowl and leave to rest on a floured work surface for 30 minutes.
- Preheat the oven to 240°C (220° fan) / 465F / gas 8.
- Pull the dough into 3 approximate long flat slipper shapes. Place on a lined baking sheet and leave to rest for 10 minutes.
- Bake in the oven for 25 minutes or until risen and golden brown. Transfer to a wire rack to cool.

SERVES 10 Apple Bread

992

- Mix the flour, salt, sugar, spices and yeast in a bowl. Add the oil then gradually mix in enough water to make a soft dough.
- Knead on a floured surface for 5 minutes until smooth and elastic. Work in the apples. Tip back into the bowl, cover loosely and leave in a warm place to rise for 1 hour or until doubled in size.
- Place in a greased 500g / 1lb loaf tin, cover loosely and leave in a warm place for 30 minutes or until the top of the dough reaches the top of the tin.
- Preheat the oven to 200°C (180° fan) / 400F / gas 6.
- Remove the covering and bake for 30 minutes or until browned and sounds hollow when tapped.
- Remove from the tin and transfer to a wire rack to cool.

Spiced Apple Bread

993

- Add a pinch of mixed spice to up the flavour.

PREPARATION TIME 2 HOURS

COOKING TIME 30 MINUTES

INGREDIENTS

450g / 15 oz / 1 ½ cups strong white bread flour
1 ½ tsp salt
2 tsp caster (superfine) sugar
1 tsp ground cinnamon
Pinch ground cloves (optional)
1 tbsp honey
1 ¼ tsp fast action dried yeast
2 tbsp vegetable oil
275ml / 10 fl. oz / 1 cup warm water
100g / 3 ½ oz / ½ cup apples, peeled, cored and finely chopped

SERVES 4 Candied Fruit Loaf

994

- Preheat the oven to 140°C (120° fan) / 275F / gas 1.
- Combine the dried fruit and peel in a bowl with the orange juice. Soak for 2 hours.
- Combine the flour, baking powder, spices, then add the butter, sugar, eggs and honey with the orange zest. Stir until thoroughly combined, then mix in the dried fruits.
- Tip into a floured loaf tin and bake for 90 minutes.
- Leave to cool for 1 hour before removing from the tin. Transfer to a wire rack and cool completely.

Candied Fruit Loaf with Jam and Butter

995

- Serve spread with butter and jam alongside tea.

PREPARATION TIME 2 ½ HOURS

COOKING TIME 90 MINUTES

INGREDIENTS

2 tbsp dried apricots, chopped
2 tbsp dates, chopped
2 tbsp prunes, chopped
2 tbsp candied cherries, chopped
1 tbsp mixed candied peel
2 tbsp sultanas
Zest and juice of 1 orange
450g / 1 lb / 2 cups plain (all purpose) flour
2 tsp baking powder
1 tsp mixed spice
½ tsp ground cinnamon
200g / 7 oz / ¾ cup butter, softened
200g / 7 oz / ¾ cup sugar
6 eggs
100g / 3 ½ oz / ½ cup honey

996

SERVES 10

Tomato Bread

PREPARATION TIME 2 HOURS

COOKING TIME 30 MINUTES

....

INGREDIENTS

450g / 15 oz / 1 ½ cups strong white
bread flour
1 ½ tsp salt
2 tsp caster (superfine) sugar
1 ¼ tsp fast action dried yeast
2 tbsp olive oil
275ml / 10 fl. oz / 1 cup warm water
100g / 3 ½ oz / ½ cup semi-dried
tomatoes, finely sliced

- Mix the flour, salt, sugar and yeast in a bowl. Add the oil then gradually mix in enough water to make a soft dough.
- Knead on a floured surface for 5 minutes until smooth and elastic. Work in the tomatoes. Tip back into the bowl, cover loosely and leave in a warm place to rise for 1 hour or until doubled in size.
- Place in a greased 500g / 1lb loaf tin, cover loosely and leave in a warm place for 30 minutes or until the top of the dough reaches the top of the tin.
- Preheat the oven to 200°C (180° fan) / 400F / gas 6.
- Remove the covering and bake for 30 minutes or until browned and sounds hollow when tapped.
- Remove from the tin and transfer to a wire rack to cool.

Tomato Olive Bread   997
- A handful of chopped black olives adds punch.

998

MAKES 12

Pitta Bread

PREPARATION TIME 2 HOURS

COOKING TIME 35 MINUTES

....

INGREDIENTS

500g / 1 lb / 2 cups strong white
bread flour
1 tsp salt
1 tsp fast action dried yeast
1 tbsp butter
300ml / 10 fl. oz / 1 ¼ cups warm
water

- Place the flour in a bowl with the salt and yeast, add the butter and water and mix to bring it together.
- Place on a floured surface and knead for 5 minutes until smooth and elastic. Return to the bowl, cover loosely and leave to rise in a warm place for 1 hour or until doubled in size.
- Tip onto a floured surface, knead for 5 minutes, then tear into 12 equal pieces. Roll them into a ball, then flatten into a round shape about 15cm wide. Place on a baking sheet and leave in a warm place for 15 minutes.
- Heat a heavy based frying pan over a medium heat and warm a little oil. Add the flatbreads, one or two at a time and cook for 3 minutes. Once blistered and darkened in patches, turn over and cook the other side.
- Split and eat immediately.

Wholemeal Pitta   999
- Use the same quantity of wholemeal flour.

1000

SERVES 4

Chipa Cheese Balls

Chipa Cheese Balls with Blue Cheese

1001

- Use gorgonzola in place of the gruyere and cheddar.

Chipa Cheese Balls with Smoky Bacon

1002

- A little finely chopped cooked smoked bacon complements the cheese.

Herby Chipa Cheese Balls

1003

- Add 1 tbsp finely chopped rosemary leaves to the mix.

PREPARATION TIME 20 MINUTES

COOKING TIME 10-15 MINUTES

INGREDIENTS

480g / 16 oz / 2 cups potato flour
100g / 3 ½ oz / ½ cup butter, cubed
2 eggs, beaten
1 tsp salt
100g / 3 ½ oz / ½ cup mozzarella, finely chopped
100g / 3 ½ oz / ½ cup Gruyère and Cheddar, grated
6 tbsp milk
Salt and pepper

- Preheat oven to 200°C (180° fan) / 400F / gas 6.
- Rub the butter into the flour using the pads of your fingertips until it resembles breadcrumbs.
- Add the seasoning, eggs, cheeses and mix well. Add the milk a little at a time until the dough comes together.
- Roll a tablespoon of dough in oiled hands and shape into a ball. Place on a baking sheet and repeat until all the mixture is used.
- Bake for 10-15 minutes until the cheese oozes and they are golden and risen.

PRESERVES

1004

MAKES 1.5KG /3 LB Strawberry Jam

- Hull the strawberries and wipe clean, then layer them in a preserving pan or large saucepan, sprinkling with sugar. Leave overnight to macerate.
- Place the pan over a low heat to melt the sugar and allow the strawberries to pulp slightly. Try not to stir as this will break the strawberries up – just shake the pan a little.
- When the sugar has completely dissolved, add the lemon juice, increase the heat and when bubbling, cook for 8 minutes then remove from the heat.
- Spoon a little onto a plate. If it wrinkles when you push it with your finger, it's set. If not, cook for 3 minutes, then repeat the test. Continue until the jam is set.
- Allow the jam to settle off the heat for 15 minutes before pouring into sterilised jars. Seal immediately with waxed lids and tie on the lids.

PREPARATION TIME 24 HOURS

COOKING TIME 30 MINUTES

INGREDIENTS

1 kg / 2 lb / 4 cups strawberries, not too ripe and soft
850g / 1 ½ lb / 3 ½ cups sugar
2 lemons, juiced

1005

Raspberry Jam **MAKES 1.5KG /3 LB**

PREPARATION TIME 24 HOURS

COOKING TIME 30 MINUTES

INGREDIENTS

1 kg / 2 lb / 4 cups raspberries, not too ripe and soft
750g / 1 ⅓ lb / 3 cups caster (superfine) sugar
Juice of 1 lemon

- Hull the raspberries and wipe clean, then layer them in a preserving pan or large saucepan, sprinkling with sugar. Leave overnight to macerate.
- Place the pan over a low heat to melt the sugar and allow the raspberries to pulp slightly. Try not to stir as this will break the raspberries up – just shake the pan a little.
- When the sugar has completely dissolved, add the lemon juice, increase the heat and when bubbling, cook for 8 minutes then remove from the heat.
- Spoon a little onto a plate. If it wrinkles when you push it with your finger, it's set. If not, cook for 3 minutes, then repeat the test. Continue until the jam is set.
- Allow the jam to settle off the heat for 15 minutes before pouring into sterilised jars. Seal immediately with waxed lids and tie on the lids.

1006

Lemon Curd **MAKES 200G**

PREPARATION TIME 5 MINUTES

COOKING TIME 20 MINUTES

INGREDIENTS

1 large lemon, grated zest plus juice
75g / 2 ½ oz / ⅓ cup caster (superfine) sugar
2 eggs
50g /1 ¾ oz butter

- Place the zest and sugar in one bowl. Place the juice and eggs in another and whisk together, then pour over the sugar.
- Add the butter, cubed up, and set over a pan of simmering water. Stir constantly until the mixture thickens and starts to look glossy – 18-20 minutes.
- Remove from the heat and cool. Spoon into a sterilised jar before storing.

MAKES 750G / 1 ½ LB # Blackcurrant and Raspberry Jam

PREPARATION TIME 10 MINUTES

COOKING TIME 30-35 MINUTES

INGREDIENTS

450g / 1 lb / 2 cups mixed
blackcurrants and raspberries
450g / 1 lb / 2 cups caster (superfine)
sugar
300ml / 10 fl. oz / 1 ¼ cups water
Juice of 1 lemon

- Discard any stalks and leaves from the fruit and place in a pan over a low heat. Do not stir, just shake the pan as the fruits collapse.
- Add the sugar, stirring very gently so as not to crush the fruit and leave for 15 minutes until the sugar has dissolved completely.
- When the sugar has completely dissolved, add the lemon juice, increase the heat and when bubbling, cook for 10 minutes then remove from the heat.
- Spoon a little onto a plate. If it wrinkles when you push it with your finger, it's set. If not, cook for 5 minutes, then repeat the test. Continue until the jam is set.
- Allow the jam to settle off the heat for 15 minutes before pouring into sterilised jars. Seal immediately with waxed lids and tie on the lids.

Mixed Currant Jam   1008

- Use the same quantity of black, red and white currants.

MAKES 1.5KG / 3 LB # Marmalade

PREPARATION TIME 2 HOURS
45 MINUTES

COOKING TIME 15-45 MINUTES

INGREDIENTS

1 L / 2 pints / 4 cups water
500g / 1 lb Seville oranges
1 lemon
1 kg / 2 lb / 4 cups granulated sugar,
warmed

- Measure the water into a large pan, then cut the oranges and lemon in half. squeeze the juice out, remove any pips and empty the juice into the water.
- Cut the orange peel into very thin shreds with a sharp knife and add to the pan.
- Bring the liquid to simmering point and simmer for about 2 hours or until the peel is completely soft.
- Pour the sugar into the pan and stir over a low heat until the sugar has dissolved. Increase the heat and boil for 15 minutes, then check to see if it has set. Spoon a little onto a plate. If it wrinkles when you push it with your finger, it's set. If not, cook for 10 minutes, then repeat the test. Continue until the jam is set.
- Allow the jam to settle off the heat for 20 minutes before pouring into sterilised jars. Seal immediately with waxed lids and tie on the lids.

Blood Orange Marmalade   1010

- Use blood oranges for a milder fruitier taste.

1011

SERVES 4 # Pears in Vanilla Tea

- Heat 1L / 2 ¼ pints / 4 ¼ cups water in a large pan until simmering. Add the sugar, tea bags, vanilla pod and seeds and the cinnamon stick and simmer for 5 minutes.
- Add the pears and simmer gently for about 20 minutes until tender.
- Remove the pears and tea bags and increase the heat. Reduce the poaching liquid to a syrupy consistency.
- Serve the pears with the syrup spooned over.

PREPARATION TIME 10 MINUTES

COOKING TIME 50 MINUTES

INGREDIENTS

4 ripe pears, fairly firm, peeled
150g / 5 oz / ⅔ cup caster (superfine) sugar
4 earl grey teabags
1 vanilla pod, split
1 stick cinnamon

Pears in Darjeeling Tea　1012

- Replace the Earl Grey tea bags with Darjeeling ones and follow the same method as above.

1013

MAKES 2KG / 4 ½ LB # Pickled Onions with Chilli and Dill

- Pour boiling water into a large bowl and submerge the onions for a minute or two. This will make them easier to peel. Drain, leave until cool enough to handle, then peel.
- Pack 2 x 1L preserving jars or the equivalent half-full with the onions and sprinkle in a little pickling spice, 1 garlic clove, half the chilli and half the dill bunch. Top up with onions and a little more pickling spice.
- Pour the vinegar over the onions right to the top so that they are completely submerged and fix the lids securely.
- Store in a cool dark place for 8 weeks.

PREPARATION TIME 20 MINUTES

INGREDIENTS

1kg / 2 ¼ lb pickling onions
1 tbsp pickling spice
1 red chilli, halved
1 bunch dill
2 cloves garlic, peeled
900ml / 2 pints / 4 cups malt vinegar

Pickled Onions without the Spice　1014

- Leave out the chilli for a more traditional version.

1015

MAKES 250G # Mango Chutney

Mango Lime Chutney
1016
- Add lime segments for added zest.

Mango Apple Chutney
1017
- Add an apple, cut into small cubes, to the mix.

Mango Pineapple Chutney
1018
- Add small cubes of pineapple – not too much – for an even fruitier chutney.

PREPARATION TIME 10 MINUTES

COOKING TIME 2-3 HOURS

....

INGREDIENTS

1 tsp cumin seeds
1 tsp fenugreek seeds
1 tsp mustard seeds
10 black peppercorns
8 cardamom pods
8 cloves
1 onion, peeled and finely sliced
4 slightly under-ripe mangoes, peeled and cut into chunks
4 cloves garlic, crushed
1 red chilli, finely chopped
2 tbsp fresh ginger, grated
350g soft light brown sugar
2 tsp salt
400ml white wine vinegar

- Heat a heavy-based frying pan and dry-fry the whole spices for 2 minutes until the aroma fills the kitchen.
- Add to a preserving pan along with all the other ingredients.
- Bring gently to a simmer, then cook for 2-3 hours until the liquid has almost evaporated and is thick and syrupy.
- Allow to cool then ladle into sterilized jars and seal.
- Label when the jars are completely cold.
- Leave for 8 weeks to mature before serving

1019

MAKES 500G / 1 LB Preserved Mushrooms

- Pour the vinegar into a pan with the salt, bay leaves, cloves, garlic and thyme. Add 150ml / 5 fl. oz / ⅔ cup water and boil.
- Wipe the mushrooms clean, then roughly chop if large. Add to the brine and simmer for 5-10 minutes.
- Remove with a slotted spoon and leave to dry on kitchen paper for at least 2 hours.
- Layer the mushrooms and oil in a sterilised jar until full and all the mushrooms are submerged. Seal the lid tightly and store in a cool dark place for 1 month.

PREPARATION TIME 15 MINUTES

COOKING TIME 10 MINUTES

INGREDIENTS

300ml / 10 fl. oz / 1 ¼ cups white wine vinegar
½ tbsp salt
2 bay leaves
3 cloves
2 cloves garlic, peeled
3 sprigs thyme
500g / 1 lb / 2 cups mixed wild mushrooms
200ml / 7 fl. oz / ¾ cup extra virgin olive oil

Spicy Preserved Mushrooms   1020

- Add a whole red chilli, pricked with a knife, to add spice.

1021

MAKES 2 KG / 4 LB Red Onion & Date Chutney

- Melt the butter in a pan and add the onions. Sprinkle over the sugar, dates, thyme, chilli and seasoning and cook for about 45 minutes until very soft and sticky and dark red.
- Add the wine, vinegar and 100ml water and simmer for about 30 minutes until the liquid has reduced to a syrupy consistency. When you can draw a wooden spoon across the pan and it leaves a clear path in its wake, it is done.
- Leave to cool, then spoon into sterilised jars and seal.

PREPARATION TIME 20 MINUTES

COOKING TIME 1 HOUR 15 MINUTES

INGREDIENTS

150g / 5 oz / ⅔ cup butter
2 kg / 4 lb red onions, peeled and thinly sliced
150g / 5 oz / ⅔ cup caster (superfine) sugar
100g / 3 ½ oz / ½ cup dates, chopped
2 thyme sprigs
Pinch chilli flakes
750ml / 1 ⅓ pints / 3 cups red wine
300ml / 10 fl. oz / 1 ¼ cups sherry vinegar
Salt and pepper

Red Onion Apple Chutney   1022

- Use the same quantity of peeled apple rather than the dates.

1023

**MAKES TWO
1 LB JARS**

Lime Marmalade

PREPARATION TIME 10 MINUTES

COOKING TIME 50-55 MINUTES

....

INGREDIENTS

16 large limes
500 g / 1 lbs 2 oz / 2 1/4 cups
granulated sugar

- Peel half of the zest from the limes. Julienne the peel and reserve to one side. Squeeze the limes into a jug; remove all the pulp and pips but reserve them.
- Pour the juice into a large bowl that can hold at least 2 litres. Make the juice up to 1.7 litres with water.
- Place the pulp and pips on a sheet of muslin and tie up into a bag using string. Place in the liquid, then cover the bowl and leave it overnight.
- The next day, pour the liquid and the muslin bag into a saucepan and cook for 35 minutes until the peel is soft.
- Preheat the oven to 170°C (150°C fan) / 325°F / gas 3.
- Place a couple of saucers in the freezer; they will be needed for testing the marmalade's setting point.
- Place two jars with their lids in the oven to sterilise. Remove the muslin bag and keep to one side until cool.
- Add the sugar to the saucepan and stir, then squeeze all the liquid contents from the bag into the saucepan.
- Boil the marmalade for 10-12 minutes. Remove from the heat and spoon a bit of the marmalade onto the cold saucers from the freezer. When the marmalade has cooled, prod it to see if a skin has formed. If so, it is ready. If not, boil for 3-4 minutes before testing again.
- When ready, remove the pan from the heat, fill the jars with the hot marmalade and seal immediately. Let the marmalade cool to room temperature before serving.

1025

**MAKES 1KG
/ 2 LB**

Piccalilli

PREPARATION TIME 20 MINUTES

COOKING TIME 25 MINUTES

....

INGREDIENTS

1 cauliflower, divided into small florets
250g / 9 oz / 1 cup small onions, peeled and roughly chopped
500ml / 1 pint / 2 cups malt vinegar
Grated nutmeg
½ tsp ground allspice
1 courgette, finely chopped
250g / 9 oz / 1 cup runner or green beans, sliced
150g / 5 oz / ⅔ cup caster (superfine) sugar
1 ½ tsp salt
1 clove garlic, crushed
1 tbsp mustard powder
¼ tsp Cayenne pepper
1 ½ tsp turmeric
3 tbsp plain (all purpose) flour

- Place the cauliflower, onion and the vinegar in a pan, then add the spices and bring to the boil. Cover and simmer for 7-8 minutes.
- Stir in the courgette, beans and sugar, garlic and salt. Cook for 5 more minutes – the vegetables should remain crisp-tender.
- Drain, reserving the vinegar.
- Mix the mustard, cayenne, turmeric and flour together, then work in 5 tbsp fresh vinegar and a little water to make a loose paste. Add a large spoonful of the hot vinegar and whisk until combined. Pour into a pan.
- Bring to the boil, whisking then gradually add the remaining hot vinegar. Boil for about 5 minutes.
- Tip the vegetables into a bowl, pour over the vinegar mixture and stir well. Spoon into sterilised jars, secure the lids and store for 3 months in a cool dark place.

Picalilli Salad

1026

- Serve alongside a salad for the perfect lunch.

1027
MAKES 2.25KG / 5LB Pickled Red Cabbage

Spicy Pickled Cabbage 1028
- Add a little dried chilli for a kick.

Red Cabbage with Dill 1029
- Add ½ bunch of dill for a Scandinavian flavour.

Red Cabbage with Ginger 1030
- Add 1 tbsp fresh ginger to the pickling mix.

PREPARATION TIME 2-3 HOURS

INGREDIENTS

1 tbsp pickling spice
1 tbsp coriander seeds
1 L / 2 ¼ pints / 4 ¼ cups malt vinegar
850g / 1 ½ lb red cabbage, cored and shredded

- Pour the vinegar into a pan with the spices and bring slowly to simmering. Leave to infuse for 2-3 hours.
- Strain into a large bowl, stir in the cabbage and combine well.
- Spoon into sterilised jars, seal and store for 8 weeks in a cool dark place.

1031

**MAKES
1 JAR**

Pickled Eggs

PREPARATION TIME 2 HOURS
20 MINUTES

....

INGREDIENTS

10 eggs, boiled and peeled
500ml / 1 pint / 2 cups white wine vinegar
1 onion, peeled and sliced
1 red chilli, halved
3 cloves garlic, peeled
1 tsp salt
8 black peppercorns

- Bring the vinegar to the boil with the flavourings and simmer for 10 minutes. Set aside and leave to infuse for 2 hours.
- Layer the eggs and spiced vinegar in sterilised jars, making sure they are submerged completely – top up with water if necessary.
- Store in a cool dark place for 1 month.

Spicy Pickled Eggs

1032

- Add a red chilli to the pickling liquid.

1033

**MAKES 1 L
/ 2 PINTS**

Home-made Tomato Ketchup

PREPARATION TIME 25 MINUTES

COOKING TIME 1 HOUR

....

INGREDIENTS

1 onion, peeled and chopped
½ fennel bulb, cored and chopped
2 sticks celery, chopped
Olive oil
2cm piece fresh ginger, finely sliced
3 cloves garlic, sliced
½ - 1 red chilli, deseeded and finely chopped
1 bunch basil leaves
1 tbsp coriander seeds
3 cloves
Salt and pepper
500g / 1 lb / 2 cups ripe tomatoes
1 x 400g can chopped tomatoes
200ml / 7 fl. oz / ¾ cup red wine vinegar
3 tbsp soft brown sugar

- Place all the vegetables except the tomatoes in a large pan with 4 tbsp olive oil, the spices and herbs, season well and cook gently for 15 minutes until softened.
- Add the tomatoes, bring to the boil and simmer until reduced by half – 30-40 minutes.
- Add the basil then blend the sauce in batches in a food processor until smooth. Push through a sieve into a clean pan.
- Add the vinegar and sugar and simmer until reduced and the consistency of ketchup.
- Adjust the seasoning, pour into sterilised bottles and store in the refrigerator.

Green Ketchup

1034

- Use green tomatoes instead of red tomatoes for a brightly-coloured variation.

1035

SERVES 4-6 Tomato Salsa

- Combine all the ingredients for the salsa and leave to infuse for at least 30 minutes in the refrigerator.
- Check and adjust the seasoning if necessary.

PREPARATION TIME 10 MINUTES

INGREDIENTS

6 ripe tomatoes, finely chopped
2 avocados, stoned and diced (optional)
1 red onion, peeled and very finely chopped
1 clove garlic, crushed
Tabasco
6 tbsp olive oil
2 limes, juiced
Salt and pepper
½ bunch coriander (cilantro), finely chopped

Tomato Mango Salsa   1036

- Surprisingly cubed mango adds a welcome fruity note to this salsa.

1037

SERVES 4 Preserved Aubergines

- Slice the aubergine lengthways 1cm thick. Brush liberally with oil, season and grill or griddle until tender and golden.
- Place the chilli, garlic, spices and oregano in a pan and cover with 200ml / 7 fl. oz / ¾ cup extra virgin olive oil and warm gently.
- Push the aubergine slices into a wide sterilised jar and pour over the oil and flavourings.
- Make sure all the aubergine is submerged, seal the lids and store in the refrigerator until needed.

PREPARATION TIME 10 MINUTES

COOKING TIME 20 MINUTES

INGREDIENTS

1 aubergine (eggplant)
Olive oil
Salt and pepper
1 red chilli, halved
2-3 cloves garlic peeled
2 bay leaves
½ tbsp coriander seeds
1 tsp cumin seeds
1 tsp dried oregano
Extra virgin olive oil

Preserved Courgettes   1038

- Courgettes can be preserved the same way if you have a glut.

1039

MAKES 1.5KG / 3 LB

Mincemeat

Sweetened Mincemeat
1040
- A small handful glace cherries sweetens the mix for children.

Mincemeat with Nuts
1041
- For a smoother texture omit the almonds.

Mince Pies in Puff Pastry with Ice Cream
1042
- Serve hot puff pastry squares, filled with mincemeat, topped with ice cream.

PREPARATION TIME 12 HOURS

COOKING TIME 20-30 MINUTES

INGREDIENTS

250g / 9 oz / 1 cup cooking apples, peeled, cored and diced
100g / 3 ½ oz / ½ cup shredded suet
175g / 6 oz / ¾ cup raisins
175g / 6 oz / ¾ cup sultanas
175g / 6 oz / ¾ cup whole mixed candied peel, chopped
Grated zest and juice of 1 orange
Grated zest and juice of 1 lemon
1 tbsp flaked (slivered) almonds
2 tsp mixed spice
½ tsp ground cinnamon
¼ nutmeg, grated
4 tbsp brandy

- Mix together all the ingredients apart from the brandy, then cover and leave for 12 hours or overnight.
- Preheat the oven 120°C (100° fan) / 225F / gas ½. Tip the mincemeat into a roasting tin, cover with foil and place in the oven to melt the suet and coat the ingredients.
- Once melted, remove from the oven, allow to cool thoroughly then stir in the brandy and spoon into sterilised jars. Cover and seal.

1043

MAKES 250G / ½ LB Marinated Olives

- Toss the olives with the flavourings, then tip into a jar or bowl.
- Cover with olive oil, seal and leave for 2 days to marinate before serving.

PREPARATION TIME 10 MINUTES

INGREDIENTS

250g / 9 oz / 1 cup green olives
3 cloves garlic, peeled
1 tbsp dried oregano
1 tsp dried chilli flakes
1 strip pared lemon zest, pith removed
Extra virgin olive oil

Olives with Orange 1044

- Add a strip of orange zest for a Provencal flavour.

1045

SERVES 4 Beetroot Jam

- Cook the beetroot in a pan of boiling water until tender when a skewer is inserted – about 1 hour.
- Remove the skins – wearing kitchen gloves – then chop the beetroot not too finely as you want some texture to the jam.
- Place in a pan with the sugar and cumin and cook until the jam is set – about 30 minutes. Spoon a little onto a plate. If it wrinkles when you push it with your finger, it's set. If not, cook for 3 minutes, then repeat the test. Continue until the jam is set. You may need to add a little water to stop it sticking.
- Once set spoon into sterilised jars and keep in the refrigerator.

PREPARATION TIME 10 MINUTES

COOKING TIME 1-2 HOURS

INGREDIENTS

2 beetroots, scrubbed and leaves removed
1-2 tbsp caster (superfine) sugar
1 tsp ground cumin
Water

Spiced Beetroot Jam 1046

- Add a little dried chilli to offset the sweetness.

1047

MAKES 4 JARS

Apricot Jam

PREPARATION TIME 45 MINUTES
+ OVERNIGHT MACERATING

COOKING TIME 20 MINUTES

INGREDIENTS

1.5kg / 3 lb ripe apricots
700-800g / 1 ⅓ – 1 ¾ lb / 3 – 3 ½
cups caster (superfine) sugar
1 vanilla pod, split
1 lemon, juiced

- Halve the fruit and reserve about a third of the stones.
- Add to a pan with the sugar – you may not need all of it, depending on how sweet the apricots are. Stir in the vanilla pod, seeds and lemon juice and leave overnight.
- Wrap the stones in a tea towel and bash with a hammer to crack and remove the inner kernels.
- Blanch them in boiling water for 1 minute, plunge into iced water, then remove the skins. Halve and add to the apricots.
- Place the pan over a low heat and stir until the sugar has dissolved. Increase the heat and boil for about 20 minutes until the mixture has thickened. This is a softer set jam so it's not necessary to get a 'set'.
- Leave to cool for 20 minutes, then spoon into sterilised jars, removing the actual vanilla pod. Cover and seal, leave to cool then store in the refrigerator.

Peach Jam   1048

- Try this with ripe peaches for a taste of summer sunshine.

1049

MAKES 1 JAR

Chocolate Spread

PREPARATION TIME 15 MINUTES

COOKING TIME 5 MINUTES

INGREDIENTS

100g / 3 ½ oz / ½ cup dark chocolate,
chopped
200g / 7 oz / ¾ cup hazelnuts
(cob nuts)
50ml / 1 ¾ oz / ¼ cup vegetable oil
1 tbsp Demerara sugar
Pinch salt

- Place the chocolate in a bowl over a pan of simmering water and stir occasionally until melted. Set aside to cool.
- Toast the hazelnuts under a hot grill for a few seconds, watching them closely.
- Crush the nuts finely in a food processor, then add the sugar and salt and combine well, scraping down the bowl as necessary.
- Add the melted chocolate until combined, then the oil in a steady stream until completely combined. Transfer to a sterilised jar and seal. Store in the refrigerator for at least 4 hours.

Spiced Chocolate Spread   1050

- A little ground cinnamon or grated nutmeg will add warmth.

1051

MAKES 1 KG / 2 LB

Apple and Raisin Chutney

Pear Raisin Chutney

1052

- Chopped peeled pear makes a more delicate version.

Mango and Apple Raisin Chutney

1053

- 2 mangos, peeled and cubed, will add sweet fruitiness.

Plum and Apple Chutney

1054

- Plums, in place of the raisins, will complement the apples.

PREPARATION TIME 30 MINUTES

COOKING TIME 1 HOUR 30 MINUTES

INGREDIENTS

1.8kg / 4 lb cooking apples, peeled cored and diced
3 onions, peeled and finely chopped
1 lemon, juiced
1 tbsp mustard seeds
850ml / 1 ½ pints / 3 ½ cups cider vinegar
450g / 1 lb / 2 cups raisins
1 tbsp fresh ginger, grated
½ tsp ground cloves
2 tsp salt
850g / 1 ½ lb / 3 ½ cups soft brown sugar

- Place the apples, onions, lemon juice, mustard seeds and ⅔ of the vinegar in a pan and boil. Reduce the heat and simmer for about an hour.
- Add the raisins, ginger, cloves, salt, sugar and remaining vinegar and simmer for at least another 30 minutes or until thickened.
- Pour into sterilised jars, secure the lids and leave to cool. Store in a cool dark place for 6 weeks.

1055

MAKES 1L / 2 LB

Summer Berry Jam

Blueberry Jam
1056
- Try with the same amount of just blueberries.

Summer Berry Jam with Blackberries
1057
- Adding blackberries instead of the cherries adds an autumnal touch.

Summer Berry Jam with Raspberries
1058
- Add raspberries for another hit of summer flavour.

PREPARATION TIME 24 HOURS

COOKING TIME 30 MINUTES

INGREDIENTS

1kg / 2 ¼ lb / 4 ¼ cups mixed strawberries, redcurrants and stoned cherries
750g / 1 ⅓ lb / 3 cups caster (superfine) sugar
1 lemon, juiced

- Hull the strawberries and wipe clean, then layer all the fruit in a preserving pan or large saucepan, sprinkling with sugar. Leave overnight to macerate.
- Place the pan over a low heat to melt the sugar and allow the fruit to pulp slightly. Try not to stir as this will break the strawberries up – just shake the pan a little.
- When the sugar has completely dissolved, add the lemon juice and tie the pips in a muslin and add to the jam. Increase the heat and when bubbling, cook for 8 minutes then remove from the heat.
- Spoon a little onto a plate. If it wrinkles when you push it with your finger, it's set. If not, cook for 3 minutes, then repeat the test. Continue until the jam is set. Remove the muslin.
- Allow the jam to settle off the heat for 15 minutes before pouring into sterilised jars. Seal immediately with waxed lids and tie on the lids.

1059

MAKES 2 KG / 4 ½ LB

Plum Jam

- Discard any stalks and leaves from the fruit and place in a pan over a low heat. Simmer with the water until just tender. Do not stir, just shake the pan as the fruit collapses.
- Add the sugar, stirring very gently so as not to crush the fruit and leave for 15 minutes until the sugar has dissolved completely.
- When the sugar has completely dissolved, increase the heat and when bubbling, cook for 10 minutes then remove from the heat.
- Spoon a little onto a plate. If it wrinkles when you push it with your finger, it's set. If not, cook for 5 minutes, then repeat the test. Continue until the jam is set.
- Allow the jam to settle off the heat for 15 minutes before pouring into sterilised jars. Seal immediately with waxed lids and tie on the lids.

PREPARATION TIME 10 MINUTES

COOKING TIME 30-35 MINUTES

INGREDIENTS

1 kg / 2 lb / 4 cups plums, stoned and halved
225ml / 8 fl. oz / 1 cup water
700g / 1 ⅓ lb / 3 cups caster (superfine) sugar

Plum Cinnamon Jam   1060

- ½ tsp of ground cinnamon is all that's needed to give a gentle hint of spice.

1061

MAKES 1.5KG / 3 LB

Pineapple Marmalade

- Cut the pineapple into small chunks, squeeze over the lemon juice and leave for 2 hours.
- Tip into a pan and bring to a simmer. Cook for 1 hour.
- Add the sugar and stir until dissolved, then bring to the boil and cook for 15 minutes then check the set. Spoon a little onto a plate. If it wrinkles when you push it with your finger, it's set. If not, cook for 10 minutes, then repeat the test. Continue until the jam is set.
- Allow the jam to settle off the heat for 20 minutes before pouring into sterilised jars. Seal immediately with waxed lids and tie on the lids.

PREPARATION TIME 2 HOURS

COOKING TIME 1 HOUR 30 MINUTES

INGREDIENTS

1 kg / 2lb / 4 cups pineapple, peeled
2 lemons, juiced
500g / 1 lb/ 2 cups granulated sugar

Pineapple Chilli Marmalade   1062

- Add ¼ red chilli, finely chopped and deseeded to offset the sweetness.

Index

Index

Index

Index